Generalized Anxiety Disorder
Across the Lifespan

Michael E. Portman, DPhil, LISW-S

Generalized Anxiety Disorder Across the Lifespan

An Integrative Approach

 Springer

Michael E. Portman, DPhil, LISW-S
Cleveland Veterans Administration
Case Western Reserve University
Cleveland, OH
USA
meport@roadrunner.com

ISBN: 978-0-387-89242-9   e-ISBN: 978-0-387-89243-6
DOI: 10.1007/978-0-387-89243-6

Library of Congress Control Number: 2008944092

Printed on acid-free paper

springer.com

Foreword

It is with great pleasure that I write this foreword for my colleague and friend Dr. Michael Portman on this new offering *Generalized Anxiety Disorder Across the Life Span: An Integrative Approach*. It is rare to find a clinician who also happens to enjoy research and is so well versed in the empirical literature on such a complex disorder. He has been able, in equal measure, to find a meaningful way to transmit in his writing this conceptual understanding in a precise and elegant manner to others. Another outstanding achievement of this book is the fact that it addresses generalized anxiety disorder (GAD) across the life span covering not only the theoretical underpinnings of GAD, but the psychosocial and pharmacological treatments – both standard ones and newer developments. There are other equally compelling areas of inquiry in this book for both the novice and seasoned psychotherapist to digest and then ideally use with their own patients. This is a rich and deeply thought out book by a highly gifted and bright new voice in the area of GAD, and for that matter the anxiety spectrum disorders.

The subject of GAD alone has generated much attention as of late, but clinicians still continue to struggle accessing the empirical data for the benefit of their patients. This publication is a much needed guide and resource, without falling prey to just being another conventional and manualized treatment approach. Even though this text eschews simple formulations, it does offer a broad and integrative perspective on the multiple options available for the mental health practitioner and others in related professions. The academic researcher and advanced graduate student in psychopathology will also benefit from this publication. In discussing the ideas behind this text with Dr. Portman over the years, I have been impressed with his initiative in seeing this publication through from its original inception. His intellectual influences are broad, and it will be apparent to anyone who has the chance to read and study carefully this work that the author has a deep grasp of his subject, and an equally great compassion for the chronically anxious sufferer.

I recommend this publication without reservation and hope that it finds a broad reading audience. It fills a much needed void in the existing literature on the topic, while making an original and profound contribution. My hope is that Dr. Portman continues in his clinical and research efforts and brings out in time his own treatment approach for those challenged with GAD. We have considered such a collaborative effort in the past, and perhaps this may be a fertile topic for another publication. In the end, whatever the future may hold, this new title is an excellent and worthwhile point of departure for this talented clinician and promising new author.

John H. Riskind, Ph.D.
Professor of Psychology
George Mason University

Editor: International Journal of Cognitive Therapy

About the Author

Michael E. Portman, DPhil, LISW-S, is a full-time staff clinical social worker at the Cleveland Veteran's Administration. He provides individual and group therapy to a patient population consisting of veterans with severe mental disorders. He is also an adjunct faculty member at Case Western Reserve University, Mandel School of Applied Social Sciences, and has maintained a private practice specializing in the treatment of mood and anxiety disorders, especially Generalized Anxiety Disorder, for ten years. In addition to his clinical experience, Dr. Portman received a Doctorate of Philosophy in Social Work from The University of South Africa, a MSW from The Ohio State University, and a M.A. in Psychology from The New School for Social Research.

Preface

Generalized anxiety disorder (GAD) is a persistent, highly debilitating, under-diagnosed, often misunderstood, undertreated and pervasive condition. In spite of advances in both psychosocial and pharmacological interventions for this disorder, namely cognitive-behavioral therapy (CBT) and antidepressant regimens (SSRIs), clinical outcomes across multiple primary and secondary measures have not been robust in nature. One of the main impetuses for writing the following book has been to present a comprehensive, albeit not exhaustive, source for clinicians by a clinician experienced in the theoretical underpinnings and treatments for GAD. The goal is not to supplant either the CBT tradition or the pharmacological one, but to extend the scope of options available to those that treat chronically anxious patients. To date, there does not exist, in the multiple sources extant on the subject, a single authored, nonedited text that encompasses the standard evidence-based treatments for GAD and newer cutting edge conceptual models and interventions for this malady.

On a more personal note, another motivating factor for this book's publication is that, as a clinician who has treated hundreds of patients with GAD with a modicum of success and witnessed firsthand the ravage this disorder can cause, it has become even more pressing (akin to a calling) to present not just "another" text on the subject, but one that does justice to the marked impairment this condition can have on the individual sufferer and the larger societal impact. In addition, even though excessive worry and chronic anxiety – the cardinal symptoms of GAD – are timely topics, especially in this age of global terrorism, economic unrest, and growing existential foreboding in the face of life's uncertainties, the reality is that in speaking to many clinicians about GAD, they simply do not know what to do in practice with patients who present with diffuse anxious symptomatology. GAD is a formidable foe for not just the sufferer, but for the practitioner, whose lives these individuals have entrusted to their care.

In attempting to write a book that remains loyal to the "empirical tradition" that is both evidence-based, yet at the same time, considers GAD's heterogeneity, the individualized needs of clinicians who treat chronically anxious patients and patients' preferences in regard to the approach that best fits their particular clinical presentation of the disorder, a balance had to be created that was quite a challenge. In the end, the book discusses in detail the "tried and tested" models and approaches to treatment for GAD; however, it has deviated from the more manu-alized how-to guide, and is more geared toward being a resource for the busy clinician treating patients with persistent worry and anxiety. It has followed the dictum that "one size does not fit all". In other words, this is not a text that endorses a monolithic, single modality approach to treating patients with GAD. On the one hand, it has an integrative flavor that may prove unpersuasive to the diehard empiricist and, on the other hand, too evidence-based for the more con-textually oriented practitioner. My hope is that even with not being able to fully satisfy all those who may align themselves within a certain "camp" in the psy-chotherapy world; it will be of benefit to the majority of those interested in this population and their ultimate well-being.

The structure of the book confirms the premise that to reach more patients with GAD and maximize clinical outcomes, increasing both evidence-based and research informed options for the novice and seasoned practitioner needs to be available in one user-friendly guide. This text is aimed to assist those in all the "helping profes-sions," which includes not just the traditional mental health disciplines, but also primary care physicians and medical specialists, who are often the first contact source for the anxiety ridden patient. Clergy, pastoral counselors and other allied health care providers may benefit from this resource as well.

The text is divided into eight clearly delineated chapters, with appendices and select assessment tools for children, adolescents, adults and older adults, references for further exploration and an index to locate particular areas of interest. The book covers GAD across the life span and integrates a broad amount of data, ranging from the historical, conceptual, and psychosocial to the pharmacological. The chap-ter topics follow in this chronology:

Chapter 1: This chapter is an overview addressing the nuts and bolts of GAD, from its historical evolution as a diagnosis, prevalence, clinical presentation, onset, course and prognosis, comorbidity, and impact on the environment. It helps the clinician get better acclimated to the subject and provides some basic facts about the disorder.

Chapter 2: This chapter discusses the most current diagnostic criteria for GAD, the challenges of properly assessing and diagnosing this disorder, and the need for reliable and valid instruments to facilitate diagnostic precision. The clinical inter-view, several structured interviews, and self-report inventories are highlighted.

Chapter 3: This chapter tackles the most well thought out conceptual models bearing on GAD. The foundational theoretical understanding for GAD stems from the pioneering work of Beck, yet other theories, including those of Barlow, Borkovec, Riskind, Dugas and Wells, are explored in depth.

Chapter 4: This chapter addresses a broad range of psychosocial interventions. Commonly known as "the talking cures," these treatments are largely cognitive behavioral in orientation or, as Norcross (2005) referred to them, as "cognitive hybrids" (cognitive permutations). However, several of them offer broader treat-ments than standard CBT, and one in particular is psychodynamic in origin. In addi-tion, some research informed models (not purely evidence-based) will be discussed, as will the influence of psychotherapy integration in the treatment of GAD.

Chapter 5: This chapter draws on the biomedical model and deals with the genetics, neurobiology, and psychotropic medications used in the treatment of GAD for adults.

Chapter 6: This chapter broaches special populations such as children, adolescents, and older adults that have, until more recently, received less attention than adults with GAD. Some descriptive phenomenology of how GAD clinically presents in these populations, assessment, diagnostic issues and both psychosocial and pharmacological interventions will be explored, as growing research is mounting to optimize their unique treatment needs.

Chapter 7: This chapter deals with several neglected topics that have important implications in the treatment of GAD. Prevention, for one, has not traditionally been the aim of health care practice, yet remains critical if we as practitioners are to stem the tide of conditions like GAD proliferating from the start. Little work in relation to prevention of GAD has been done to this point. Anxiety is not culture bound; however, the bulk of the research has been conducted on Western samples. Non-Western patients with GAD also suffer, but present in many cases with a different set of symptom clusters. This information is important for clinicians to keep in mind when treating others who come from different cultural groups. It requires a different perspective and unique sensitivity when encountering such patients. In addition, another challenging topic – the "treatment resistant" patient with GAD – has been a source of complication for clinicians and is a ripe area for ongoing research. GAD could be conceived as treatment resistant by definition, given the difficulty in achieving significantly positive outcomes for a sizeable number of patients. Yet in principle, not all patients with GAD are in actuality resistant to treatment. However, for those who are partial responders or nonresponders, there are interventions, both psychologic and pharmacologic, that have shown some initial promise with the treatment refractory GAD patient. These will be explored in greater depth.

Chapter 8: In this chapter future directions and recommendations in the study and treatment of GAD are elucidated. For example, Barlow's unified protocol, motivational interviewing, and well-being therapy are three of a number of interventions and conceptualizations that may enhance treatment for GAD and other disorders.

Having outlined the basic contents of this text, clinicians from different disciplines and theoretical persuasions, after reading this work, may still be left with unanswered questions, concerns, or feedback. This author makes no case for mind reading the voices of his colleagues' reactions to this publication and welcomes inquiries from others. Not only will it enhance the learning curve of this clinician but also, should the volume resurface in updated editions, the collective mouthpiece of one's peers can only further refine the original offering. This clinician can be reached at meport@roadrunner.com for comments, or just the quick exchange of an idea or two. This book is the product of years of clinical work with patients who suffer from GAD, combined with extensive research to address the needs of clinicians seeking guidance on how to offer the highest quality care to chronically anxious patients. If it has accomplished the goal of being helpful to my fellow practitioners, this endeavor will have been a successful one.

Acknowledgments

No accomplishment, great or small, exists in isolation from the help of others. This project of writing a book for GAD would not have been made possible if it had not been for the backing of Springer and a phenomenally gifted and creative editorial staff. I first thank Ms. Sharon Panulla, a seasoned editor, who first read the proposal for this book on GAD and gave it the green light. From the beginning Sharon believed in my work, and it was passed on over time to the highly capable editor for this particular undertaking, Ms. Jennifer Hadley. Ms. Carol Bischoff was also instrumental in seeing this project come to fruition. Together this team of professionals gave me the opportunity to demonstrate my passion and commitment to the topic of generalized anxiety disorder.

In addition, the crux of my interest in psychotherapy came from my loving parents – my father, the doctor, and my mother, the artist. This combination of parental influences has slowly, but profoundly, shaped my intense passion for ideas and concern for the welfare of others. My parents embody the best of both the scientist and artist in me, and I am grateful for this gift. Two younger brothers and their families have also always been supportive of their loved one "the psychotherapist," never quite knowing what to say when others ask them if they themselves feel like they are "lying on the couch," so to speak, in my presence. Invariably, you should all be encouraged by the fact that an ethical therapist neither practices on, nor officially treats, his relatives.

There have been many colleagues along the way who have sent articles, responded to endless e-mails, and offered sage advice on various aspects of GAD and psychopathology. Two world renowned experts on GAD, Dr. John Riskind, who wrote the foreword to this publication and, Dr. Thomas Borkovec, have been wellsprings of knowledge, and without them this book would still be a pile of papers in an old drawer. They have been mentors in the most humble of ways, assisting a seasoned clinician, yet budding researcher, indirectly get a book deal with their unwavering support. Dr. Riskind, behind the scenes, gave someone feedback that I could do a good job writing a book; while a brief e-mail letter from Dr. Borkovec to this author reaffirmed my commitment to this project. Three other international experts, Dr. Ann Marie Albano, who provided guidance on GAD in children and adolescents, and Drs. Julie Wetherell and Melinda Stanley, who were most helpful in offering feedback and materials about GAD in the elderly, were instrumental in enhancing my knowledge and clinical base. Finally, the influence of Drs. Aaron Beck, David Barlow, Otto Kernberg, Paul McHugh, Rudolph Hoehn-Saric, who wrote an endorsement, and Douglas Mennin, have not gone unnoticed, influencing me in more subtle, yet profound directions. Professor Wilfried van Delft, my doctoral dissertation chairperson at the University of South Africa, deserves a special mention of gratitude for his civility and patience. In addition, a special thanks to my colleagues at the Cleveland Veterans Administration and Case Western Reserve University interns. The thought leaders of the psychotherapy integration movement, which include Drs. Stanley Messer, who kindly added another official endorsement, George Stricker, Hal Arkowitz and Barry E. Wolfe, also merit a heartfelt thanks for their constructive feedback and support. To all the others who have offered their encouragement in one way or another, I am deeply appreciative and touched by the kindness.

Many patients with GAD have put their faith and trust in my capacity to offer them a respite of relief from the nagging worry and anxiety that pervades this painful disorder. In unique ways, each of them has ideally made me a better clinician and person. This book may help the clinician, but is devoted to those who suffer.

My wife Riva, the bastion and anchor of my life, lives with a man who cannot share with her any specifics about the details of a good part of his life. She is more patient and loving than any man deserves, especially this one. Her brilliance as a web designer has helped shape the contours of this publication, making it not just a substantive work, but an aesthetic one. Few men can say that their spouse is a true woman of valor. To my children, Yoni and Sarah Tova – words cannot express the patience required beyond your years, as their father moves from one intellectual undertaking to another. My hope is to resume and become a bigger and brighter presence in your lives, sooner than later.

To the Creator of the world, there are no words of gratitude large enough to thank for bringing all those mentioned in this acknowledgement into my life at the most opportune of times. The continuous blessings of life, love, work, and worship are beyond the expressions of one person. Without You nothing is absolutely meaningful or worthwhile.

Contents

Chapter 1
Nature of Generalized Anxiety Disorder

Over the last 10–15 years, generalized anxiety disorder – commonly referred to as GAD – has mystified both researchers and clinicians. GAD has been a topic of heated debate in the mental health field. It bears repeating that this disorder is a highly misunderstood (Kasper, 2004), commonly occurring, chronic, disabling, diagnostically independent, and severe condition. GAD, compared with other anxiety disorders, has also been understudied (Dugas, 2000). Once considered a mild disorder of the "worried well," GAD has proven to be much more complex and elusive in nature (Rickels & Rynn, 2002; Sanderson & Andrews, 2002). The early paucity of research was due in part to multiple changes in diagnostic conceptualizations (Nutt, Argyropoulous, & Forshall, 2001; Pollock & Kuo, 2004), low interrater reliability (Barlow & Di Nardo, 1991; Di Nardo, et al., 1983), and imprecision in identifying target symptoms of the disorder (Rickels & Rynn, 2001). In other words, clinical recognition and research have been hampered by the shifting and diffuse nature of the disorder's symptoms, changes in diagnostic criteria over time, and high rates of psychiatric and medical comorbidity (Hoge, Oppenheimer, & Simon, 2004). Finally, the enigmatic quality of GAD, with its ubiquitous clinical presentation of "anxious apprehension" and "hyperarousal" (Barlow, 1988, 2002), has only served as a further impasse in developing systemic treatment approaches, targeting not only simply symptom reduction of worry and anxiety, but broader improvements and indices in overall functioning.

However, one caveat – recent advances in the understanding of the disorder's symptomatology, pathogenesis, and management (Nutt, Rickels, & Stein, 2002) have garnered for GAD, a heightened sense of renewed identity, respectability, and legitimacy by primarily academic psychiatrists and psychologists. This recent upsurge in attention to its assessment, diagnosis, and treatment has been considered a paradigm shift in furthering a deeper appreciation of GAD as an important diagnostic entity.

GAD is an intriguing affliction for other reasons. The ubiquity of worry and anxiety so common to GAD is found in all, or at least most, of the other emotional and psychiatric disorders. These symptoms are not only fundamental aspects of the human condition; they cause considerable subjective suffering and are associated with profound disability and distress (Pollack, 2006). Yet, according to two leading scholars (Hoehn-Saric & McLeod, 1991), teasing out normal worry and anxiety from pathological worry can be a challenge, as there is not always a distinct boundary

M.E. Portman, *Generalized Anxiety Disorder Across the Lifespan*,
DOI: 10.1007/978-0-387-89243-6_1, © Springer Science + Business Media, LLC 2009

that separates one from the other. Starcevic (2005) adds that the clinical features of GAD, such as worry and anxiety, can be hard to discriminate because of the heterogeneous quality of the disorder. Anxiety and depression also occur together with increased frequency and can make things difficult from a diagnostic perspective. Tyrer (2001) has referred to this enmeshment of anxiety and depressive symptoms common in GAD and other disorders as "cothymia."

Pollock and Kuo (2004) have taken notice of some other characteristics of GAD worthy of attention. First, those who suffer from pathological forms of worry and chronic anxiety do seek treatment, but the treatment is often inadequate, and help-seeking, when pursued, is often delayed for years. In addition, "very few people with pure GAD seek treatment" (Kessler, Walters, & Wittchen, 2004, pp. 45–46). This is unfortunate, given our growing conceptual understanding of GAD and the burgeoning number of more effective and creative treatment approaches that have emerged over the last few years. Second, subsyndromal forms of GAD are common. Third, it is often the more emotionally paralyzing depressive symptoms that sequentially follow years of GAD that generally drive patients into professional treatment seeking, not the GAD alone (Wittchen et al., 2002). Last, which will be broached in greater detail throughout this text, is that optimal treatment may need to incorporate individualized pharmacotherapy and/or psychotherapy regimens for acute and long-term management. Now the chapter turns to the contextual surround behind GAD, giving the clinician a window into the historical evolution of the diagnosis.

Historical Overview

Anxiety has been observed for centuries (Nutt et al., 2001) and witnessed since time immemorial. It was not until Feuchtersleben (1847, cited in Berrios & Link, 1995) hypothesized that anxiety was the cause of various organic maladies, such as heart and digestive illnesses, that the concept began to take on the semblance of scientific verbiage. Prior to that, anxiety had been romanticized and mythologized, and was more of a way of describing an emotional state of melancholia (Berrios & Link, 1995) than a condition worthy of study. In addition, in the early 1800s, anxiety was treated by physicians as separate physical symptoms, and attempted remedies focused on alleviating independent somatic complaints. Morel (1866, as cited in Nutt et al., 2001) attempted to tie together seemingly unrelated symptoms of anxiety into a unitary syndrome, and argued that these various manifestations could give rise to changes in the autonomic nervous system, producing mental symptoms called "emotional delusions."

Perhaps the single most influential event in the history of anxiety came with the publication of a seminal paper by Freud (1894) on neurasthenia, which provided, for the first time, a dynamic and descriptive approach in clarifying the concept of anxiety. Freud teased out neurasthenia and detached from it a specific syndrome now called "anxiety neurosis." At that time, hysteria and hypochondriasis were considered the traditional neuroses and viewed as psychogenic in origin, while obsessional states and the new anxiety neurosis had, according to Freud, an organic basis. This clinical position remained dominant throughout the larger part of the twentieth century. It was not based on hard scientific evidence, but more on insight and clinical observation. The brilliance of Freud's term anxiety neurosis not only contributed to anxiety symptoms being seen as primarily somatic in nature, but also allowed for reflections and intimations that anticipated much of the later diagnostic schemes that were to follow. Terms such as "free floating anxiety," which would later be a precursor for GAD, and other defining features of anxiety neurosis, such as excessive worry, general irritability, anxious expectation, chronic apprehension, anxiety attacks, and phobic avoidance, were all the result of Freud's keen power of perception and discernment.

Anxiety neurosis continued to be a unitary category until Klein (1964), a psychiatrist and psychopharmacologist, delineated panic from a general anxiety syndrome, based on their differential response to imipramine. Panic conditions, according to his research, responded to this antidepressant, whereas GAD sufferers did not. Even though later evidence would disconfirm this (Johnstone et al., 1980; Kahn et al., 1986; Rickels, Downing, Schweizer, & Hassman, 1993), and other counter arguments were put forward to keep GAD where it was, the advent of the *Diagnostic and Statistical Manual of Mental Disorders* (third edition) *DSM-III* (American Psychiatric Association [APA], 1980) allowed Klein's views about a generalized persistent anxiety condition to be incorporated into the classification system. But, it took time and multiple diagnostic reconceptualizations for this to become a reality (Nutt et al., 2001; see Table 1.1).

In retrospect, *DSM-I* (APA, 1952) and *DSM-II* (APA, 1968) catalogued psychopathology as secondary to anxiety, and anxiety became the cause of mental instability. In addition, based on remnants of Freudian metapsychology, the psychopathology of all biopsychosocial disturbances was caused by intrapsychic conflict. The *DSM-III* heralded in a new age for GAD, but not without a struggle. A summary of this debate can be found in Spitzer, Williams, and Skodol (1980). On the one side, the atheoretic camp wanted a criterion-based system; on the other side were those who pressed for a guide that had a psychodynamic perspective. In the end, the atheoretic group won the day, making it possible to base particular disorders on an individualized cluster of symptoms, and not on a single theoretical model. From the mid-1980s it also became clearer that chronic worry, accompanied by persistent anxiety, was to

Table 1.1 Evolution of the concept of anxiety disorders

1800s	Independent symptoms
1866	Morel – one syndrome
1894	Freud
1964	Klein – different syndromes
1980	*DSM-III*
1992	ICD-10
1994	*DSM-IV*

become the defining feature of GAD, establishing an important place in our understanding of psychopathology (Hoge et al., 2004). This ultimately led the path for GAD to be separated in *DSM-III* from panic, due to its unique clinical presentation, and given increased status with subsequent text revisions in *DSM-III-R* (APA, 1987), *DSM-IV* (APA, 1994), and *DSM-IV-TR* (APA, 2000). The criteria changes in the diagnosis of GAD included a decrease in emphasis over time on somatic symptoms, a 6-month duration, excessive anxiety, restlessness, fatigue, impaired concentration, irritability, muscle tension, sleep disturbance, and pathological uncontrollable worry over a number of different domains and activities (e.g., work, finances, health, etc.). Other criteria were also required to make the diagnosis, which contributed to a disorder now being perceived as anything but mild, but quite to the contrary, severely impairing (Brawman-Mintzer, 2001). Erickson and Newman (2005) confirmed GAD as being a debilitating "stand alone" psychiatric disorder. However, challenges have not gone away for the disorder, as "the diagnostic criteria of GAD have continuously evolved over the past 30 years, making consistent research efforts difficult" (Pollock & Kuo, 2004, p. 4).

Despite these roadblocks, there is agreement among clinicians and researchers regarding target symptoms for GAD (Brown, Di Nardo Lehman, & Campbell, 2001; Starcevic & Bogojevic, 1999), yet some critics still feel that the current classification has its shortcomings (McHugh, 2001; Rickels & Rynn, 2001). GAD has become a reliable diagnosis, but was almost excluded from the *DSM-IV* on account of poor reliability (Brown, Barlow, & Leibowitz, 1994), and its validity still conjures up unresolved questions (Nutt et al., 2001). Some still feel that GAD remains ill-defined (Tyrer & Baldwin, 2006). Part of the problem may be the confusing nosology – "tension disorder" may be a more useful name (Stein, 2005). On the more optimistic side, Mennin, Heimberg, and Turk (2004) argue that GAD has taken time to establish its validity. In spite of it often being maligned and subject to vilification in earlier versions of the *DSM* as a residual category, the disorder has survived, and the present nomenclature in the *DSM-IV-TR* is a more valid one. The authors also add that the most current conceptualization has reframed *DSM-IV*, revising the text to better reflect more current research into the nature of GAD and its basic mechanisms. These better-refined areas pertaining to prevalence rates, comorbidity, and other demographic topics will now be more fully explicated.

Prevalence

Anxiety disorders are the most common psychiatric disturbances. Prevalence rates are high, yet less than 30% seek treatment (Pollock & Kuo, 2004). In using *DSM-IV* data from the Australian National Survey of Mental Health and Well-Being (Hunt, Issakidis, & Andrews, 2002), 1-month prevalence for GAD was 2.8%, and 12-month prevalence was 3.6%. According to the National Comorbidity Survey (NCS-R), lifetime prevalence rates of 5.7% were found by Kessler et al. (2005), which used the *DSM-IV* criteria (APA, 1994). GAD has the highest prevalence rate among all the anxiety disorders (Robins & Regier, 1991), with rates ranging from 4.1 to 6.6%. The risk of developing GAD for women is twice that of men (Ormel et al., 1994),

> To date, examination of the association between sociodemographic features and an increased incidence of GAD have found gender to be the most highly correlated characteristic. As with many other anxiety disorders, GAD is much more common in woman than in men. In both clinical (Woodman, Noyes, Black, Schlosser, & Yagla, 1999; Yonkers, Warshaw, Massion, & Keller, 1996) and community samples (Wittchen, Zhao, Kessler, & Eaton, 1994), GAD rates were found to be approximately double in women (Holmes & Newman, 2006, p. 104).

The lifetime prevalence rates for women in community samples were 7%, compared to 4% for men. It was found that the rates for GAD were particularly elevated for women older than 44 years (Halbreich, 2003; Wittchen et al., 1994). In a cross-cultural survey, the World Health Organization found rates of 9.2% among women and 5.7% among men (Maier et al., 2000). "In clinical settings, 55–60% of those diagnosed with GAD are female and in epidemiological studies about two thirds of the adults with GAD are female" (APA, 1994, as quoted in McLellarn & Rosenzweig, 2004, p. 386). In summary, women are twice as likely to develop GAD. The possible explanations "for this discrepancy include hormonal differences, cultural pressures and a higher rate of reporting anxiety" (Roe-Sepowitz, Bedard, & Thyer, 2005, p. 18; see Table 1.2).

In looking at trends related to socioeconomic status (SES), GAD was found to be more common in those with lower SES backgrounds (Corcoran & Walsh, 2006). The authors offer the reason for this to be the greater number of stressors affecting those in poverty. In addition, those with higher SES are, in general, better educated, have higher job levels, and as a result, have increased access to treatment. It would then make sense that the unemployed and women who work only at home would

Table 1.2 Disorder distribution among US adults

Disorder	Total US population affected		
	Number (in millions)	Percentage	Gender
Generalized anxiety disorder	4	2.8	Women are twice as likely as men to be afflicted
Obsessive compulsive disorder	3.3	2.3	Equally afflicts men and women
Panic disorder	2.4	1.7	Women are twice as likely as men to be afflicted
Posttraumatic stress disorder	5.2	3.6	Women are more likely than men to be afflicted
Social phobia	5.3	3.7	Equally afflicts men and women
Specific phobia	6.3	4.4	Women are twice as likely as men to be afflicted
Total all/any phobia	14.8	10.3	

© John Wiley and Sons. Roe-Sepowitz, D.E., Bedard, L.E., & Thyer, B.A. (2005). Anxiety. In C.N. Dulmus & L.A. Rapp-Paglicci (Eds.), Handbook of preventive interventions for adults (pp. 13–26). Hoboken, New Jersey: John Wiley and Sons. Reprinted with permission.

be more vulnerable to experience GAD. The National Comorbidity Study (Kessler et al., 1994; Wittchen et al., 1994) confirmed these findings with higher rates among those not working outside the home, homemakers, and one atypical finding of those who reside in the Northeast. No direct links to race, education, income, or religion could be established in the National Comorbidity Survey study.

In looking at other variables related to prevalence rates, such as marital status, GAD was more prevalent in those who had previously been married, than in those who are either currently married or have never been married (Corcoran & Walsh, 2006). Kessler, Keller, and Wittchen (2001) revealed that unmarried status, racial minority (they did not specify which race), and low SES were predictors of vulnerability to GAD. Another confirming assessment concluded that GAD particularly affects individuals who are unmarried, a racial minority, and belong to low SES (Grados, Leung, Ahmed, & Anega, 2005). In an Australian National Survey, Hunt et al. (2002) found that being separated, divorced, widowed, and unemployed were risk factors in developing GAD. Blazer, Hughes, George, Swartz, and Boyer (1991) concluded that GAD is common among the separated, divorced, or widowed persons, in contrast to the married or never married. In their study GAD may occur more often among those in the lower SES.

GAD is highly prevalent in primary care settings (Ormel et al., 1994; Roy-Byrne & Katon, 1997; Schonfeld et al., 1997). In a more recent research article by Wittchen (2002), GAD was the most frequently seen disorder in primary care, rarely diagnosed correctly, and not managed appropriately in terms of psychosocial and pharmacological treatments (Wittchen et al., 2001). In addition, GAD sufferers report to mental health services less often than those with other anxiety disorders seeking similar treatment (Kennedy & Schwab, 1997; Roy-Byrne, 1996).

Rickels and Rynn (2001), two of the leading experts on GAD, make a compelling case that the disorder continues to be unduly biased, favoring those GAD sufferers who present with the benchmark "pathological worry" – a central psychic symptom. These individuals are referred to by Rickels as "psychologizers" and are overrepresented in clinical research studies. In contrast, the bulk of GAD sufferers are in actuality "somaticizers," presenting mostly in primary health care settings with a constellation of physical complaints, such as autonomic hyperarousal, muscle tension, hypervigilance, and other bodily preoccupations (Judd et al., 1998). In summary, if we look across a number of variables, GAD is prevalent and well represented in medical clinics with significant frequency in the general population. Now we turn to the clinical presentation of GAD, which manifests itself in unique ways, depending on many factors.

Clinical Presentation

GAD has a complex clinical picture and is the most common presentation of all the anxiety disorders (Tyrer, 1999). According to Durham and Fisher (2007), subthreshold presentations of GAD are much more the norm than episodes of the disorder. In other words, many patients with GAD have a chronic condition that may not fully meet the diagnostic criteria, but can persist in this less severe form for years. The core features for meeting full diagnostic criteria of GAD, which have been alluded to before, consist of the following: (1) excessive worry and anxiety occurring more days than not for a period of 6 months, (2) impairment in social and occupational functioning, (3) difficulty in controlling the worry, and (4) frequency, intensity, and duration are out of proportion to the probability of the feared event (Schulz, Gotto, & Rapaport, 2005). The authors go on to use the pejorative term "worry warts" (Schulz et al., 2005) as a description of GAD patients' thought processes, but do acknowledge accurately that the worry and anxiety do often occur in light of no external triggers, and often without a persistent focus on anything. In addition, GAD sufferers viscerally experience their anxiety; they are impaired by it and their quality of life is compromised.

Many GAD patients complain of somatic symptoms (Schulz et al., 2005; see Table 1.3), even though paradoxically excessive cognitive activity in the form of uncontrollable worry has become the classic symptom of the illness. Other cognitive symptoms besides worry, poor concentration, indecisiveness, and perceptual distortions do occur with frequency, but fewer than 20% of patients will present with these types of psychological concerns (Ballenger et al., 2001). Somatic dominance can present in rather atypical presentations to medical providers, such as noncoronary chest discomfort and pain, irritable bowel syndrome, dizziness, nausea, and hyperventilation

Table 1.3 Common somatic symptoms of generalized anxiety disorder

Muscular
   Back and neck pain
Gastrointestinal
   Upset stomach
   Nausea
   Heartburn
   Belching
   Flatulence
   Diarrhea
   Dry mouth
   Abdominal pain
Cardiovascular
   Shortness of breath
   Tachycardia/Palpitations
   Chest pain
Other somatic symptoms
   Fatigability
   Perspiring
   Frequent urination
   Dizziness
   Tension headaches
   Tremor

© Primary Psychiatry. Schulz, J., Gotto, J.G., & Rapaport, M.H. (2005). The diagnosis and treatment of generalized anxiety disorder. Primary Psychiatry, 12 (11), 58–67. Reprinted with permission.

syndrome (Nutt et al., 2001). Additionally, the same authors conclude that the main organ systems affected by chronic anxiety are the cardiovascular, digestive, and respiratory ones, which reflect that physical symptoms are often dominant in nature.

Given the frequency of the somatic presentation in GAD, it is the most common disorder that presents to primary care physicians (Wittchen et al., 2002). It is associated with chronic physical conditions that reduce the chance that it will be diagnosed correctly. This ultimately will worsen the prognosis for the patient with GAD. According to Wittchen et al. (2001), who reinforce the above findings by arguing that GAD is the most frequent anxiety disorder seen in primary care (more than 50% of all anxiety disorders), and it is rarely diagnosed correctly (only 28% were accurately diagnosed as having GAD by their general practitioner). More often than not, a diagnosis of the disorder is made 5–10 years after the onset of symptoms (Rogers et al., 1999).

Generalized anxiety disorder has often been described as the "basic anxiety disorder" and as having gateway status to other anxiety disorders (Brown et al., 1994). Holmes and Newman (2006) describe the primary element of anxiety and diffuse uncontrollable worry, based on the research findings, as the defining features of the disorder.

Many GAD sufferers describe themselves as always nervous and on edge, with autonomic and motoric evidence of fear (Marten et al., 1993), and are often not able to remember a time when they did not feel this way. Patients with GAD worry about multiple domains, such as family, money, work, health, and a litany of other "realistic" concerns, such as perception by others, achievement, danger, and safety (Deffenbacher & Suinn, 1987). GAD sufferers view the world as a dangerous place, are prone to being hypervigilant, and use worry as a coping strategy to avoid these painful thoughts and feelings (Borkovec & Roemer, 1995). Chronic vigilance, scanning, and muscle tension are commonly experienced physiologically by GAD patients. "This suggests that GAD patients often fail to process evidence that the world offers them" (Holmes & Newman, 2006, p. 103). This failure to process

Table 1.4 Symptoms and behaviors associated with generalized anxiety disorder

Excessive physiologic arousal
Muscle tension
Irritability
Fatigue
Restlessness
Insomnia
Distorted cognitive processes
Poor concentration
Unrealistic assessment of problems
Worries
Poor coping strategies
Avoidance
Procrastination
Poor problem-solving skills

© American Family Physician. Gliatto, M.E. (2000). Generalized anxiety disorder. American Family Physician, 62 (7), 1591 –1600, 1602. Reprinted with permission.

evidence, meaning the facts of life, refers to their inability to see and experience the world in an objective manner. A summary of symptoms and behaviors associated with GAD have been collected and summarized in a compact chart by Gliatto (2000; see Table 1.4). Patients present with a wide range of symptoms and degrees of severity (Hoehn-Saric & McLeod, 1991).

The extent of the overall worry is not in proportion to what would be reasonable, or that is relative to the situation (Pollack, 2006). Dugas et al. (1998) suggest that patients with GAD tend to worry about highly unlikely or remote events more than other anxious individuals. They live in the future, not in the present moment, and do a great deal of "what if"? This is "generalized" to almost all aspects of their lives (Dugas & Robichaud, 2007). "For example, they may have nonspecific concerns about some existential and philosophical issues (such as the meaning and purpose of life and death) or state they are anxious about everything" (Starcevic, 2005, p. 104). In addition, GAD sufferers worry more about minor events, than both nonclinically anxious individuals and people with other anxiety disorders (Brown, Moras, Zinbarg, & Barlow, 1993; Hoyer, Becker, & Roth, 2001). Even though they may worry about everyday realistic concerns, Starcevic (2005) adds that we need to begin focusing on how GAD sufferers worry, not just what they worry about.

Onset, Course, and Prognosis

Even though the diagnostic criteria have tightened over the years, GAD has an insidious onset and a chronic unremitting and recurrent course, and prognosis is poor (Kessler et al., 2001). GAD does not just appear out of nowhere, but is slow and subtle, and stealthily builds a constellation of anxious symptoms (Anderson, Noyes, & Crowe, 1984). Onset may be as early as 13 years of age for GAD to be the primary disorder (but can start earlier), and occur as late as age 30, when presentation is secondary to other disorders (Rogers et al., 1999). Pollack (2006) has the onset for GAD in the late teens and early twenties, but it can date back to childhood. Onset can occur at any age. Mean age of onset is estimated at 21 years, and the average length of particular episodes has been estimated to be 20 years (Yonkers, Warshaw, Massion, & Keller, 1996). Given the propensity of GAD sufferers who first present to primary care physicians, it should come as little surprise that the average age they are referred to a mental health specialist is in middle age (Ballenger et al., 2001).

It has been suggested that the onset for GAD is bimodal in distribution – one occurring at an earlier point without a precipitating event and heightened exposure to domestic disturbances in childhood, contrasted by a later onset GAD, where there are more commonly precipitating adverse life experiences (Hoehn-Saric, Hazlett, & McLeod, 1993). Others have noted this early vs. late onset and argued that earlier onset GAD has a more chronic course. This has led some experts to speculate that it is a lifelong disorder (Rapee, 1991). Given this reality, just as in more character-based disorders, 80% of GAD cases fit this profile of having a gradual onset that lacks a precise starting point (Noyes et al., 1992; Sanderson & Barlow, 1990). This is in marked contrast to later onset cases of GAD that are the result of adverse life stressors and where the individuals have more robust person-alities (Hoehn-Saric, 2005). The two presentations have been highlighted elsewhere by other scholars in the field (Brown, 1997; Starcevic, 2005).

The course for GAD tends to be chronic (Fricchione, 2004), causing lifelong problems, yet symptom severity does wax and wane around social and environmental stressors (Blazer et al., 1991). The mean duration is 6 years, but generally the course is a chronic one (Hoge et al., 2004). It is in most cases a lifelong condition if left untreated. However, GAD often lingers quietly, even after successful treatment (Noyes et al., 1992; Yonkers et al., 1996). There is still very little known about the long-term course of GAD (Grados et al., 2005). Nonetheless, treatment should be on the longer side in order to maximize resolution of symptoms, soften functional disa-bility, and lengthen the intervals between episodes of the illness (Keller, 2002).

Prognosis is complicated by comorbidity with anxiety, depressive and personality disorders, high symptom severity, higher levels of neuroticism, poor social adjustment, low SES, and being unemployed (Durham, 2007; Tyrer, 1999; Yonkers, Dyck, Warshaw, & Keller, 2000). Long-term remission rate is low for GAD, at 38% (Yonkers et al., 2000). In a 12-year follow-up, called the Nottingham Study (Tyrer, Seivewright, & Johnson, 2004), 59% of patients originally diagnosed with GAD (using *DSM-III* criteria) were symptomatic at follow-up. The Harvard–Brown Anxiety Research Program concluded that 60% of GAD patients had active GAD at 2-year follow-up, and at 5-year follow-up 66% had either GAD or GAD in partial remission (Yonkers et al., 1996). The conclusion was an obvious one – GAD is persistent. Kessler et al. (1994) found that two out of five seek treatment for their GAD, and rates of full and/or partial remission in the long term (5 years or more) are rather disappointing, at 38–41%. In the Epidemiologic Catchment Area Study (Yonkers et al., 2000), 40% had the diagnosis for 5 years, and among those who remitted, 27% relapsed within 3 years.

An ambitious study by Rubio and Lopez-Inbor (2006), in a 40-year follow-up, found an overall improvement of GAD with age. By age 50, 38% had recovered from GAD; while at age 60, 88% had a total recovery. In other words, GAD tended to start disappearing around age 50, but was replaced by somatization disorder (undifferentiated). Worse outcomes in this study were caused by the lack of regular treatment compliance, female gender, and onset before the age of 25 years.

In spite of the somewhat encouraging results of the last study, GAD is a severe illness with an early or later onset, a course that is often protracted, and with a prognosis that is, for the most part, on the poor side.

Comorbidity

Generalized anxiety disorder is highly comorbid with other mental disorders (Kessler et al., 2001). Pure GAD is a rare disorder and 90% of patients have another diagnosis (Nutt et al., 2001). In the National Comorbidity Study Replication, the rate of current comorbidity among individuals with GAD is 85%

(Kessler et al., 2005). This does not include the factoring in of a host of comorbid medical conditions, which frequently coexist with GAD. Approximately 80% of GAD cases, when referred to mental health professionals, have another co-occurring anxious personality disorder and other anxiety and depressive disorders (Maier et al., 2000). Comorbidity might be the highest in patients with GAD (Kessler et al., 1994; Noyes, 2001). Noyes also noted that comorbidity with other conditions brings with GAD greater symptom severity, increased interference with daily activities, more help-seeking behavior, increased use of medications, more laboratory tests, increased hospitalizations, increased conflict with others, and poorer outcomes for the condition.

In terms of the aggregation of GAD with specific comorbid disorders, Yonkers et al. (1996) reported that 52% of the GAD sample met criteria for panic disorder with and without agoraphobia, 32% were socially phobic, and 37% had major depressive disorder (MDD). Judd et al. (1998) found GAD plus MDD to be 62%, and with dysthymia 39%. Wittchen and Jacobi (2005) supported the relationship between GAD and MDD, finding that three out of five patients have both disturbances. Once again, Judd et al. (1998) found that depression is the most common comorbid disorder with GAD, numbering two out of three patients. The predominance of co-occurring GAD plus MDD has been challenged, as other research (Borkovec, Abel, & Newman, 1995; Brawman-Mintzer et al., 1993; Brown & Barlow, 1992) supports social anxiety disorder being the most comorbid disorder with GAD. Personality disorders are thought to coexist in close to 60% of patients with GAD (Grant et al., 2005; Zimmerman, Rothschild, & Chelminski, 2005). Comorbidity with GAD and a personality disorder is a major barrier to recovery (Tyrer et al., 2004; Yonkers et al., 2000). In an intriguing two-study investigation by Schut et al. (2001), the relationship between worry and compulsive checking was explored. It was found that compulsive checking in a subset of patients is more common in GAD. The authors also recommended that a more detailed measure of OCD could have proved useful in the studies, and targeting compulsive checking behavior in GAD may therefore lead to improved effectiveness in treatment protocols.

One note of importance and interest is that in most cases of comorbidity, GAD is often temporally primary to other disorders, especially mood disorders (meaning it is the disorder that starts first) (Kessler et al., 2001, 2004). Yet, in a prospective longitudinal cohort study out of New Zealand (Moffitt et al., 2007), a contrary finding was found in comorbid GAD–MDD – in 37% of cases anxiety either preceded or was concurrent with depression, whereas in 32% of cases depression preceded or was concurrent with anxiety. In other words, anxiety occurred first in about one third of all cases and depression occurred first in another one third of cases. This challenges the prevailing notion that GAD precedes depression and/or develops into depression. It also suggests that the GAD–MDD comorbidity rates may be more underestimated than first thought, creating an even greater mental health burden. In summary, GAD is a highly comorbid disorder that occurs in varying degrees with a wide range of different Axis I and Axis II diagnoses. Finally, it bears repeating that "regardless of comorbid conditions, prognosis in general for GAD is not good" (Holmes & Newman, 2006, p. 108).

Impact on Self, Others, and Society

There is significant impairment in broad social functioning in multiple life roles in patients with GAD (Hoge et al., 2004). The disorder interferes with their life activities and role functioning (Kessler et al., 2001). In addition, there is a substantial reduction in quality of life (Turk, Mennin, Fresco, & Heimberg, 2000), and the suffering is enduring and subjectively felt as disabling (Wittchen, 2002). The suffering can be misleading and minimized by both the sufferer and others, as GAD patients can often act, and still be highly impaired (Turk & Wolanin, 2006). It is still viewed by many as a mild disorder, in spite of it being associated with poor quality of life and subtleties in impairment for a subset of those with GAD (Dugas & Robichaud, 2007; Henning, Turk, Mennin, Fresco, & Heimberg, 2007). A study by Stein and Heimberg (2004) found that GAD is associated with decreased likelihood of satisfaction with family life, lack of a sense of overall well-being and in one's primary activity. Henning et al. (2007) concluded that severe dysfunction occurred across multiple areas, but in romantic relationships in particular (28.8% of the sample), there existed the greatest disability. Another intriguing finding is that there was greater impairment at work and social functioning than at home and with family responsibilities. Finally, satisfaction with the quality of life was decreased in nine different domains, including the following: self-esteem, goals and values, money, work, play, learning, creativity, friends, and relatives.

In relation to impaired social functioning, the rubric of work and vocational functioning has been a fertile area for research, and is a central area that comes to mind for exploration. There are similar findings with regard to work productivity (which is diminished), as well as other areas of interpersonal challenges (Wittchen, Carter, Pfister, Montgomery, & Kessler, 2000). The World Health Organization's Collaborative Study on Psychological Problems in General Health Care (Ormel et al., 1994) pooled data from 14 countries and found that 38% of those with GAD had a moderate–severe impairment in occupational role functioning. In addition, the study also concluded that 6.3 days per month were lost in the work place because of the disability from GAD. Given the intractability of the disorder, there is significant vocational impairment as measured by the following: decreased rates of employment, decreased coping, decreased productivity, increased missing of work, and increased likelihood of receiving public assistance (Wittchen et al., 2000). "The anxiety associated with GAD is debilitating, causing many with the disorder to be unable to go to work" (Holmes & Newman, 2006, p. 131).

In relation to health costs and the larger societal effects and burdens, GAD is at least as impairing as other chronic mental illnesses, such as depression (Wittchen et al., 2002). There is a high degree of professional health seeking, high use of medications, and increased preoccupation with one's health (Hoehn-Saric, 2005). GAD sufferers tend to view themselves as being in poor health (Katon et al., 1990). Patients with GAD have been found to be frequent utilizers of primary medical care resources to the point of overutilization of these services, rather than seeking out mental health specialists (Maier et al., 2000; Roy-Bryne & Katon, 1997). In addition, the cost to society in terms of use of excessive health care has profound effects

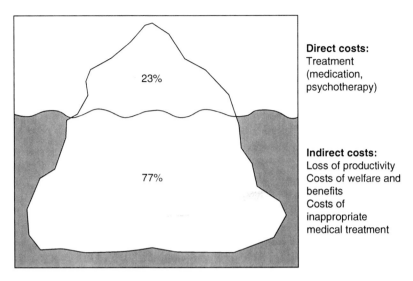

Fig. 1.1 Costs of generalized anxiety disorder: the iceberg
© Martin Dunitz/Informa Healthcare. Nutt, D., Argyropoulous, S.V. & Forshall, S. (2001). Generalized anxiety disorder: diagnosis, treatment and its relationship to other anxiety disorders (3rd ed.), England: Martin Duntiz, Informa Healthcare. Reprinted with permission.

(Nutt et al., 2001, see Fig. 1.1). The impairment secondary to the condition, rather than the actual treatment costs, better accounts for the social burden. In other words, greater utilization of general medical services (Ballenger et al., 2001) rather than high treatment costs is the consistent pattern found in the literature. Finally, Greenberg et al. (1999) felt that work productivity, instead of absence from work, is a better assessment of the financial costs resulting from GAD. Needless to say, work productivity is decreased and less efficient in terms of both quality and quantity of input and output of those who suffer from GAD.

As mentioned earlier, one of the cardinal symptoms of GAD is excessive worry. One of the particularly sensitive and preoccupying worry domains is being overly concerned about the welfare and health of significant others. Yet, with all this worry about family and marital life, "there is evidence that such marital problems are somewhat specific to GAD reactive to other anxiety disorders" (Holmes & Newman, 2006, p. 131). Spouses with GAD reported more conflictual marriages than spouses with agoraphobia (Friedman, 1990). Wives with GAD revealed being more dissatisfied with their marriages than those without GAD and other anxiety disorders (McLeod, 1994). In a sample of 4,933 married couples, marital discord was independently and strongly associated with GAD, more so than MDD, mania, dysthymia, social phobia, simple phobia, panic disorder, and alcohol dependence (Whisman, Sheldon, & Guering, 2000). In terms of family life, GAD adversely affected overall family relationships (Holmes & Newman, 2006). In one study, Ben-Noun (1998) found that when parents had GAD, there were increased rates of dysfunctional relationships with their spouses and children. Pollack (2006) concluded that the disorder causes significant interference with family functioning. In addition, having GAD was a predictor of increased odds of becoming separated or divorced (Hunt et al., 2002).

The most frequent worry, according to some researchers, relates to interpersonal challenges (Breitholtz, Johansson, & Ost, 1999), which translates into problematic relationships and the maintenance of these types of worries and behaviors. The level of social disability associated with GAD is comparable to that seen in people with chronic somatic disease (Kessler et al., 2001). GAD is a strong predictor of a lack, and in some cases an absence, of close relationships (Sanderson, Wetzler, Beck, & Betz, 1994). Pincus and Borkovec (1994) found increased interpersonal distress and rigidity in different situations. Not only does GAD adversely affect family and marital life, but it also impacts peer relationships. Some reviews have revealed that those who suffer from GAD have restricted expression, affect and empathy, and avoid displaying emotional vulnerability (Newman, 2000a; Newman, Castonguay, Borkovec, & Molnar, 2004). "Such restriction in affective involvement suggests the potential usefulness of psychotherapies that increase access to pleasurable experiences and assist in emotional processing in general and interpersonal contexts in particular" (Steketee, Van Noppen, Cohen, & Clary, 1998, p. 134).

Overall, many spheres of a person's life are negatively affected – not only do individuals with GAD suffer, but family, friends, and others are infected, so to speak, and nonadaptively influenced as well (McLellarn & Rosenzweig, 2004). In a recent review of the literature (Hoffman, Dukes, & Wittchen, 2008), the authors made a compelling and humane case that, given GAD's considerable human and economic costs, quality of care initiatives implemented to increase awareness and improve treatments for those suffering with MDD should be expanded to better treat those with GAD. This requires, according to leading figures, in this area (Wittchen et al., 2002), early recognition before substantial complications begin, appropriate combinations of acute and long-term management strategies to stem the tide of suffering caused by GAD and comorbid disorders, and reduction of the accompanying disability as a major source of relapse. Doing so softens the burden of GAD on the individual and society.

Conclusion

Diverse topics have been covered in this chapter. The attempt has been made, in large part, to dispel any remaining doubts the clinician may have about the severity and complexity of GAD as an independent disorder with serious individual and societal impact. Millions of individuals are afflicted with this condition worldwide. Even though we mainly looked at demographics in America, challenges of comorbidity, impairment, and decreased quality of life, to name just a few, invariably translate into poor prognosticators for GAD and are far reaching. By having given the reader some historical background, it should become clearer that the disorder has come a great distance in being better understood and legitimized in academic and clinical circles. Yet, it does remain a difficult condition to treat for the many reasons outlined in this chapter. At this point, the reader should now be better acquainted with the basics of GAD, as we move into the more delicate and difficult area of assessing and diagnosing GAD. In turn, with precise identification of GAD, this can help maximize the prospects of enhanced efficacy from both a psychosocial (Chap. 4) and pharmacotherapeutic perspective (Chap. 5). However, before outlining the burgeoning approaches to treat GAD, assessment and diagnostic issues are taken up next.

Chapter 2
Diagnosis and Assessment

There is little debate about at least one topic – GAD is one of the most difficult disorders to assess and diagnose with any significant consistency (Holmes & Newman, 2006). The reasons for this barrier in establishing a clear and precise diagnosis are the following: (1) complexities in the interpretation of *DSM* criteria, (2) symptoms overlap with other disorders, (3) questions regarding diagnostic threshold, and (4) patient variability in reporting symptoms (Brown, Di Nardo, Lehman and Campbell 2001). Turk and Wolanin (2006) echo the above conviction, by arguing that assessment and diagnosis of GAD have been impeded by the consistent evolution of the diagnostic criteria with each revision of the *Diagnostic and Statistical Manual of Mental Disorders* (DSM), hampering development of theoretical models and retarding development of instruments consistent with these models. Of all the anxiety disorders, GAD is one of the least reliably diagnosed (Di Nardo, 1993). Owing to these challenges, some researchers have recommended the use of two independent structured interviews in order to obtain an accurate diagnosis (Borkovec & Newman, 1998; Borkovec & Whisman, 1996). Given these constraints, Holmes and Newman (2006, p. 109) write, "Clearly there are subtleties in the diagnostic criteria and symptom picture of GAD that need to be taken into consideration during assessment." Tyrer and Baldwin (2006) feel that anxiety has easily detectable symptoms; the inherent difficulty lies in the interpretation.

There is no disputing the fact that anxiety, and more particularly GAD (at least on the surface), can be perceived as a shared and intrinsic human response that can universally be experienced during times of stress as a threat or challenge (McLellarn & Rosenzweig, 2004). Therefore, assessment and diagnosis of GAD needs to focus on the magnitude (intensity, pervasiveness, and persistence) of the worry and anxiety reported. In a previous discussion, complications can arise in locating the often blurred boundaries between normal and pathological worry and anxiety with other diagnoses (Barlow, 1988, 2002), and the symptom overlap between GAD and depressive disorders (Brown, Marten, & Barlow, 1995; Holmes & Newman, 2006). In the end, making the delicate, yet painstaking diagnosis favoring GAD over other disorders is often left to the discretion of the treating clinician (Hoehn-Saric, Borkovec, & Nemiah, 1995; Lipschitz, 1988). What makes these diagnostic quagmires easier to navigate is a solid understanding of the most recent criteria for the

M.E. Portman, *Generalized Anxiety Disorder Across the Lifespan*,
DOI: 10.1007/978-0-387-89243-6_2, © Springer Science+Business Media, LLC 2009

...order (to be taken up next), and reliable and valid assessment instruments in the hands of a skilled clinician.

DSM-IV-TR: Diagnostic Criteria for Generalized Anxiety Disorder

What is generalized anxiety disorder (GAD) from a diagnostic point of view? In the *DSM-IV-TR* (American Psychiatric Association [APA], 2000; see Table 2.1) there are highly defined criteria that can assist the clinician in answering this question, making the step to diagnosing GAD that much easier. Without a thorough knowledge of these criteria, the assessment of the diagnosis is doomed to fail. That is what belies the rationale for placing the diagnostic criteria for GAD in this publication first, before spending an extended period of time focused on assessment.

Table 2.1 *DSM-IV-TR* diagnostic criteria for generalized anxiety disorder

A	Excessive anxiety and worry (apprehensive expectation), occurring more days than not for at least 6 months, about a number of events or activities (such as work or school performance).
B	The person finds it difficult to control the worry.
C	The anxiety and worry are associated with three (or more) of the following six symptoms (with at least some symptoms present for more days than not for the past 6 months). *Note:* Only one item is required in children.
	(1) Restlessness or feeling keyed up or on edge
	(2) Being easily fatigued
	(3) Difficulty concentrating or mind going blank
	(4) Irritability
	(5) Muscle tension
	(6) Sleep disturbance (difficulty falling or staying asleep, or restless unsatisfying sleep)
D	The focus of the anxiety and worry is not confined to features or an Axis I disorder; e.g., the anxiety or worry is not about having a panic attack (as in panic disorder), being embarrassed in public (as in social phobia), being contaminated (as in obsessive–compulsive disorder), being away from home or close relatives (as in separation anxiety disorder), gaining weight (as in anorexia nervosa), having multiple physical complaints (as in somatization disorder), or having a serious illness (as in hypochondriasis), and the anxiety and worry do not occur exclusively during posttraumatic stress disorder.
E	The anxiety, worry, or physical symptoms cause clinically significant distress or impairment in social, occupational or other important areas of functioning.
F	The disturbance is not due to the direct physiological effects of a substance (e.g., a drug of abuse, a medication) or a general medical condition (e.g., hyperthyroidism) and does not occur exclusively during a mood disorder, a psychotic disorder, or a pervasive developmental disorder.

At the heart of GAD is excessive anxiety and worry ("apprehensive expecta-tion"), lasting for at least 6 months, occurring more days than not, about a number of events and activities (e.g., work, school, performance). In addition, three of six symptoms need to be present (restlessness, easily fatigued, poor concentration, muscle tension, and sleep disturbance) to make the diagnosis. The disorder causes significant distress or impairment in functioning. Worry or anxious apprehension is not the result of another disorder or related to any organic cause.

From the above criteria listed, Dugas and Robichaud (2007) argue that GAD is more streamlined and independent as a disorder. In addition, the term "unrealistic" was dropped and replaced with "difficult to control" worry. Worry themes are not unusual or odd in and of themselves (Starcevic, 2005). It now becomes a quantitative difference in worry frequency and intensity, focusing on why (matter of degree), how (Starcevic, 2005), and not the content per se of the worries. The somatic criteria were also decreased, and there is less focus on symptoms deriving from the autonomic nervous system. The coined term "the walking wounded" (Dugas & Robichaud, 2007), not the "worried well," seems to be a more apt description of what is going on with these patients phenomenologically. In other words, these authors feel that worry is a universal experience that GAD sufferers endure "silently" (this clinician's emphasis) to a greater degree than non-GAD individuals.

In regard to teasing out GAD from other diagnoses, it becomes imperative to differentially rule out GAD from other potential candidates. GAD can commonly be mistaken for hypochondriasis, social anxiety disorder, obsessive–compulsive disorder, posttraumatic stress disorder, major depressive disorder, dysthymic disorder, panic disorder, personality disorders, and other psychiatric and medical conditions. Three excellent references (Dugas & Robichaud, 2007; Nutt et al., 2001; Rygh & Sanderson, 2004) do a comprehensive job of helping the clinician make the appro-priate differential diagnosis of GAD from comorbid diagnoses.

Suffice it to say, for our purposes, GAD can be discriminated from the diagnoses mentioned above, based on a few key, but important, differences. These conclusions are drawn from varied sources and through clinical experience with these patients. Regarding GAD vs. hypochondriasis, the health worry in GAD is one of a number of different worry domains, and involves less likelihood of focusing on minor physical symptoms, whereas in health anxiety, it is the main preoccupying concern of having a serious disease that is central to the diagnosis. Little to no reassurance can assuage someone suffering from hypochondriasis. In the case of GAD vs. social anxiety disorder, both disorders can cause the sufferer to worry about the perception of others. However, in GAD there is considerably less overt behavioral avoidance, compared with social anxiety disorder. With social anxiety, the antici-pation of being judged or having to face the public and perform in front of others is much more terrifying than with those who have GAD. When comparing GAD and obsessive–compulsive disorder, we find that in GAD the worries are ego syntonic (congruent with reality/about real-life happenings), whereas in obsessive–compulsive disorder the obsessions are ego dystonic (incongruent with real life to the point of being odd or horrific). In addition, combined with the obsessions in obsessive–compulsive disorder, there are often compulsions (rituals to reduce anxiety) that are less common in GAD, even though compulsive checking can accompany GAD (Schut et al., 2001). Nutt et al. (2001) go so far to say that GAD can be viewed as a cognitive variant of obsessional checking. This is an intriguing conceptualization worthy of further exploration and research. In the case of GAD and panic disorder, GAD symptoms of worry are more persistent around life circumstances, whereas panic symptoms of "heightened anxiety" tend to be discrete or acute episodes, and comprise greater autonomic hyperactivity concerning fear of misperceived and catastrophic physical sensations. Posttraumatic stress disorder's main symptom is the experiencing or reliving of a past major trauma or stressor. Even though GAD sufferers often report having experienced several traumas in their lives, they are not as self-absorbed with the trauma or fearful of talking about it with the clinician, than those having PTSD. Most PTSD patients avoid facing the trauma or abuse, and a sequelae of symptoms flare up when encouraged to discuss and process the event(s).

Another area of contention diagnostically, is whether GAD is more akin to a personality disorder, rather than an Axis I symptom-based disturbance. Akiskal (1998) feels that GAD has a prominent anxious temperament component, similar to a personality disorder. It is not inaccurate to point out that the traits of GAD can be highly inflexible and pervasive across a wide range of situations. Shapiro (1965, 1989) has called this a "neurotic style." The ICD-10 (World Health Organization, 2007) (the European equivalent of the *DSM*) does refer to an "anxious personality disorder" which has never gained a strong foothold in the *DSM* classification system, in spite of some discussions about the conceptualization. In viewing GAD this way, one could make a claim that all aspects of the personality and character seem to be adversely affected by the disorder and may prove to be responsive to process oriented treatment (Kernberg, personal communication, 2007; Portman, 1995). Blashfield et al. (1994) claim that GAD is associated with severe character pathology, such as mistrust, suspicion, hostility, irritability, and obsessive–compulsive personality disorder.

Yet, accumulating evidence does not seem to support GAD as a personality disorder, given research bearing on comorbidity rates and the fact that pure GAD is as impairing as other anxiety and depressive disturbances (Kessler, Walters, & Wittchen, 2004). Together, this data and other empirical support beyond the scope of the present publication appear to confirm GAD's status (despite the critics) as an independent Axis I diagnosis (Brawman-Mintzer, 2001; Kessler et al., 2004). This does not preclude the fact that GAD is responsive to effective treatments, aside from standardized CBT, that target personality correlates and broader indices of functioning, which will be discussed in a later chapter.

Given that the most frequently comorbid and difficult differential diagnosis takes place with GAD and mood disorders, it is essential to have a good command of their commonalities and differences. What they have in common is an overlap in somatic symptoms (sleep disturbance, lack of concentration, and fatigue). However, worries in GAD are about potentially threatening future events happening (sometimes consisting of negative events about the past), while in depression, ruminations tend to focus on the failings of the past. In addition, self-esteem in GAD is selectively low, and in depression the erosions of the self are on a more global scale (Beck, Emery & Greenberg, 1985). Muscle tension is more unique to GAD, whereas anhedonia (loss of pleasure in things and persistent feelings of sadness) predominates in depression. Yet, dysphoric mood can also accompany GAD when the chronicity and magnitude of the illness are more pronounced. McHugh and Slavney (1998) refer to this as "dysphoric anxiety." In major depressive disorder, the mood disturbance lasts at least 2 weeks, whereas with dysthymic disorder (a less severe, though more chronic form of depression), the duration persists for a period of at least 2 years. GAD symptoms have to be present for at least 6 months to make a diagnosis. In many cases, GAD is often temporally first to mood disorders in order of occurrence. When they do co-occur, the outcome is much greater symptom and functional severity. One other difference regarding GAD is that life event exposure to danger is a predisposing risk factor, contrasted by depressive illness, where events are more inclined to be related to loss. In both cases of GAD and depression, the disorders share a course that is generally chronic, highly destabilizing, and severe in nature. Depression is often perceived by the public as more debilitating, while the worry and anxiety in GAD tends to be viewed as more "normal" and common. Either way, GAD and depression are inherently challenging conditions for the sufferer and clinician, in spite of public perception.

Assessment

Many different assessment tools have been used for the purpose of assessing the presence of GAD, which can include a clinical interview/evaluation, structured interviews, and self-report measures and inventories. However, in many clinical settings, such as private practices, agencies, and clinics, clinicians rely almost exclusively on one-to-one sessions to (1) assess for the diagnosis, and (2) determine patient's posttreatment outcomes (Rygh & Sanderson, 2004). Unfortunately, GAD is too difficult a condition to diagnose accurately without using formalized assessment measures, such as structured and unstructured instruments (Antony, Orsillo, & Roemer, 2001; Brown, O'Leary, & Barlow, 2001; Davey & Wells, 2006).

> Belzer and Schneier (2006, p. 26) bring the point home by stating that "given its prevalence and associated impairment, the significant burden imposed on health care resources, accurate assessment of GAD and its severity by mental health and primary care clinicians is an increasingly important goal. Reliable diagnosis and assessment of disorder severity can guide the nature, frequency and duration of therapeutic interventions. Moreover, accurate assessment of initial disorder severity provides a benchmark from which ongoing evaluation of treatment effectiveness can proceed".

One of the initial standard practices in assessing GAD and other psychiatric disorders is to rule out any medical comorbidity from the start (Fricchione, 2004). This is especially true when the medical conditions are associated with anxiety, and can often include cardiac, pulmonary, neurologic, endocrine illnesses, and even hypothyroidism (Goldberg & Posner, 2000).

In addition, substance abuse should be excluded, as cocaine, other stimulants, caffeine, drug withdrawal, (alcohol, opiates, benzodiazepines), over-the-counter and prescribed medications can mimic anxiety symptoms (Pollack, Smoller, & Lee, 1998). Rosenbaum, Pollack, Otto, and Bernstein (1997) argue that medical illnesses, accompanied by anxiety, often have an onset after 35 years of age, no personal/ family history, no current increase in stress, little or no avoidance of anxiety-provoking situations, and poorer response to anxiolytics. In the case of GAD, teasing the disorder out from a medical condition requires that a history and complete physical examination be performed. In a previous discussion, some detail was devoted to discussing the challenges of establishing a differential diagnosis when the potential exists for there to be the co-occurrence of other psychiatric disorders. These should also be definitively ruled out, if there is no support for their presence. Assessment for suicide risk should be screened in suspected cases of GAD, given the strong association with depression (Olfson, Weissman, Leon, Sheehan, & Farber, 1996).

Even though PCPs and other medical specialists must take the lead in attempting to rule out GAD from other possible medical conditions, coordinated care between physicians and nonmedical mental health clinicians plays a vital role in exchanging collateral information and forming a collaborative multidisciplinary relationship. Generally, the more professionals involved in the care of a patient with GAD, the better, as this can assist in facilitating a smoother assessment process for such a complex and challenging diagnosis. However, one of the problems with this idealized picture is that GAD is not well recognized in the primary care setting (Hoge, Oppenheimer, & Simon, 2004). In a German survey of 20,000 primary care patients, PCPs recognized and diagnosed pure GAD 34% of the time, and 44% were either treated or referred to a nonspecialist (Wittchen et al., 2002). It seems to suggest that the seemingly vague nature of the symptoms and common somatic clinical presentations confound PCPs. This is troubling because of the reality that it is the most frequent anxiety disorder seen in primary care practice (Sherbourne, Wells, Meredith, Jackson, & Camp, 1996). Stein (2005), a world-class psychiatrist and expert on anxiety, argues that assessment of the disorder requires addressing both the acute and chronic psychic and somatic symptoms of tension and avoidance behaviors, such as worry. Some assessment tools to aid the PCP in better detecting GAD will be discussed in the near future.

For the mental health clinician there are also challenges in correctly assessing GAD. In spite of the hypothesis that mental health specialists (including psychiatrists) should be better equipped than their colleagues in primary care in assessing GAD, this is not always the case. Roemer and Medaglia (2001) discuss a host of targets that ideally need to be assessed for GAD. Many of these are missed, even by skilled clinicians. Some of these targets are more obvious, like worry and anxiety (both psychic and somatic), yet familiarity with associated features (tension, trouble sleeping, fatigue) and teasing out comorbid symptoms (social anxiety, panic, obsessive–compulsive, depressive) are often what create confusion. In addition, the occurrences, frequency, controllability, pervasiveness of worry, and maintenance factors associated with worry are also emphasized by the authors as important in the assessment process. Turk and Wolanin (2006) also make a case that assessing comorbid symptoms, degree of impairment, quality of life, and measures of change during treatment that are consistent with contemporary theoretical models is of critical value. Now we turn to the varied assessment instruments used to assess and diagnose GAD.

The Clinical Interview

The clinical interview may still have its place as a point of departure in the assessment of GAD. The verdict, as we shall see, does not seem to favor its use (especially as a sole means of assessment). Many clinicians feel that in the first few sessions, it is important to establish rapport and, in a more informal sense, attempt to elicit information from the patient. Loosely structured clinical interviews appear to be used with the greatest frequency by practitioners in private practice and various outpatient settings (Rygh & Sanderson, 2004).

One type of clinical interview, called the Life Context Interview, attempts to address GAD over the life span by assessing onset, circumstances, duration, course, life events associated with exacerbations, coping efforts, and previous treatments (Rygh & Sanderson, 2004). According to Durham and Fisher (2007), asking the right questions can help establish the right disorder, even when others coexist. They argue that the somatic symptoms of GAD are more straightforward, whereas the cognitive ones require more determination and probing to get to the root of GAD. Dugas and Rochibaud (2007), in their clinical protocol, spend two full sessions on information gathering related to each major worry topic. According to these experts in the field, the clinical interview should focus the assessment on the patient's worry in an attempt to establish a diagnosis, rather than concentrating on somatic symptoms. At a later point, GAD somatic symptoms (such as muscle tension), impairment and distress become areas of inquiry to learn more about the patient in order to gain a deeper diagnostic perspective.

This information gathering assessment enhances the clinician's confidence in diagnosing GAD, builds the therapeutic alliance, and gives a more complete picture of the patient. In spite of the advantages that an unstructured clinical interview may hold for some clinicians, and the fact that they are common in the settings described, they are too prone to error (bias of the clinician, lack of awareness of the patient presenting for treatment) (Garb, 1998). The biases of both clinician and patient may direct the interview, and vital information may be missed or deemphasized (Miller, 2003). The general consensus is that unstructured clinical interviews are not well suited for assessment and diagnosis purposes in the case of GAD (Turk & Wolanin, 2006).

Structured Interviews

There are several advantages to structured clinical interviews. The most advantageous reasons for their use in assessment are the following: (1) have established psychometric properties, (2) provide structure for a thorough assessment of diagnostic conditions – not left up to subjective judgment, (3) a few provide severity ratings – allow for more specific treatment planning and outcome measures, and (4) can be less flexible and labor intensive, but the positives outweigh the disadvantages (Miller, 2003; Miller, Dasher, Collins, Griffiths, & Brown, 2001; Turk & Wolanin, 2006).

The two most widely used structured interviews to assess GAD are The Anxiety Disorders Schedule for *DSM-IV* (ADIS-IV; Brown, Di Nardo, & Barlow, 1994) and The Structured Clinical Interview for *DSM-IV* (SCID-IV; First, Spitzer, Gibbons, & Williams, 1997). There is also the lifetime version of the first scale, called the Anxiety Disorders Interview Schedule for *DSM-IV* Lifetime Version (ADIS-IV-L; Di Nardo, Brown, & Barlow, 1994). In terms of the SCID-IV, there is also a newer version that conforms to *DSM-IV-TR* (APA, 2000), called the SCID-I/P (First, Spitzer, Gibbons, & Williams, 2001).

The ADIS-IV is the preferred choice of the two in assessing GAD. It assesses for onset, remission, temporal sequence, and existence of comorbid disorders (i.e., anxiety, depressive, substance abuse) and symptom intensity for associated/core features of GAD (even when the condition is subsyndromal) (Holmes & Newman, 2006). In other words, the ADIS-IV is a comprehensive diagnostic assessment tool for each anxiety disorder (Turk, Heimberg, & Mennin, 2004). The GAD section of the ADIS-IV (Brown et al., 1994) includes questions related to excessive and uncontrollable worry in multiple life domains (health, work, finances) and associated *DSM-IV* symptoms (like the full scale). Clinician severity rating (CSR) is based on a 0–8 scale. A rating of 4 or higher indicates a diagnosis of GAD. In cases of multiple diagnoses with ratings over 4, the highest clinician rating score is viewed as the primary diagnosis. Brown et al. (2001) found good interrater reliability for ratings of excessiveness of worry, uncontrollability of worry, and associated symptoms (e.g. muscle tension). Good interrater reliability was also found for the clinician severity rating for GAD ($r = 0.72$). They also found fair to good reliability for the current principle diagnosis ($k = 0.67$), current clinical diagnosis ($k = 0.65$), and fair interrater reliability for GAD as a past diagnosis ($k = 0.65$). In summary, the ADIS-IV is the gold standard for structured clinical assessment of GAD (Turk & Wolanin, 2006).

The SCID-IV is a common structured assessment tool for Axis I disorders. It is limited in scope in assessing *DSM-IV* criteria and may not be that reliable with regard to diagnosing GAD (Holmes & Newman, 2006). It does assess a broader range of disorders than the ADIS-IV; however, it does not provide dimensional severity ratings for either diagnoses or symptoms (Turk et al., 2004). Zanarini et al. (2000) found that $k = 0.63$ for a diagnosis of GAD and test–retest reliability is $k = 0.44$ for a diagnosis of GAD. It appears that, due to the low interrater reliability, more research is needed in this area.

Given the length of these two structured interviews, and due to copyright laws, they are not included in the appendix of selected assessments for GAD in this publication. However, the interested clinician can find out more about these instruments (based on their credentials and skill set) and avail themselves of detailed information via Oxford Press for the ADIS-IV, and the American Psychiatric Association for the SCID-IV. They can also be purchased at these publishing houses.

This clinician has a preference for using the ADIS-IV in the assessment and diagnosis of GAD. Yet, each clinician will need to decide for themselves which instrument speaks to them and best fits the needs of their patients. In the end, assessment for GAD is enhanced using structured clinical interviews.

Self-Report Measures

There are several reasons to use self-reports and inventories in the assessment of GAD, which include the advantages of brevity, ease of administration, and decreased demand on human resources (Belzer & Schneier, 2006). Many self-report measures exist, but few with the function of actually diagnosing GAD (Holmes & Newman, 2006). A summary of several of the more popular ones are listed below. The following self-report measures have proven the most accessible and helpful to this clinician.

Depression Anxiety Stress Scales (DASS; Lovibond & Lovibond, 1995)

The Depression Anxiety Stress Scales (DASS) is a 42-item, self-report instrument designed to measure the negative emotional states of depression, anxiety, and stress. Each of the three DASS scales contains 14 items, divided into subscales of 2–5 items with similar content. Subjects are asked to use 4-point severity and frequency scales to rate the extent that they have experienced depression, anxiety, or stress over the past week. The DASS has excellent reliability on all three scales (Depression = 0.91, Anxiety = 0.84, Stress = 0.90). In particular, what is pertinent for our purposes is that "the Stress scale as a whole comprises a coherent set of symptoms, which in appropriate circumstances, permit a sharper differentiation than the Anxiety scale, and a closer link with stressful life events" (not uncommon in GAD) (Lovibond & Lovibond, 1995, p. 34). The architects of this inventory also add that the Stress scale measures a syndrome distinct from depression and anxiety and quite similar to the *DSM-IV* diagnosis of GAD (see Appendix A).

Penn State Worry Questionnaire (PSWQ; Meyer, Miller, Metzger, & Borkovec, 1990)

The Penn State Worry Questionnaire (PSWQ) is a widely used measure, but is not meant to be diagnostic in nature. It is a 16-item trait measure of clinical worry. This self-report inventory assesses the typical tendency of an individual to worry, as well as the degree of excessiveness of worry. The respondents are asked to rate each item on a 5-point scale ranging from *not typical at all* to *very typical*. Scores range from 16 to 64, with higher scores reflecting greater worry. It has good internal consistency using a sample of patients diagnosed with GAD having a coefficient alpha = 0.86 (Brown, Antony, & Barlow, 1992). The PSWQ also has good test–retest reliability (r = 0.92) (Meyer et al., 1990). In all, this measurement has good psychometric properties and sensitivity to treatment change and is a good choice for research and clinical studies – assessing the intensity of pathological worry (Turk et al., 2004) (see Appendix A).

Generalized Anxiety Disorder Questionnaire (GADQ-IV; Newman et al., 2002)

The Generalized Anxiety Disorder Questionnaire (GADQ-IV) is a nine-item, Likert scale measured screening for GAD based on the *DSM-IV* diagnostic criteria. It has good psychometric properties, with specificity = 89%, sensitivity = 83%, and 2-week test–retest reliability = 92% (Newman et al., 2002). The GADQ-IV is a good initial screening device for GAD – to tease out those not meeting *DSM-IV* criteria and before a costlier structured interview is used for further assessment (Holmes & Newman, 2006). The scale measures excessiveness and uncontrollability of worry, and severity of related somatic symptoms. For scoring purposes, a cutoff score of 5.7 has been the standard in assessing whether individuals have GAD, rather than matching responses (Newman et al., 2002). Further research is needed to address its validity and sensitivity as a measure of treatment outcome (Turk et al., 2004) (see Appendix A).

Several self-report inventories measure quality of life or similar indices of well-being. Given that quality of life has been shown to be compromised in GAD patients, a measure of these indices can be helpful in the assessment process. The three most popular, Satisfaction with Life Scale (SWLS; Diener, Emmons, Larsen, & Griffin, 1985), Quality of Life, Enjoyment, and Satisfaction Questionnaire (Q-LES-Q; Endicott, Nee, Harrison, & Blumenthal, 1993), and the Quality of Life Inventory (QOLI; Frisch, 1994), can be incorporated in the assessment process. All of these scales have good psychometric properties, and both the SWLS (see Appendix A) and QOLI are this clinician's preference. The SWLS is not registered in the public domain and can be easily downloaded, making its use in assessment more user-friendly than the other instruments. Many favor the QOLI, given that it is the most comprehensive measure of overall quality of life, as the scale addresses 16 critical areas. Another scale that has received far less attention, called Scales of Well-Being (PWB; Ryff, 1989), has good reliability, theoretical ties to the positive psychology movement and well-being therapy; yet there is only preliminary evidence of validity for this measure and it can be somewhat cumbersome and time-consuming to complete.

Many other measures exist as well, and knowledge and use of these will, in large part, depend on the clinician's theoretical persuasion and penchant for a particular instrument that derives from that conceptual model. For example, The Meta-Cognitions Questionnaire (MCQ; Cartwright-Hatton & Wells, 1997) measures beliefs about worry and metacognitive processes, while The Anxious Thoughts Inventory (AnTI; Wells, 1994), distinguishes between type I and type II worries; both have their derivation in the metacognitive model, to be discussed in the next chapter. The same can be said for The Intolerance of Uncertainty Scale (IUS; Buhr & Dugas, 2002) that targets how an individual responds to uncertainty. This scale also stems from a particular conceptual model. Another measure related to a theoretical model is experiential avoidance that is common in GAD, which can be assessed using The Acceptance and Action Questionnaire (AAQ; Hayes et al., 2004).

Several other inventories are worthy of mention, which are the following: The Worry Domains Questionnaire (WDQ; Tallis, Eysenck, & Matthews, 1992) measures the content of worry; The Why Worry? (WW; Freeston, Rheaume, Letarte, Dugas, & Ladouceur, 1994) and revised Why Worry II Questionnaires (WW-II; Holowka, Dugas, Francis, & Laugesen, 2000) measure metaworry; and The Consequences of Worrying Scale (CWQ; Davey, Tallis, & Capuzzo, 1996) measures the consequences of worry.

One would think that the topic of assessment for GAD and related constructs would be an exhausted one at this point. However, some recent assessment instrumentation has been undergoing development in order to add precision in the identification of GAD. These tools may ultimately prove more useful to PCPs and medical specialists than to mental health professionals, who need quicker and more efficient ways to identify and treat patients with GAD who present in primary care settings.

Argyropoulous et al. (2007) have developed a specific 18-item self-rated instrument for the measurement of GAD, that is based on *DSM* criteria. The tool is called The Generalized Anxiety Disorder Inventory (GADI), and was tested on 197 outpatients and 522 clinical subjects in four studies. The scale comprises three factors – cognitive, somatic, and sleep symptoms. The GADI has measurement precision (akin to reliability) in all three factors, and convergent and divergent validity. It accurately distinguishes GAD patients from nonpatient controls. The scale was constructed because of the researchers' conclusions that current instruments have inherent limitations or do not conform to the current concept of the condition. They argue that the PSWQ, for example, does not measure GAD and conceptualizes the disorder as a personality trait (worry), rather than a fluctuating state. The GADQ-IV does not give a definite numeric score to assess severity, even though it is accurate in detecting and diagnosing GAD.

Notwithstanding these critiques, the GADI is still in its infancy. In spite of claims of being easy to complete, having good reliability, and being able to assess a general GAD factor, plus three other factors, it professes to track changes in GAD over time. It is not intended to replace the diagnostic interview, albeit the claim is made that it might be used for that purpose in the future (the authors are unclear whether this refers to the clinical interview or the more structured interviews). Clearly, more research is needed to obtain test–retest reliability and determine whether the term "precision" is in actuality the same as reliability. This scale, if better refined, may be equally useful to clinicians at some point, not just medical providers.

The Generalized Anxiety Disorder Severity Scale (GADSS; Shear, Belnap, Mazumdar, Houck, & Rollman, 2006) is a simple six-item interview assessment that evaluates the severity of each GAD DSM-IV symptom. It is intended for researchers and clinicians in primary care settings. The sample for the GADSS came from four primary care facilities, with patients having the diagnosis of GAD or panic that participated in a collaborative study. They were then evaluated at a 12-month follow-up. The inventory is an attempt to rate the severity of GAD over the telephone with patients who already have an established diagnosis. It purports to have high internal consistency and good validity and sensitivity to change. The scoring ranges, on a 5-point scale, from 0 (*none*) to 4 (*very severe*). For the sake of brevity and efficiency, in the primary care setting it may have some value, as it addresses a target worry list plus situations that are focuses of worry. Additionally, six items bearing on this identified worry are flushed out in detail. However, subjective self-reporting (especially over the phone) may create inherent biases and doubts about its generalizibility to the real world. The authors do address this last concern. Ironically, there are still no results for test–retest reliability, no replication to date of the findings, and an ongoing need for a GAD specific rating scale.

The final scale is the seven-item brief self-report anxiety scale called the GAD-7 (Spitzer, Kroenke, Williams, & Lowe, 2006). Of the three inventories just discussed, the GAD-7 appears to have the most reliability and validity. The scale has excellent internal consistency and good test–retest reliability. The goal of the GAD-7 is to identify possible cases of GAD and assess the severity of the disorder. Given the high prevalence rates of GAD in general medical practices, a quick clinical measure for GAD is an imperative. The scores for the inventory are 5 (*mild*), 10 (*moderate*), and 15 (*severe*). A cutoff point for GAD is 10 or above. The main strengths of the GAD-7 are its generalizibility to primary care, it being validated in a large sample, and the fact that it is brief and efficient in purpose. It may once again prove helpful in a busy clinical setting – medical and mental. Similar to any relatively new instrument, the GAD-7 must be used more extensively, with clinicians and patients providing increased feedback. The researchers also feel that it may need further evaluation to confirm probable diagnoses, given that the type of study was cross-sectional and it only focused on one diagnosis, namely GAD. I do not see the focus on one diagnosis as being a limitation. Further research to examine changes in severity of anxiety over time seems a more legitimate concern, and potential limitation of the instrument. Overall, this is a simple, but impressive self-report inventory for GAD.

Conclusion

In this chapter many different assessment tools were broached in depth to aid the clinician with the challenges in identifying and diagnosing GAD. Clinical interviews help build rapport and establish the therapeutic alliance, but structured interviews, in particular, and self-report inventories are significantly more effective in pinpointing the diagnosis and comorbid conditions. Even though I favor giving one structured interview (preferably the ADIS-IV) and several self-report inventories (DASS, PSWQ, GADQ-IV, SWL), which includes at least one that measures an index of quality of life; other practitioners may have different preferences.

However, one must be careful as a clinician – there is still an inherent danger that by choosing measures with poor psychometric properties and minimizing formalized assessment, ongoing treatment will be seriously compromised. Some will argue that, either way, the diagnostic criteria of the current *DSM-IV-TR* does not capture what happens in real life clinical settings with patients, or that these same patients being seen in actual practice are more severely ill than research subjects. However true these assertions may be, in part by using multiple measures that target not just worry and anxiety, but broader areas of functioning, this can enhance the prospects that a more heterogeneous patient population can be identified with greater accuracy. Finally, treatments can start to fulfill their promise to chronically anxious patients, guided by more clearly defined assessment strategies, with increased diagnostic precision and ideally clinical acumen to attempt the daunting task of maximizing clinical outcomes.

Conceptual models that form the theoretical underpinnings of treatment "protocols" (a term used loosely in this text), can now be broached with greater breadth and specificity to demonstrate how theory clearly impacts clinical practice. Next, we turn to these important conceptual contributions that have deepened our understanding of the pathogenesis of GAD, and continue to play a vital role in informing treatment choices.

Chapter 3
Conceptual Models

Chronic worry has been the focus of psychological theories of GAD. This excessive cognitive activity has been viewed by most theorists as not being accompanied by heightened physiological symptomatology emanating in the autonomic nervous system – hypervigilance, increased motor tension, or behavioral inhibition. According to Akiskal (1998), emotionality is a core feature of an anxious temperament, rather than the core feature of GAD. In other words, this anxious temperament is a personality trait that reflects episodes of GAD, where somatic arousal occurs with acute and chronic symptoms. Rickels and Rynn (2001) argue that there is the danger of conceptual oversimplification when GAD is predominantly viewed as a disorder of maladaptive processing that leads to worry. They make a case that somatic, not just cognitive, symptoms are both features of GAD, depending on the particular individual.

Theories of GAD need to account for the cognitive, biological maintaining factors plus proximal environmental stressors and developmental vulnerabilities (Goldberg & Goodyear, 2005). Erickson and Newman (2005) echo this point – when it comes to GAD diagnostic criteria, there are extra diagnostic problems that involve dysregulation of multiple cognitive, physiologic, and behavioral systems. This is congruent with conceptualizations of GAD that are part of various cognitive and behavioral theories. These theories explain the reciprocal interactions that take place between cognitive, affective, physiologic, and behavioral domains in these vicious maladaptive cycles. Covin, Ouimet, Seeds, & Dozois (2008) add that, due to inconsistencies in the diagnostic criteria over the years, conceptual models of GAD and their assessment and evaluation have lagged behind those of other anxiety disorders. However, the following conceptual models for GAD address many different features of the disorder, but do continue to primarily focus on worry, a cognitive/psychic symptom, as the cardinal target of this disorder.

Beck's Model

There are not enough words of gratitude that can be expressed to Dr. Aaron Beck for enhancing our understanding of the foundational cognitive processes underlying the anxiety disorders, which includes those regarding GAD. Clinical trials have

M.E. Portman, *Generalized Anxiety Disorder Across the Lifespan,*
DOI: 10.1007/978-0-387-89243-6_3, © Springer Science + Business Media, LLC 2009

taken place for close to three decades, dating from 1980 to the present, which have shaped standard therapies for GAD, and focused on the premise that pathological anxiety derives from the misperception of danger, resulting from distortions in the way information is perceived. This core idea is based on procedures and principles of cognitive therapy as applied to appraisal of threat (Beck, Emery & Greenberg, 1985). Beck, in his classic text, which is clearly one of the seminal tomes on anxiety, states that GAD sufferers view the world as a dangerous place, and in order to avoid possible danger or to plan ways to deal with the occurrence of danger, they feel that it is imperative to constantly scan the environment for cues of threat. The goal of this model in a practical sense is to identify these automatic thoughts and core beliefs about self/world/other ("the cognitive triad"), and confront maladaptive beliefs about worry. By challenging these beliefs, the GAD sufferer creates alternative interpretations and more logical analyses of worry probability via gathering of objective evidence tests of negative forecasts.

Rygh and Sanderson (2004) agree with this author that Beck is the most influential theorist on anxiety disorders. Beck states that "schemas," which are overactive in anxiety disorders such as GAD, underlie perceptions of danger. Perceptions of danger are filtered through these schemas, leading to cognitive distortions in thinking that require the Socratic method, which makes use of both cognitive interventions and behavioral experiments to confront distorted thinking and danger schema (Beck, Emery & Greenberg, 1985).

In Beck's work (Beck, Emery & Greenberg, 1985), there is a discussion of precipitating psychological factors, such as increased demands (greater expectations, increased responsibilities, overall increase in energy output). These factors involve an increased threat to core values and often deplete coping resources. Second, there is an interaction of precipitating factors with previous problems. According to Beck, in cases of GAD, the problems reported by the patient did not start with the precipitating events, but date back in time to earlier developmental periods. The precipitating stressors are only as potent as the specific vulnerabilities that strike the particular individual. The primary pathology is in the cognitive apparatus. Symptoms that result from the above are manifold and can affect the cognitive, affective, and behavioral systems. These include inability to relax, anxious affect, motoric mobilization, activation of the sympathetic nervous system or the parasympathetic nervous system, poor concentration, cognitive impairment, fear of losing control, fear of being rejected, and difficulties in communication. In chronic anxiety disorders, anticipatory anxiety seems to have been present most of their lives. Beck feels that in GAD, the origins of the current symptoms often precipitate reactivation of challenges that involved relationships with others (this is a precursor of some newer conceptual models on GAD), and are relevant to identity, mastery, autonomy, and health. There is also the fear of not being able to cope with the expectations imposed by self and others.

Beck does differentiate GAD from depression. In GAD, appraisals are more selective – anxious patients see some hope for the future, do not view personal shortcomings as irreversible, are tentative, anticipate possible danger to self (goals, objectives, ability to cope, health, survival) and others, have some avoidance, perceive only certain events going badly, often have energy, but are resistant to their wishes and there is the expectation of "future" failure. Depression has more global self-appraisals and pathology, and is largely about the perceived failures of the past.

Bear in mind that when Beck's views about the subject of anxiety and GAD came out, GAD was not viewed as an independent diagnostic anxiety disorder. This did not seem to pose a barrier to Beck, who saw beyond fixed diagnostic boundaries and was able to capture the core features of GAD in a precise and phenomenologically rich manner.

Other scholars influenced by Beck (Riskind, 2004; Riskind & Williams, 2005) have revisited his thinking, and confirmed the importance of these contributions that stress the centrality of cognitive processes as mediators of psychopathology and anxiety (GAD) for a whole new generation of clinicians and researchers. For example, maladaptive variants of cognitive structures, called "danger schemas," guide information processing and are biased in GAD (Riskind, 2004). Beck and his colleagues suggest that "worry" is an attempt to cope with this fear (Beck & Clark, 1997; Beck, Emery & Greenberg, 1985). Finally, for the purpose of Beck's model, individuals with GAD are likely to react to their initial appraisals of potential threat by engaging in increased cognitive avoidance (i.e. worry) and/or emotional avoidance (e.g., faulty emotional regulation strategies) at the expense of enhancing their attention to additional environmental information or veridical situational contingencies, indicating that the potential threat is in actuality benign or dissipating (Riskind & Williams, 2005).

Barlow's Emotion Theory

Barlow (1991, 2002) posits that generalized anxiety (anxious apprehension) and panic (or fear) are two distinct and independent broad-based phenomena present in all anxiety disorders to a greater or lesser degree. Barlow's emotion theory focuses on generalized anxiety as the major feature of all anxiety disorders. There is a synergy that takes place between a generalized biological vulnerability (genetic contribution) and a generalized psychological vulnerability (diminished sense of control) (Barlow, 2002). In addition, congruent with Barlow's contributions on the subject, early experiences, which have been shaped by uncontrollable or unpredictable events plus overprotective/intrusive/punitive parenting styles, lead to low perception of control, increased neurobiological activity, and a varied output of nondifferentiated somatic outputs. The children are impeded in their ability to assume personal control of events and subsequently develop an external locus of control (life is perceived as being determined by outside of oneself). This is the major psychological vulnerability factor that contributes to the formation of anxiety disorders. Anxious apprehension (negative affect) becomes the cognitive filter that is characterized by a state of hopelessness to control and a heightened arousal or readiness to counteract this state of loss of control. What this ultimately culminates in is a nonadaptive cycle, where there is limited perceived control, lack of predictability combined with hyperarousal. Coping may also include avoidance of cues, as well as "worrying," which serves as a strategy that reduces negative affect through misguided attempts to plan or solve problems. In turn, the later developmental period is influenced by the chronic effects of this early activation, and the pattern becomes a persistent one, leading to GAD in some cases.

Barlow (2002) adduces that the generalized psychological vulnerability (chronic cognitive biases) creates a neurotic temperament. As mentioned, the synergistic combination of a generalized biological factor, which forms the genetic influence, added to the generalized psychological one of early experiences and vulnerabilities, more than likely lead to GAD and the depressive syndromes.

Over the years Barlow has taken his earlier theoretical offerings and extended them into a unified treatment protocol for the emotional disorders (Allen, McHugh, & Barlow, 2008; Barlow, Allen, & Choate, 2004; Ehrenreich, Buzzella, & Barlow, 2007; Moses & Barlow, 2006). These include the anxiety and depressive disorders and others where emotional dysregulation (Campbell-Sills & Barlow, 2007; Ehrenreich, Fairholme, Buzzella, Ellard, & Barlow, 2007) plays a central role. The range of this contribution, in its more evolved form, by Barlow is still in its infancy, but based on recent research, it could change the way clinicians and researchers look at psychopathology and the emotional disorders. It may well move us beyond fixed diagnostic syndromes into at least serious discussions about dimensional ones (Brown & Barlow, 2005), and then approach them based on what they have in common etiologically. This etiological model, called the "tripartite model," and existing evidence for it have been reviewed elsewhere (Barlow, 1991, 2000, 2002; Suarez, Bennett, Goldstein, & Barlow, 2009), and more will be discussed about the practical implications of Barlow's theory and empirical support for the unified treatment protocol later in this publication. Needless to say, this is cutting-edge research with broad treatment implications for not just GAD, but well beyond this disorder.

Cognitive Avoidance Theory of Worry

At the heart of this theory lies the fact that the primary function of worry is a cognitive avoidance response to danger (Sibrava & Borkovec, 2006). Borkovec is the architect of this theory. The central cognition of GAD is, "the world is potentially dangerous and I may not be able to cope with whatever comes from the future, so I must anticipate all bad things that might happen so that I can avoid them or prepare for them" (Sibrava & Borkovec, 2006, p. 239).

Worry serves as a cognitive avoidance strategy in three ways: (1) worry suppresses anxious arousal, (2) worry functions as an attempt to prevent or prepare for future negative events, and (3) worry focuses on superficial events which distract from more pressing emotional concerns (Borkovec, Newman, Pincus, & Lytle, 2002). These deeper level concerns are predominantly interpersonal in nature, and anxious arousal associated with addressing these potentially painful unresolved challenges becomes an effective coping response (in the short run), further conditioned through a process of negative reinforcement (Borkovec, Ray, & Stober, 1998). It seems that one of the functions of worry by individuals who have GAD is to avoid uncomfortable emotions (Borkovec, Alcaine, & Behar, 2004). There is no actual present moment or imminent danger, and the threat is in the future (if at all) or in the mind of the sufferer – little behavioral avoidance exists, and worry becomes the "only" seemingly reasonable coping strategy (Borkovec & Newman, 1998). In other words, GAD patients live multiple emotional and psychophysiological lives up in their heads, even though most will not happen in reality (Sibrava & Borkovec, 2006).

Worry involves primarily verbal-linguistic thought, rather than imagery – when we worry we are doing self-talk, that is talking to ourselves (Borkovec & Inz, 1990; Borkovec, Robinson, Pruzinsky, & DePree, 1983). In addition, GAD patients report greater weighted negative thought that normalizes after psychotherapy (Freeston, Dugas, & Ladouceur, 1996).

One other interesting finding, which has been part of this theory and subject to debate, is that GAD sufferers have increased muscle tension at rest and in response to threat, but worry dampens many other somatic reactions (Hoehn-Saric & McLeod, 1988; Hoehn-Saric, McLeod, & Zimmerli, 1989; Sibrava & Borkovec, 2006). Marten et al. (1993) argue that autonomic symptoms are not reported by most GAD subjects, but this does not mean they are not present in this population (Rickels & Rynn, 2001). However, even with data that GAD sufferers do experience somatic symptoms, empirical evidence supports the fact that worry suppresses aversive stimuli and thereby reduces somatic activation (Borkovec, Lyonfields, Wiser, & Deihl, 1993; Castaneda & Segerstrom, 2004).

In a comprehensive review of this theory (Borkovec et al., 2004), it was concluded that worry is a negatively reinforced cognitive avoidance response. In the same article, Borkovec continued to summarize the already extant data that worry suppresses somatic activity (meaning that worry helps one avoid dealing with future events and allows one not to face emotionally charged topics). This, in turn, decreases emotional processing and increases anxious meanings. These topic-related GAD fears often center on past traumas (Roemer, Molina, Litz, & Borkovec, 1997), childhood relationships (Cassady, 1995; Zuellig, Newman, Alcaine, & Behar, 1999), and current interpersonal ones (Borkovec et al., 1983; Roemer, Molina, & Borkovec, 1997). This decrease in emotional processing and increase in anxious meanings is relevant to the other anxiety disorders, and can play a negative role in one's physical health. This culminates in an absence of a present-moment focus of attention. The message of this approach is that, in the short term, GAD patients can avoid and hide, but to function more effectively and meaningfully in the real world, they must ideally face their fears head on and either accept or master them.

Riskind's Model of Looming Vulnerability

The model of looming vulnerability is aimed to specifically pinpoint fear-provoking threat cognitions and cognitive styles that will be important in inducing anxiety and worry (Riskind, 2004). According to this model, a great deal of attention has focused on worry, affect, and avoidance in the research, but much less empirical attention has been directed to the cognitive underpinnings of the appraisals that drive the threat that inheres in GAD. In this model, anxiety is initiated and maintained by fear-provoking imagery and appraisals that signify threats are quickly escalating. This rapid intensifying of threat leads to nonadaptive attempts to neutralize this via strategies such as worry and experiential avoidance.

The "Looming Cognitive Style" (LCS) is a distinct danger schema that some individuals develop, which produces a unique risk for GAD and other anxiety disorders. It induces, in those individuals who are vulnerable, a proclivity to formulate mental representations of expectations that manifest threats as rapidly intensifying and involving risk (Riskind, Williams, Gessner, Chrosniak, & Cortina, 2000). It is a negative cognitive style. In GAD there are danger schemas and cognitive vulnerabilities. This model of looming vulnerability speculates that the tendency to worry and both cognitively and experientially avoid painful emotions, so characteristic of GAD (Freeston, Rheaume, Letarte, Dugas, & Ladouceur, 1994; Roemer & Orsillo, 2002), is located in the LCS. When GAD sufferers are threatened with greater degrees of intensification in their perceived threat level as predicted by this theory, they engage in overcompensatory self-protective responses, such as worry and avoidance (Riskind & Williams, 2005, 2006).

The LCS is both a cognitive antecedent and maintaining factor in GAD. In GAD, the LCS can be characterized by the following: (1) the generation of continuous streams of threatening catastrophic images, leading to worry and cognitive avoidance as protective strategies; (2) increases in animated fear-inducing mental scenarios, images, and expectations of being overtaken by rapidly intensifying risks and dangers – emotion regulation then becomes a challenge with faulty strategies to regulate it; (3) fostering of schematic processing bias for processing threatening materials in ambiguous ways with enhanced focus on such materials; and (4) the absorption, when activated, of attentional control resources cognitively vulnerable individuals need to cope when confronted with negative emotions (Riskind, 2004).

The looming vulnerability model (Riskind & Williams, 2005) extends the traditional cognitive model of anxiety (Beck, Emery & Greenberg, 1985). It focuses on dynamic danger content, rather than static forecasts of threat. In addition, the model suggests that individuals worry, experience anxiety and fear, and engage in self-protective strategies to the degree that they appraise danger as either impending or in the process of unfolding.

In regard to GAD, these individuals with such a cognitive vulnerability are likely to perceive the world as highly unpredictable and increasingly intensifying in danger, and to view the self as way underprepared to cope with threat (Riskind, Williams, & Joiner, 2006). With GAD, the sense of danger is fine tuned, and these individuals are both fearful and vigilant for threat. There is a chronic and extreme overactivation of danger-related schemas (Beck & Clark, 1997; Riskind, 2004; Riskind & Williams, 2005). Patients with GAD experience an ongoing stream of threatening automatic thoughts that serve as a catalyst for "worry triggers," leading to pathological worry. The LCS is related to worry (Riskind et al., 2000), interpersonal and attachment challenges (Williams & Riskind, 2004), and emotional dysregulation (Riskind &

Williams, 2005). Ultimately, mental control mechanisms are impaired, which are required to deal with upsetting thoughts and increasing hypervigilance for threat-related information, leading individuals to engage in faulty, catastrophic, looming mental stimulations of even relatively benign events and stimuli (Riskind & Williams, 2005). The LMS confers this type of vulnerability to GAD (Riskind, 2005).

In the end, pathological worry, interpersonal problems, and lack of emotional regulation often become nonadaptive self-protective measures to mitigate the looming threat of impending danger and doom. Riskind's model is a tremendously valuable conceptual contribution to understanding the theoretical underpinnings (especially the "cognitive style") of GAD, and has been neglected for far too long in the literature. The inclusion of the model in this chapter attempts to rectify the act of omission.

The Role of Intolerance of Uncertainty

The role of intolerance of uncertainty is a cognitive model developed in a preliminary test by Dugas, Gagnon, Ladouceur, and Freeston (1998) that comprises four components: intolerance of uncertainty, erroneous beliefs about worry, poor problem orientation, and cognitive avoidance. The results of this study found that all the main components of the conceptual model were related to the discriminant function and intolerance of uncertainty, which distinguished GAD patients from nonclinical subjects. Intolerance of uncertainty is the pivotal component and belief that directs the way individuals process information from their environment. The authors of this model further define this fundamental tenet as a "dispositional characteristic" that results from a set of negative beliefs about uncertainty and its consequences. In addition, intolerance of uncertainty is upsetting, stressful, causes dysfunction, and is viewed as being unfair by the GAD sufferer, not to be certain about the future (Dugas & Robichaud, 2007).

Empirical support for the model has been forthcoming in many different studies. Dugas, Marchand, and Ladouceur (2005) compared 17 patients with noncomorbid GAD vs. 28 patients with noncomorbid PDA (panic disorder with agoraphobia), and concluded that only intolerance of uncertainty showed evidence of diagnostic specificity (intolerance of uncertainty scores were higher in the GAD sample relative to the PDA sample). This study lends further support to the link between intolerance of uncertainty and GAD. In other research, Freeston et al. (1994) found intolerance of uncertainty to be highly related to worry (a central symptom of GAD). In comparing GAD vs. other anxiety disorders, intolerance of uncertainty was more highly related to GAD (Ladouceur et al., 1999). The greater severity of GAD, the more difficult it was found to be for individuals to tolerate intolerance of uncertainty (Dugas et al., 2007). Intolerance of uncertainty was more highly related to worry than to obsessions and panic symptoms (Dugas, Gosselin, & Ladouceur, 2001). A similar outcome implied that intolerance of uncertainty was more related to worry than to depression (Francis & Dugas, 2004). Dugas, Langlois, Rheaume, and Ladouceur (1998) found that changes in intolerance of uncertainty preceded changes in levels of worry for 11 of 16 patients, whereas changes in worry preceded change in intolerance of uncertainty for only 1 patient. Finally, Koerner and Dugas (2006), in summarizing much of the evidence, demonstrated a direct link between intolerance of uncertainty and worry. This also confirmed another finding, based on the research, that uncertainty and ambiguity are considerably more unpleasant for GAD sufferers than for those with other anxiety disorders (Dugas et al., 2005).

In terms of the other components of the model, data also support their validity. For example, GAD subjects reported stronger beliefs about worry than did nonclinical worriers (Ladouceur, Blais, Freeston, & Dugas, 1998). Dugas et al. (1998) found that GAD patients had more negative problem orientation. High levels of intolerance of uncertainty and negative problem orientation deeply impact, in an aversive way, GAD sufferers' ability to deal with (not necessarily solve) day to day problems (Dugas & Robichaud, 2007). Cognitive avoidance, which was confirmed in Borkovec's model presented earlier in this chapter, adds to the complexity of challenges facing those who struggle with GAD.

Overall, this conceptual model has extensive evidence to support its hypotheses. It is an important addition to the bastion of relatively newer theories that can account for the underlying dynamics behind GAD, namely, intolerance of uncertainty.

Metacognitive Model

The metacognitive model is the brainchild of Wells (1995a and 1995b, 1997). It is based on the distinction between two types of worries – type 1 (worries about everyday events and physical sensations) and type 2 (worry about worry – both positive and negative appraisals of worrisome activity) (Wells, 1999). GAD is associated, in particular, with type 2 worries. The main principle behind this model is that erroneous metacognitive beliefs about worry are a central cognitive factor in pathological worry (Wells, 2004; Wells & Carter, 2006). Normal worries (type 1) lead to GAD when type 2 worrying becomes activated in response to worry and its associated anxiety symptoms. In GAD, these negative metacognitive beliefs center on two main themes: (1) beliefs about the uncontrollability of worry, and (2) beliefs about the dangerous consequences of worrying for mental, physical, and/or social functioning. Empirical support for the model comes from multiple sources (Cartwright-Hatton & Wells, 1997; Wells, 2005, Wells & Carter, 2001; Wells & Papageorgiou, 1998).

An excellent introduction to the model can be found in Wells (2002). In this review, some additional themes behind the metacognitive model are delineated in depth. For instance, individuals with GAD make use of worry to cope with the threat of danger and its perceived uncontrollability. Positive metacognitive beliefs about the value of worry can become reinforced and lead to worry sequences ... "what if?" It is not until negative metacognitive beliefs about worry are activated that pathological worry turns into GAD. In addition, individuals' behavioral responses and thought control strategies are two other mechanisms that can further contribute to the maintenance of the problem. For example, behavioral avoidance, constant reassurance seeking, checking and not attending to the triggers that motivate worry may be ways GAD sufferers temporarily disrupt the worry sequence, which is not necessarily pathological unless overutilized (Wells, 1994, 2006a and 2006b). This does little in the long run to challenge appraisals of threat or adaptively decrease negative beliefs about worry (worry is uncontrollable, worry is dangerous) (Wells, 2005).

In a more recent offering by Wells (2007), he argues that standard CBT with its traditional schemas explains the negative content of thought, but does not account for the presence of worry. In other words, according to Wells, it is the fact that worry arises from positive and negative metacognitions that leads to a particular style of cognitive thinking ("metacognitive"). Positive metacognitions use worry as a coping mechanism, whereas negative ones, which are more intractable and can lead to GAD, are about the uncontrollability and pernicious effects of worry. Wells asserts that his model extends cognitive theory beyond pure CBT, in that there is a failure of CBT to modify negative beliefs about worry.

In closing, this is a sophisticated and abstract model with solid evidence behind it; however, its complexity is a mixed blessing. It requires an equally sophisticated and seasoned clinician and patient, who possess the capacity for abstraction to fully appreciate and make use of this model to expand their understanding of GAD.

Conclusion

In this chapter many different and unique conceptual models (more commonly referred to as "theories") were addressed to broaden the clinicians' understanding of GAD. All of the models presented were predominantly "cognitive" in nature, and many have extended their theoretical applications into more formalized evidence-based treatment approaches. However, as the next chapter will demonstrate, cognitive dominance in theory does not always translate into psychosocial treatments in practice that lead to the most robust outcomes for GAD sufferers. Therefore, in spite of the conceptual contributions discussed here (which are significant), challenging this hegemony of a monolithic single modality "one size fits all" treatment for GAD in the following chapter becomes an important corrective and redressing of the current imbalance.

With the help of many diverse thought leaders in the fields of psychotherapy, anxiety disorders, and GAD, the road can take more than one path in not only understanding, but treating patients with this disorder. Some of the psychosocial treatments that follow are outgrowths of the models previously discussed, while others open new vistas to widen our lenses, not with the goal of abandoning the tried and tested, but to expand the horizon for enduring change. The tried and tested have empirical value, not to be traded in on a whim for the untested (Beck, e-mail communication, 2007), and integration of approaches for their own sake with little clinical benefit has minimal value (Barlow, e-mail communication, 2007). Yet, having said that, we, as clinicians, can draw from the empirical research, our clinical experience and the preferences of patients to avail ourselves of what best enables those who suffer from GAD to reach their fullest potential.

Chapter 4
Psychosocial Treatments for Those with Generalized Anxiety Disorder

We live in a pluralistic world, and GAD is a heterogeneous disorder (Hoehn-Saric, 2005). Given these realities, GAD sufferers, not unlike others who are challenged by vulnerable and often debilitating conditions, present a need by researchers and the clinicians who take care of them, to accommodate treatments to the individual sufferer's clinical needs (Havens, 2004). In other words, the scope of therapy needs to be widened, whether it is cognitive in nature (Safran, 1998) or some other approach. A new publication by Hazlett-Stevens (2008) offers an excellent review and manual of various psychological approaches to GAD, and some of the most common stumbling blocks in the treatment of this population. Even though it is largely informed by CBT, it is a highly worthy addition to the literature for the clinician and advanced graduate student.

Messer (2002), a pioneer in the psychotherapy integration movement, has had a profound influence on this writer and the present publication. He writes one of the most insightful and humane statements regarding clinical practice. "In terms of clinical practice, the medical model in which empirically supported treatments are based says, 'Seek a therapist who uses techniques with demonstrated ability to alleviate your condition,' whereas the contextual model (common factors) advises, 'Seek an interpersonally competent therapist who uses a treatment approach you find compatible with your worldview.'" (Messer, 2004, p. 582). This does not preclude, in his estimation, using an evidence-based approach, but factors in to a greater degree the quality of the therapist–patient relationship.

The psychotherapy debate between those who favor evidence-based treatments, defined by randomly controlled trials (RCTs) (Chambless & Hollon, 1998; Sanderson & Rego, 2000), and those who are seemingly more in favor of factoring contextual variables into the equation (Bohart, 2000; Levant, 2004), has only served, according to some experts (Parloff, 1979), to create an internecine feud that has not taken the field in any significantly positive direction. Some have argued to the contrary (Messer, 2004), that the debate has brought many central issues of great consequence to the forefront about the true calling of the psychotherapeutic enterprise.

In the end, this is not an either or choice that clinicians need to make when it comes to the treatment of GAD, but one that can encompass the best of those that

M.E. Portman, *Generalized Anxiety Disorder Across the Lifespan*,
DOI: 10.1007/978-0-387-89243-6_4, © Springer Science+Business Media, LLC 2009

are evidence-based, and still selectively evaluate the merits of other approaches that are more research-informed (but fall short of the standards set by the evidence-based proponents). They can then be incorporated in a judicious manner. Norcross (2002) refers to these later approaches as empirically supported relationships (ESRs), focusing less on disorders per se, but rather on people and relationships. These approaches also tend to be more process-oriented and less amenable to manipulation in the laboratory and research clinic.

Having said all that, this publication does still favor an evidence-based approach to the treatment for GAD, as demonstrated in the particular choices of approaches up for examination. Yet, it does not look askance at certain contributions made that are the product of years of informed research and clinical experience. It would be akin to throwing the baby out with the bath water.

The psychosocial treatments that are broached in this chapter range from standard CBT to advances in emotion regulation and acceptance/mindfulness. Some have established themselves as already empirically effective for GAD; others have preliminary data awaiting further confirming evidence. The remainder clearly have heuristic appeal and efficacy without being manualized, or finding themselves in a position that can either endorse or support empirical replication of their findings.

Cognitive Behavioral Therapy

There is little debate that cognitive behavioral therapy (CBT) is an effective therapy for generalized anxiety disorder (GAD) (Durham, 2007). It has been the most extensively studied treatment for GAD (Borkovec, Newman, & Castonguay, 2003), and is still considered by many as the "first line" psychosocial treatment (Erickson & Newman, 2005). According to Durham and Fisher (2007), there have been more than 30 clinical trials (1/2 used *DSM* criteria) and CBT was the main focus. The dispute over CBT is more generally about its effectiveness, not the treatment itself. Research outcomes report that only 50% of patients with GAD demonstrated significant benefits in achieving symptom relief, comparable to those nondiagnosed individuals (Newman, 2000a, 2000b). Needless to say, based on this data, there is room for improvement and the need for augmentation of current cognitive behavioral therapeutic strategies.

In addition, there is not one CBT approach, but many that stress different components. CBT often includes multiple treatment components that target various symptom domains (Erickson & Newman, 2005). However, as a rule, the commonalities between them far outweigh the differences. For the sake of simplicity, CBT is a broad-based "coping skills" approach that challenges distortions in thinking and attempts, in the process, to improve the individual's ability to think more rationally and act in an increasingly adaptive manner. Needless to say, as we proceed, the specifics of a few well-known CBT treatments will be spelled out in greater detail. Yet, at the heart of CBT is the fundamental belief that cognitive processes mediate either functional or nonfunctional patterns of thinking, behaving, and feeling that underlie psychiatric conditions.

Historically, the first clinical trials to assess the effectiveness of CBT in the treatment of GAD began with non *DSM*-defined "general anxiety" (Newman & Borkovec, 2002, p. 167). These early studies (Barlow et al., 1984; Barlow, Rapee, & Brown, 1992; Blowers, Cobb, & Matthews, 1987; Butler, Cullington, Hibbert, Klimes, & Gelder, 1987; Lindsay, McLaughlin, Hood, Espie, & Gamsu, 1987), that combined anxiety management packages, including some mixture of cognitive therapy (CT), behavior therapy (BT), cognitive–behavioral therapy, and relaxation therapy (RT), demonstrated greater improvements vs. nondirective ones and a wait-list control. There was a failure to show differential efficacy among the various treatments, except in two studies where Borkovec et al. (1987) and Butler, Fennell, Robson, & Gelder (1991) showed that the inclusion of a cognitive component produced even more superior results. They also concluded that CBT was superior to BT and a wait-list control on measures of cognition, mood, and anxiety. Harvey and Rapee (1995) confirmed that specific interventions, such as cognitive structuring and relaxation techniques, decreased GAD symptoms at a far greater rate than did nondirective treatments.

In some other earlier studies, Borkovec and Costello (1993) found greater gains in the short run and with longer term follow-up for CBT vs. nondirective and applied relaxation (AR). Chambless and Gillis (1993), in a seven-study meta-analysis, concluded that CBT produced more substantial reductions in anxiety than a wait list or placebo. Borkovec and Whisman (1996), in a study of 12 different CBT protocols, demonstrated that treatment led to clinically significant changes with sustained improvement for up to a year. They also concluded that, in using multicomponents of CBT, it produced the best long-term results (relaxation training addressed physical symptoms, and cognitive restructuring targeted cognitive features of GAD such as excessive worry). A contrary finding found no difference between AR and CT (Ost & Breitholtz, 2000). However, in this study, no control group was used. In a recent meta-analysis (Siev & Chambless, 2007), where the effects of CT and RT were examined, studying GAD vs. panic disorder, the findings supported the above research – namely, that for GAD, CT and RT were equivalent in efficacy. However, for panic disorder CT outperformed RT.

In looking at the evidence to further investigate the relative degree of effectiveness of CBT for GAD, Fisher and Durham (1999) reviewed six clinical trials during the time period 1990–1998, and found an overall recovery rate of 40%, whereas CBT plus AR led to a 50–60% recovery at a 6-month follow-up. Borkovec and Ruscio (2001) reviewed outcomes of 13 controlled clinical trials that included CBT, CT, BT, placebo, nonspecific treatment, and psychoeducation. CBT produced the most intermediate and long-term improvements in decreasing anxiety and depressive symptomatology in GAD sufferers vs. other treatments. In addition, CBT in particular, exhibited greater effects than either CT or BT alone. In a follow-up with a slight twist in the use of certain interventions, Borkovec, Newman, Pincus, and Lytle (2002) compared three therapy conditions: one condition using AR and stimulus control desensitization, the second condition using CT, and the third was a combination. The conclusion was that no more than 50% of all the patients in the three conditions achieved high end-state functioning. All three were equally effective treatments. This study did not seem to support the prior existing evidence that long term maintenance for GAD is best produced by a combined CBT approach that targets multiple domains. Yet, a more promising outcome did occur in this research – CBT yielded strong durable treatment effects at a two year follow-up. On the flip side, absence of treatment for GAD shows little change – spontaneous remission rates are 25% (Ballenger et al., 2001).

In an 8- to 14-year follow-up of two clinical trials (Durham, Chambers, MacDonald, Power, & Major, 2003), 50% had an initial response to CBT, 33% had some improvement, and the rest suffered from recurrent anxiety and disability. The 30–40% that fared poorly had the most complex symptom presentation. The conclusion from these studies were that treatment gains following CBT proved to be less enduring than was assumed. From the findings, it also was discovered that some do well in the short run, but relapse under stress; for others the course is a chronic one. Finally, in summary, the majority of GAD patients in both studies remained symptomatic at long-term follow-up.

In more recent research, Lang (2004) showed that CBT is effective using cognitive restructuring, relaxation, worry exposure, behavior modification, and problem-solving. Struzik, Vernani, Coonerty-Femiano, and Katzman (2004) demonstrated that CT and CBT showed the most promise in resolving and maintaining treatment gains in the long term. It is useful alone and in combination with pharmacotherapy. Linden, Zubraegel, Baer, Franke, and Schlattmann (2005), in a controlled clinical trial, tested CBT in a GAD sample based on *DSM-IV* criteria with 72 outpatients. Thirty-six patients were put in a CBT-A group and 36 patients in a contact control group (CCG). The control group were treated afterwards with CBT and called CBT-B group. Results found a 6.4% reduction in symptoms in the CCG group vs. a 35.4% reduction in the CBT-A group and a 47.3% reduction in the CBT-B group, as measured by the Hamilton Anxiety Observer Rating Scale (Hamilton, 1959). On the Spielberger State-Trait Anxiety Inventory (Spielberger, 1983), there was a reduction of 2.7% seen in CCG, 14.6% in CBT-A, and 11.6% in CBT-B. According to the Clinical Global Impression Rating (Guy, 1976), 65.6% were moderately ill at the end of CCG posttreatment, while the rate was 37.4% for CBT-A and 15.7% for CBT-B. Overall, CBT treatment exhibited statistically significant clinical improvement. The improvements remained enduring over an 8-month follow-up period.

Westen and Morrison (2001), in a much cited meta-analysis of RCTs (most were CBT) for panic disorder, GAD, and depression, confirmed that for GAD and depression, only 40% benefited. The findings also concluded that none of the CBT components evidenced long-term treatment gains from posttreatment to follow-up. Their conclusion was that treatment effects do not persist dramatically after treatment. They encouraged testing different treatments for the disorder. In a more recent meta-analytic review (Gould, Safren, Washington, & Otto, 2004), where 15 studies were evaluated, it was found that, on average, the combined packages of CBT did produce large effect sizes. In addition, combined treatments had a modest advantage over single component treatments. Two other meta-analyses (Covin, Ouimet, Seeds, & Dozois, 2008; Norton & Price, 2007) support the assertion, showing strong effect sizes of CBT for GAD. In the later meta-analysis, which focused on CBT for pathological worry, CBT was effective in the short and long run. Treatment gains were maintained for up to a year. Younger adults benefited to a greater degree than older adults. In spite of the effectiveness and tolerability of CBT for GAD, the outcomes are not robust (Gould et al., 2004; Rapee & Barlow, 1991).

In other words, CBT packages may reflect large effect sizes on average, yet the reality is that many patients do not return to a "well" status – that is a high end-state functioning determined by falling within normal limits on several outcome measures. One of these outcome measures is GAD severity (in spite of a sizeable population of sufferers no longer meeting the diagnostic criteria for the disorder after treatment). Roemer, a leading authority on CBT treatment for GAD writes, "In my opinion, the standard CBT model largely leads to efficacious treatments. The issue is solely that it hasn't been efficacious enough" (Roemer, e-mail communication, 2007).

In summary, researchers confirm the wide ranging findings supporting CBT as an effective and validated treatment for GAD. "However, it is important to reiterate that a large percentage (~30–50%) of those with GAD do not significantly benefit from the most effective treatments" (Rygh & Sanderson, 2004, p. 10). Investigations of the efficacy of CBT for GAD have also lagged well behind progress for CBT in the treatment of the other anxiety disorders (Brown, Barlow & Liebowitz, 1994; Gould et al., 2004; Norton, Asmundson, Cox, & Norman, 2000).

In terms of specific CBT treatments that reflect the best this approach has to offer, this clinician has a preference for these offerings (Brown, O'Leary, & Barlow, 2001; Dugas & Robichaud, 2007; Newman & Borkovec, 2002). They will be highlighted with greater specificity, especially the one espoused by Newman and Borkovec (2002), as the discussion progresses. There are also other effective CBT packages (Leahy, 2004; Rygh & Sanderson, 2004). Yet, in spite of their potential value and interest to the clinician, they do not add significant novelty beyond the first three mentioned in this section on CBT.

In a nicely summarized chapter by Newman and Borkovec (2002), the essential techniques of a CBT approach for worry and GAD are spelled out in clear detail. The components of their approach, which targets cognitive, imaginal, and physiological responses (Newman, 2000a, Newman & Borkovec, 1995) to constantly perceived threat, are the following: (1) self-monitoring, (2) stimulus control methods, (3) relaxation techniques (i.e., diaphragmatic breathing, progressive muscle relaxation, and AR), (4) self-control desensitization, and (5) CT. These interventions are in the arsenal of most, if not all, CBT clinicians for the treatment of GAD. Even though some researchers and clinicians stress one component over another, all of them attempt to decrease symptoms at the cognitive, physiological, and behavioral level (Rygh & Sanderson, 2004).

A brief overview of each technique will shed some light on a cognitive behavioral therapist's modus operandi. Self-monitoring refers to the client being able to pick up internal and external cues that trigger anxiety. "In CBT more emphasis is placed on internal cues than external ones" (Newman & Borkovec, 2002, p. 152). Stimulus control methods are aimed at reducing "worrying." The main technique used is to schedule worry time. Patients are instructed to worry only during prescribed periods of time. Relaxation methods are a core part of any CBT protocol. The central function is to reduce somatic tension and increase autonomic flexibility. The range of relaxation techniques can help therapists tailor them to the unique needs of the particular patient. Diaphragmatic breathing shifts the breathing away from the chest to slower paced, more relaxed, diaphragm producing breaths. Progressive muscle relaxation takes the patient through the 16 different muscle groups, where tensing and relaxing of these muscles assist the individual patient in their "letting go" of anxiety (Bernstein, Borkovec, & Hazlett-Stevens, 2000). A mindfulness and acceptance-based approach (Roemer & Orsillo, 2002), which will be discussed later, has been helping patients focus less on worry and more on the present moment. Applied relaxation is used when patients start to feel initial twinges of anxiety cues or subtle tension. It can be used on a moment-to-moment basis as needed by the patient. Self-control desensitization was designed for particular disorders such as GAD (Goldfried, 1971), where phobic stimuli and avoidance are less of a challenge. It is an imaginal technique, aimed at countering images that decrease worrying and promote increased emotional processing.

Cognitive therapy often uses cognitive restructuring, which is at the core of this approach. The premise behind it is based on the principle that interpretations of situations and events determine our emotional states. It is a structured and directive intervention, where therapists challenge automatic thoughts that lead to various distortions. In the process, a patient begins to learn to generate more positive and realistic appraisals of self, others, and the world (Beck, 1976; Beck et al., 1985). In cognitive–behavioral therapy, which has extended the scope of CT to account for the more behavioral therapy side of the therapeutic action, behavioral experiments and other techniques are used to facilitate change (Beck, 1995; Ledley, Marx, & Heimberg, 2005).

Another approach that is a standard CBT one (Brown, O'Leary, & Barlow, 2001) is a protocol for GAD that consists of 12–15 sessions held weekly (last 2 weeks are held bi-weekly). The target of treatment is excessive and uncontrollable worry, and the accompanying hyperarousal symptoms that are frequently present (tension-related CNS symptoms). The treatment follows a highly structured manualized procedure that can be easily duplicated. There is a therapist guide (Zinbarg, Craske, & Barlow, 2006) and a patient workbook (Craske & Barlow, 2006) that derive from this approach. This CBT psychosocial treatment has the following process of treatment: (1) initial session, which is psychoeducational about CBT and rapport building; (2) CT based on Beck et al. (1985); (3) questionnaires that are filled out, such as the ADIS-IV, PSWQ, DASS; (4) worry exposure, which is a unique component where spheres of worry are identified and imagery training is used; (5) relaxation training, such as progressive muscle relaxation, is incorporated; (6) worry behavior prevention, such as "compulsive checking" and others, should be made into a list, and the individuals, over time, should "prevent" themselves from engaging in them to extinguish the behaviors; (7) time management helps to structure time to decrease "anxious apprehension"; and (8) problem-solving is geared towards setting achievable and realistic goals, allocating responsibility, and staying on task in order to decrease perfectionism and catastrophizing. In a nutshell, this is another well thought out CBT treatment approach.

Another more cutting-edge model, calling itself a CBT approach for GAD, has gained popularity and empirical status, but targets primarily intolerance of uncertainty (Dugas & Robichaud, 2007; Robichaud & Dugas, 2006). The ultimate goal for patients with GAD is to learn to better tolerate uncertainty. In the most recent refinement of this treatment (Dugas & Robichaud, 2007), the therapy followed distinct modules, such as psychoeducation and worry awareness training, uncertainty recognition and behavior exposure, reevaluation of the usefulness of worry, problem-solving training, imaginal exposure, and relapse prevention. In the relapse phase, and at other points in treatment, assessment tools congruent with the model, such as the IUS (Buhr & Dugas, 2002), The Why Worry? (Freeston, Rheaume, Letarte, Dugas, & Ladouceur, 1994), and The Why Worry-II (Holowka, Dugas, Francis, & Laugesen, 2000), are used to evaluate treatment outcomes.

There have been some exceptions to the more modest past clinical findings in improvement rates (as measured by no longer meeting criteria for the illness) using this CBT informed therapy, that targets primarily intolerance of uncertainty. These outcomes have been somewhat atypical, but in fairness to the data and for the sake of presenting a more balanced view on CBT, the results are being factored in for consideration. Two studies (Dugas et al., 2003; Ladouceur et al., 2000) provided significant research evidence to support the efficacy of this treatment. Ladouceur et al. (2000), in a randomly controlled clinical trial with 26 patients (CBT, $n = 14$; wait-list control, $n = 12$) consisting of ~12–16 sessions meeting the criteria for GAD, demonstrated some rather significant findings. At the end of treatment, 77% of patients (20 of 26) no longer met the criteria for GAD, and this outcome did not change at a 12-month follow-up. Conclusions of the study supported the theory that intolerance of uncertainty closely paralleled changes in symptoms during treatment and follow-up. It was found that three fourth were GAD-free and 60% reached high end-state functioning. Intolerance of uncertainty is an important target treatment. The authors still argued that "the percentage of participants having reached high endstate functioning at posttreatment in the present study is superior to those previously studied. But given that the specific criteria for determining endstate functioning were different in these studies, caution is advised in making such direct comparisons" (Ladouceur et al., 2000, p. 10).

Another more recent study (Dugas et al., 2003), using intolerance of uncertainty as the target variable, reinforced the above findings. The treatment was offered in group cognitive behavioral therapy of 5–6 groups with 4–6 participants, totaling 52 patients ($n = 25$, treatment group; $n = 27$, wait-list control) with GAD for 14 weekly 2-hour sessions by two clinical psychologists. The percentage of patients no longer meeting criteria for GAD were 60% at posttest, 88% at 6 months, 83% at 12 months, and increased to 95% at a 2-year follow-up. Criteria for both high responder status and high end-state functioning were modest, being 52% (25 subjects) at posttreatment, 48% (20 subjects) at 6-month follow-up, 59% (24 subjects) at 12-month follow-up, and 62% (24 subjects) at 24-month follow-up.

There was also more subject dropout in the CBT group modality than in the earlier individual CBT study.

It is important to bear in mind that the results and outcome measures in both studies were standardized clinician ratings of GAD symptoms and the rather narrow self-report measures of pathological worry. It is possible that, by using these limited criteria (Orsillo, Roemer, Lerner, & Tull, 2004) alone for outcome measures, the clinical findings were higher than usual for those not meeting diagnostic criteria for GAD. In addition, the impact of the treatment in both studies on a broader range of social functioning (i.e., life satisfaction, social, occupational impairment) (Roemer & Orsillo, 2002) was not explored, further lending evidence that the results, however high diagnostically after treatment, were still limited in scope.

It could be that targeting intolerance of uncertainty in this largely CBT approach appears to have stronger effects in decreasing pathological worry and somatic symptoms, than those CBT packages that do not include interventions to target intolerance of uncertainty. Either way, this is a promising approach that extends the more standard CBT model into new and potentially more effective directions for patients with GAD.

Metacognitive Therapy

The treatment using metacognitive therapy has been evaluated in an open trial, with community outpatients having a primary diagnosis of DSM-IV GAD (Wells & King, 2006) and in a randomized trial (Wells et al., in prep.). In the former study, recovery rates were 87.5% at posttreatment and 75% at 6- and 12-month follow-up on measures of trait anxiety in the open trial. The protocol for the treatment was once a week for 12 weeks, yet 6–12 sessions are not uncommon. Successful outcomes are measured by the absence of prominent positive and negative beliefs about worry on the Generalized Anxiety Disorder Scale (GADS; Wells, 1997), and relapse prevention strategies are well integrated into treatment. "The RCT is complete and being written up. The study compared MCT with AR and metacognitive therapy was deemed superior. MCT led to 80% recovery, as measured by Penn State Worry Questionnaire and 80% recovery as measured by trait-anxiety using Jacobson's criteria on these measures posttreatment" (Wells, e-mail communication, 2008).

Other common assessment tools used in this approach are the SCID (First, Spitzer, Gibbon, & Williams, 1997), ADIS-IV (Di Nardo et al., 1994), GADQ-IV (Newman et al., 2002), PSWQ (Meyer, Miller, Metzger, & Borkovec, 1990), BAI (Beck, Epstein, Brown, & Steer, 1988), and the BDI-II (Beck, Steer, & Brown, 1996). The treatment focus is twofold: (1) modifying negative beliefs about the uncontrollability of worry, and (2) modifying negative beliefs about the danger of worry and positive beliefs about worry. An excellent overall introduction to the metacognitive model can be found in Wells and Carter (2006).

The approach follows a series of treatment phases that are spelled out in different sources (Wells, 2006a, 2007; Wells & Carter, 2006). A case formulation is a critical starting point, where the patient is asked about recent episodes of distressing worry (structured questions are used), type I worries plus anxiety symptoms and type II worries, which mirror negative beliefs. The next stage, called socialisation, is where the clinician presents the formulation that worry is not inherently a problem, but certain beliefs about it and nonadaptive coping strategies (seeking excessive reassurance from others, obsessive checking) can create barriers to recovery. The rationale of metacognitive therapy is discussed, as is the nature of positive (type I) and negative beliefs about worry (type II). The focus is on negative beliefs about worry (type II – meta-worry about worry), and this is the key target area of this approach. In addition, behaviors (decrease reassurance seeking and obsessive checking) and thought control strategies (thought-suppression experiments – worry postponement in order not to control worry, changing negative beliefs about worry) are highlighted with the goal of modification of negative metacognitive beliefs concerning uncontrollability of worry and danger metacognitons. Dangers of worrying can encompass physical, psychological, and social functioning of the individual GAD patient. GAD at this point is often conceptualized as a specific phobia – meaning a specific fear of worrying.

Many varied verbal and behavioral techniques are incorporated throughout this treatment. Once the negative beliefs about worry are sufficiently addressed (which are the ones most responsible for the maintenance of GAD), modifying positive metacognitive beliefs (last one third of treatment) becomes a central part of this approach. The modification of positive beliefs about worry increases flexibility and cognitive strategies for dealing with threat. Relapse prevention is used in the last two sessions to review patient's level of beliefs in the (1) usefulness of worry, and that (2) worry is uncontrollable and dangerous (which should by now be easily challenged and under the patient's metacognitive control). Avoidance of worry situations, which in the past served as worry triggers, are also explored and determined whether they will continue to pose challenges. Relapse prevention forms a blueprint for what was accomplished in metacognitive therapy, and the patient is asked to write a narrative summary of his or her learning experiences that can be accessed for future reference and to avert potential problems down the road.

More specifics, about a study discussed earlier in this section, are now elaborated on at this point. In an open trial by Wells and King (2006), based on an empirically supported metacognitive model (Wells, 1995a, 1995b) and a cognitive manualized therapy for anxiety disorders (Wells, 1997), ten patients with DSM-IV GAD were assessed pre- and postmetacognitive therapy at 6- and 12-month follow-up. Self-report measures, weekly sessions, and homework assignment were components of the treatment. Significant improvements occurred at posttreatment, with large effect sizes (ranging from 1.04 to 2.78) in worry, anxiety, and depression. In nine cases these changes were lasting ones. Recovery rates were 87% at posttreatment and 75% at 6 and 12 months. In a randomized-controlled trial, metacognitive therapy was compared to AR, and MCT demonstrated more robust clinical outcomes vs. AR (Wells et al., in prep.). Metacognitive therapy produced recovery rates of 80%, with a further 10% showing improvements on the basis of trait anxiety scores.

Metacognitive therapy is effective and has empirical validation for the treatment of GAD. It should be considered one of the first line psychosocial treatments for this disorder. However, many clinicians and patients alike may find the approach a little too abstract and not easy to translate from theory into practice. This clinician has found the approach helpful in his own work with GAD patients, but it does take some patience in learning to master the approach.

Supportive–Expressive Psychodynamic Therapy

Supportive–expressive psychodynamic therapy (Crits-Christoph, Connolly, Azarian, Crits-Christoph, & Shappell, 1996; Crits-Christoph, Connolly Gibbons, & Crits-Christoph, 2004) is an effective, brief, focal, and interpersonally oriented treatment for GAD. It relies on one theoretical paradigm – a relational psychodynamic approach. It addresses cognitive factors, such as worry and interpersonal challenges first broached in Borkovec, Robinson, Pruzinsky, & DePree (1983). The approach has been developed, in large part, because of the researchers' belief that existing treatments have been insufficient – namely CBT (Chambless & Gillis, 1993) and pharmacotherapy (Rickels et al., 1982). In addition, GAD is a persistent disorder, has major public health concerns, causing significant impairment (Crits-Christoph, Crits-Christoph, Wolf-Palacio, Fichter, & Rudick, 1995), and psychodynamic approaches are commonly used by therapists (Jensen, Bergin, & Greaves, 1990), thereby suggesting their utility.

The model is based on the premise that worry serves a defensive function, and the effect of traumatic experiences common to GAD are largely interpersonal in nature. These relational patterns are cyclical and maladaptive, leading to "core conflictual relationship themes" (CCRT). These CCRTs are composed of a wish and/or desire, the perceived response of another person and the self-response. When fears increase, GAD sufferers prefer not to think about the CCRT, and defense mechanisms are activated that increase worrying as a way to avoid thinking about these more basic, yet important aspirations and desires. However, the nonadaptive relational patterns, though mostly unconscious, are still apparent, as undue cognitive and somatic distress persists as defensive responses.

The treatment model has a supportive component to bolster self-esteem and adaptive abilities, and an expressive component to express thoughts/feelings and increase insight interpersonally. It is an adaptation from Luborsky's (1984) general supportive–expressive (SE) manual. SE consists of 50-min weekly individual therapy sessions, lasting for 16 weeks with four phases – early, middle, termination, and a monthly booster phase that continues for 3 months. The goals of therapy are to change the CCRT through building the therapeutic alliance, increasing self-esteem, changing behaviors, and reducing symptoms.

Empirical findings for this approach have been mixed thus far, as there have been two SE studies for GAD. The first study (Crits-Christoph et al., 1996) was a preliminary, open trial of 16 weekly sessions of SE focal psychotherapy followed by three monthly booster sessions for patients with GAD. The sample for the initial study consisted of 26 patients with *DSM-IV* criteria GAD, where 23 of them completed 12 weeks of treatment, but were all evaluated at 16 weeks. There were 65% of the patients who presented with a comorbid Axis I diagnosis, and 42% had an Axis II diagnosis at intake. Empirical data demonstrated statistically significant changes at 16 weeks across all outcome measures. At the termination phase, 79% of patients no longer met the criteria for GAD. Scores on the Hamilton Anxiety Rating Scale and the Beck Anxiety Inventory decreased considerably. The conclusion from this preliminary excursion is that SE may prove to be a promising treatment for GAD. In the second study (Crits-Christoph, Connolly Gibbons, Narducci, Schamberger, & Gallop, 2005), 16 weekly sessions of either SE therapy or supportive, nondirective therapy were compared in a pilot randomized trial. Interpersonal problems only modestly changed during the course of SE therapy. However, the SE approach was statistically and clinically superior to supportive therapy with symptomatic remission rates. It appears that targeting interpersonal problems in GAD may have only limited success in SE, compared to a more integrative approach that builds CBT, interpersonal and experiential techniques into it (Newman, 2000a, 2000b; Newman, Castonguay, Borkovec, & Molnar, 2004). This integrative approach will be discussed at a later point in this chapter.

Supportive–expressive psychodynamic therapy has proven effective in reducing rates of remission in GAD patients, but has been less successful in its primary goal of decreasing interpersonal challenges in this population. Questions remain for the future of this approach, such as the following: (1) Should the length of treatment be extended? (2) What about combining medication with SE? and (3) What about refining SE to better target the interpersonal problems that are most common in GAD (such as in the overly nurturant domain)? The overly nurturing GAD patient did particular poorly in the SE approach (Crits-Christoph et al., 2005).

In conclusion, one could argue, based on the data, that supportive–expressive psychodynamic therapy works well for a subset of GAD patients, but has a minimal effect on others. In other words, the architects of SE for GAD would claim that there is some benefit, but not one reaching a level of significance (especially in relation to interpersonal issues). Perhaps this may change, as the SE treatment for GAD is further refined over time. Either way, it may have some value in that it does offer an alternative conceptual and treatment package to the heavily CBT-dominated models and approaches already in existence for GAD.

Integrative Psychotherapy

In an article by Schottenbauer, Glass, and Arnkoff (2005), it was found that studies consistently demonstrate that 33–50% of American clinicians consider themselves to be either "eclectic" or "integrative" in their theoretical orientation (Glass, Victor,

& Arnkoff, 1993; Norcross, Hedges, & Castle, 2002). Psychotherapy integration is believed, in widening circles by experienced clinicians, to improve the effectiveness of therapy (Wolfe, 2001). The reality is that there is a large theoretical and clinical body of literature in this area, yet subsequent empirical research on psychotherapy integration has lagged behind other, more standardized, approaches for many years (Arkowitz, 1997; Glass, Arnkoff, & Rodriguez, 1998). This trend is changing, as empirical literature in the area of psychotherapy integration is growing. Two evidence-based experts on CBT and GAD write, "on a final note, the field seems to be moving towards integrative therapies for GAD" (Dugas & Koerner, 2005, p. 77).

Over the last 5–10 years, a number of researchers, with a primarily CBT orientation, have become increasingly disenchanted with the treatment outcomes for GAD *DSM-IV* criteria clinical samples. It has been argued in this text that CBT is effective for GAD based on empirical data (Borkovec & Newman, 1998; Borkovec & Ruscio, 2001). "Despite its therapeutic value, there is room for improvement in CBT for GAD. Replicated findings show that at best, it leads only to an average of 50% of clients achieving high end state functioning" (Newman et al., 2004, p. 322). Given the overall findings, some investigators have argued that GAD may be the most difficult anxiety disorder to treat (Brown, Barlow, & Liebowitz, 1994).

One area that has started to attract clinical attention and garner supporting evidence in the treatment of GAD is targeting interpersonal problems and emotional processing in this population (Newman, Castonguay, & Borkovec, 1999). The impetus to address relational issues in GAD stems in part from the findings, that on posttherapy and follow-up clinical improvement, dimensions of interpersonal problems had a predictive effect (Borkovec et al., 2002). Borkovec, one of the leading experts in the world on psychosocial treatments for GAD, has been a growing proponent for integrative therapy of this disorder. In a review article of CBT findings to date, Borkovec et al. (2003) began to outline what an integrative approach would look like in theory and practice (CBT with integrations from interpersonal and experiential therapies). This paper summarizes the components (i.e., self-monitoring, relaxation training, CT, rehearsal of coping responses, scheduling of pleasant activities, stimulus control techniques, establishing a brief worry period, reducing intolerance of uncertainty) used in their CBT model. It also targets maladaptive relationship patterns (Borkovec et al., 2002), resolves "alliance ruptures" (Safran, Muran, & Samstag, 1994), and deepens emotional processing (Greenberg, Rice, & Elliot, 1996).

The integrative treatment for GAD involved sequential combining of 55 min of CBT, followed by 55 min of interpersonal/emotional processing (I/EP). The main goal of this approach was to determine whether additive components to CBT from different theoretical orientations would improve outcomes for GAD. Preliminary research in the evolution of this integrative approach seemed to suggest a role for CBT plus I/EP in the treatment of GAD. Finally, the optimal goal for these researchers was to compare CBT plus I/EP vs. CBT plus supportive listening (SL).

Two follow-up articles, that are more comprehensive in scope (Castonguay, Newman, Borkovec, Grosse Holtforth, & Maramba, 2005; Newman et al., 2004), take the previous research one step further, by discussing integrative therapy for GAD with greater specificity and sophistication. The standard CBT protocol has been broached earlier in this paper under the section on cognitive behavioral therapy (Newman et al., 2002), and will not be reiterated at this point. Both of these articles focus on the techniques, processes of change, and subsequent findings that result from having used an integrative approach for GAD. However, the later publication (Castonguay et al., 2005) also has more updated clinical studies, theoretical constructs, treatment components, and directions for further research possibilities. The defining paper and exposition of the integrative approach from a conceptual and pragmatic point of view, is an article by Borkovec and Sharpless (2004). The lead author shared with this clinician his belief that the above publication best expressed his views on the subject of CBT, GAD, and integrative therapy (Borkovec, e-mail communication, 2007). Another excellent review by Behar and Borkovec (2005) addresses many cutting-edge issues in similar areas bearing on the nature and treatment of GAD.

In terms of specific I/EP techniques, they can be categorized as targeting problematic relationship patterns and facilitating emotional processing. The techniques used for challenging maladaptive patterns are the following: (1) exploring past and current relationships, (2) teaching patients alternative ways to handle interpersonal relationships, and (3) making use of the patient–therapist relationship.

Emotional processing techniques are based on the work of Greenberg and Safran (1987), Greenberg et al. (1996), and Safran and Segal (1990). In the case of exploring past and current relationships, the task for the clinician is to get a sense of the patient's interpersonal history. Open-ended questions tend to help the GAD sufferer focus their attention on their relationships, rather than on themselves or other persons. In addition, the discovery that what may have once been viewed as relationally adaptive is no longer a healthy interpersonal mode. This, in turn, can create new patterns of relating that are more positively reinforcing. Finally, taking responsibility for their role in relationships, in both adaptive and nonadaptive ways, can increase awareness and lay the groundwork for helping GAD sufferers later with emotional processing.

Assisting patients to change these maladaptive patterns can start with social skills training. Role playing has the potential to challenge the "all or none thinking" that often comes with those who suffer from GAD in their dealings with others. Homework can also be assigned to practice new behaviors outside of therapy, as therapists can actually see whether real life interactions are changing for the better as a result of the therapeutic interventions. Making use of the patient–therapist relationship assumes that maladaptive patterns of relating are played out in the context of the therapy relationship. Safran and Segal (1990) argue that therapists need to be able to identify these unhealthy relational patterns, and stop the patient from acting in these habitually aversive ways by not meeting their expectations. The therapist can now self-disclose how the patient's interpersonal style is making them feel, thereby increasing the patient's awareness, and using the therapist as a model for more appropriate relating to others (Safran & Muran, 2000). This requires particular empathy and sensitivity on the therapist's part, the reason being that a therapist is encouraging the patients to take a closer look at themselves and their potentially less flattering side.

At this point, "alliance ruptures" are common, as patients can become defensive, irritable, hostile, evasive, aggressive, and avoidant. Safran, Crocker, McMain, and

Murray (1990) suggest that patients first be invited to talk about their negative reactions. Second, the therapist attempts to empathize with the patient's perceptions and emotions. Finally, the last step is to "disarm" (Burns, 1999), which means to find some element of truth in the patient's reactions, even if it seems an unreasonable one. This last technique gives the patient the impression that the therapist is open-minded, and takes some responsibility for the lack of connection in their relationship. In many ways, this can promote positive interpersonal change, by creating a safe milieu for the patient to feel vulnerable and still be accepted by another.

The other component of this treatment for GAD focuses on encouraging the patient to experience, deepen, and express his or her emotions. "Specifically, evidence now suggests that GAD clients largely ignore their emotions and indeed may be fearful of many of them, including positive ones" (Castonguay et al., 2005, p. 245). In facing these painful emotions, GAD sufferers are often confronting material that has been cognitively avoided in the form of chronic worry. This cognitive avoidance through worry forms the basis of Borkovec's avoidance theory of worry, and can be countered with techniques that help patients stay with their current feelings. "The use of emotional processing techniques is also based on Greenberg and Safran's view that emotion provides information about a person's needs" (Newman et al., 2004, p. 341). Patients are encouraged to get in touch with their feelings and attempt, with the therapist's guidance, to process and deepen unfinished and unprocessed emotions. Terms, such as unfinished business, internal conflicts, and problematic reactions, are used to facilitate the above dynamics. For example, Greenberg et al. (1996) use the technique of "systematic evocative unfolding" to address problematic reactions when patients are confused about their responses. Patients are asked to take themselves back to the situation that evoked the reaction, and play it out in their imagination. This re-experiencing can help patients better express and take responsibility for their emotions, while gaining access to once inaccessible emotions. Unfinished business-dealing with unresolved feelings towards another person are addressed with the empty chair technique. The patient expresses feelings, while imagining another person sitting opposite them in an empty chair. Internal conflicts are also referred to as a self-evaluative split. The patients learn to gain increased insight into their feelings and needs and own their internal conflict by distinguishing the two separate parts of themselves, and engaging in reciprocal dialogue with each part.

Before presenting the empirical findings on the integrative therapy approach just presented on GAD, an interesting aside is in order at this juncture. Castonguay et al. (2005) have called their integrative model that addresses both the interpersonal problems and emotional challenges endemic to GAD sufferers, as cognitive–behavioral assimilative integration. They point out that "their integrative approach is based on the assumption that clinical improvement is due in part to principles of change that cut across different forms of therapy" (p. 242 and as cited in Castonguay, 2000). In speaking about these processes of change cutting across different forms of therapy, Castonguay and his colleagues rely on Goldfried's model (Goldfried, 1980; Goldfried & Padawer, 1982). These processes of change are as follows: (1) creation of positive expectations for the patients, (2) a provision for a new perspective, (3) a corrective experience and ongoing reality test, and (4) the use of the therapeutic relationship.

The results of the CBT plus I/EP combination have been finally collected (Newman, Castonguay, Borkovec, Fisher, & Nordberg, 2008) in an open trial of integrative therapy for GAD. The findings have demonstrated some encouraging empirical results for an integrative treatment approach for GAD. In this open trial, 18 adult subjects meeting *DSM-IV* criteria for GAD received 14 sessions of CBT plus I/EP. Three participants received 14 sessions of CBT plus supportive listening for training purposes. With all subjects in the study (except for the three in the training protocol), 50 min of CBT was followed by 50 min of I/EP. At the end of the 2-hours of treatment 10 min was given to complete process measures. Even though the findings were preliminary in nature, effect size between pre- and posttreatment outcome measures appeared to be superior to those found in past studies conducted with standard CBT. It appeared from the results that integrative therapy significantly decreased symptoms of GAD at posttreatment and at 1 year follow-up. Interpersonal problems, which are often refractory after standard CBT, also improved significantly at the end of treatment and were maintained at 1 year follow-up.

In a more ambitious randomized clinical trial, 70 GAD patients, upon completion, will have been assigned to one of two treatment groups – CBT plus I/EP or CBT plus SL. "So far these results show that those in the integrative treatment have better endstate functioning at 2-year follow-up than those in CBT plus supportive listening but endstate functioning is not significantly different at any other time point. So there is some evidence that integrative treatment is better than CBT alone, at least in the long run" (Newman, e-mail communication, 2008). This qualified statement does not negate the positive findings from the open trial on integrative therapy or definitively conclude that there is little or no therapeutic merit to this approach. It only implies that to date, there may be room for improvement and potential refinement of this psychosocial treatment for GAD. Final results are being calculated from the RCT and therefore still in process.

One of the most comprehensive integrative models to date has been developed by Wolfe (1992, 1994, 1995, 2001, 2003, 2005). The strength of the model lies in its problem specificity (addressing the full spectrum of anxiety disorders, including GAD), etiological theory, and clinical treatment strategies. It is an amalgamation of psychodynamic, behavioral, cognitive, experiential, and humanistic concepts and interventions. Pharmacotherapy is not a focus of this model. Wolfe (2005) has authored a book, which can give the clinician a window into his well thought out approach. This work is the culmination of a 30-year career as a clinician, thought leader of the psychotherapy integration movement, a former research psychologist at The National Institute of Mental Health (NIMH), a college professor and, at present, a full-time director of an integrative therapy training institute.

Wolfe's integrative framework relies on clinical acumen and a "research informed", not empirically validated, assimilative approach (Wolfe, 2001). Other prominent researchers (Borkovec & Castonguay, 1998; Messer, 2001) make a case that therapeutic models do not necessarily have to be all inclusive with empirically supported treatments to be considered bona-fide effective therapy approaches. "At different points in therapy, with different patients, it is possible that insight-oriented, behavior modifying, awareness enhancing or schema-modifying techniques might be used with anxiety disorders" (Wolfe, 2005, p. 184). Having concluded this section on integrative therapy with Wolfe's clarion call to being open (yet selective) as clinicians, we now turn to another psychosocial treatment approach called emotion regulation therapy (Mennin, 2001, 2004, 2006; Mennin, Heimberg, Turk, & Fresco, 2002, 2005; Mennin, Turk, Heimberg, & Carmin, 2004). This treatment model and approach has some parallels to those found among the integrative ones, but because of its uniqueness in that the focus is on "emotion" and its dysregulation, it has been afforded its own heading.

Emotion Regulation Therapy

What differentiates emotion regulation theory from the models discussed so far is that this emotion-focused perspective's aim is to elucidate "the nature of the emotional experience that prompts individuals with GAD to engage in avoidance strategies such as worry" (Mennin et al., 2004, p. 67). The therapeutic approach and interventions unique to emotion regulation therapy (ERT) will be discussed in due course. At the heart of ERT is the hypothesis that emotions are dysregulated in individuals with GAD. This implies that those with GAD have marked challenges understanding their emotional experience, are highly emotionally sensitive, and concurrently have few skills to modulate emotional states. Worry is conceptualized as a nonadaptive cognitive way to maintain homeostasis by regulating and fixing problems that are accompanied by aversive emotional experiences. These emotional deficits in GAD and their unearthing hold the key for a more profound understanding of the cognitive, behavioral, interpersonal, and biological aspects of the disorder (Mennin et al., 2004). Mennin and colleagues (2002, 2004) feel convinced that an emotion regulation perspective could be the "tie that binds" the various dimensions of GAD together, including their unpredictable emotionality. In other words, from an ERT perspective, GAD sufferers are prone to have more intense and reactive emotional experiences, making the attempts at trying to modulate them a particularly daunting task.

Additionally, there are various skills used by ERT clinicians to help modulate emotions that seemingly are not learned by GAD sufferers because of a confluence of factors, such as genetics and an emotionally impoverished early environment (Saarni, 1990, 1999). Saarni refers to these skills to respond emotionally and apply the knowledge to relationships with others, while modulating and regulating one's emotions, as "emotional competence." In a nutshell, worry and other cognitive control strategies are used to suppress a range of emotions at the expense of learning the requisite skills to solve problems. The result is that cognitive information is assimilated, rather than the raw emotional experience. There is preliminary data (Mennin, 2001) to confirm that chronic worriers have more difficulty vs. a control group of nonchronic worriers in regulating their emotions.

ERT for GAD integrates components of standard CBT, experiential exercises to address emotional avoidance, and short-term psychodynamic therapy (Fosha, 2000; McCullough et al., 2003), which tackles the inherent interpersonal deficits (Borkovec et al., 2002) from an emotion-focused point of view. ERT is composed of four distinct phases: (1) psychoeducation, monitoring and taking a developmental history, (2) skills training in somatic awareness and emotional knowledge, utilization and regulation, (3) use of these skills to confront core thematic issues using experiential exposure exercises, and finally, (4) progress review, relapse prevention, and terminating processing (Mennin, 2004).

In a more fleshed out version of the therapy protocol (Mennin, 2006), ERT is administered over 20 sessions in a 16-week period. To be more exact, the first four weekly sessions (phase 1) are still psychoeducational about GAD, focus on functional patterns of worrying, emotions in past and current situations, and self-monitoring of worry episodes. The following four weekly sessions (phase II) are geared towards the development of somatic awareness and emotion regulation skills. The next eight sessions occur twice weekly within a 4-week period (phase III), and these "intensive" sessions are the core of ERT. These sessions focus on the application of newly learned skills to emotionally evocative themes. The final four sessions (phase IV) are conducted weekly. These sessions concentrate on termination of treatment, the therapeutic relationship, relapse prevention, and future goals. Mennin (2006) feels strongly that emotions and their regulation can play a highly significant role in complex, chronic, and often treatment-refractory forms of anxiety such as GAD. One encouraging sign among many in relation to ERT is the "view that recovery from worry is best achieved when effective emotion regulation skills are attained. Hence the goal of treatment extends beyond symptom reduction" (Mennin et al., 2004, p. 81).

The evidence for ERT has been growing over the years, and funding to support the research hypotheses and measure clinical outcomes and change processes are underway. This integrative emotion-focused therapy may ultimately add a new and promising path in the understanding and treatment of GAD. Now it is crucial to take a closer look at the existing and ongoing empirical research for ERT. Three studies by Mennin et al. (2005) provide some initial support for an emotion dysregulation model of GAD. Study 1 demonstrated that students with GAD reported higher intensity of emotions, poorer understanding of emotions, increased reactivity to emotional experience, and decreased ability to self-soothe after negative emotions, compared with controls. Study 2 replicated the findings with a clinical sample. Finally, in Study 3, it was found that students with GAD, not controls, displayed heightened increases in self-reported physiological symptoms after listening to emotion-inducing music than after neutral stimuli.

In a study by Salters-Pedneault, Roemer, Tull, Rucker, and Mennin (2006), additional preliminary evidence was found for an emotion regulation deficit model of GAD. Three hundred twenty-five participants were involved in research that examined the relationship between emotion regulation deficits and GAD-related outcomes in an analogue sample. The findings were consistent, in that emotion dysregulation was associated with chronic worry and with analogue GAD-status. In addition, deficits in emotional clarity, acceptance of emotions, ability to engage in goal-directed behaviors when distressed, impulse control, and access to effective regulation strategies were all related to worry and analogue GAD.

In more recent research, Decker, Turk, Hess, and Murray (2008) concluded that, relative to controls, individuals having a diagnosis of GAD reported more intense daily emotional experiences (Mennin et al., 2004). However, in contrast to earlier research (Mennin et al., 2004), those with GAD did not show poor emotional differentiation, and were able to make use of several emotion regulation strategies to a greater degree than did controls. This study lends some support to the emotion regulation model, but seems to suggest that GAD sufferers may indeed possess and, in actuality, make use of the capacity to differentiate their emotions, thereby potentially decreasing heightened emotional reactivity. In another study by Novick-Kline, Turk, Mennin, Hoyt, and Gallagher (2005), individuals with GAD scored significantly higher than controls on emotional awareness. This is not consistent with earlier research that shows that GAD sufferers have difficulties in their ability to identify and describe their emotions (Mennin et al., 2005; Turk, Heimberg, Luterek, Mennin, & Fresco, 2005). To be more precise, in the study by Turk et al. (2005), the findings replicated earlier ones, in that both in GAD and social anxiety disorder (SAD), emotion dysregulation were common phenomena. Another revealing difference between GAD and SAD was that GAD patients have increased emotional intensity and fear of the experience of depression than those with SAD. Finally, it was found that GAD individuals reported greater emotion impulse strength than did controls or persons with SAD. This palpable sense of increased emotional intensity was associated with a greater likelihood to engage in nonadaptive strategies, such as worry to regulate emotions.

The verdict is still out, based on some conflicting research findings that appear to challenge some of the more cherished assumptions of this emotion-based approach. However, at present, participants are being selected for a random controlled trial on ERT and the empirical data should be out within the year (Mennin, e-mail communication, 2008). The results of this study are highly anticipated, as this should give ERT the empirical evidence needed to either more definitively support its approach or, if not, make the necessary modifications to enhance its relevance in the treatment of patients with GAD. An emotion-focused approach has not just novelty, in a cognitively dominated field regarding GAD, but can offer sufferers enhanced self-mastery to better manage their emotions without necessarily presuming that they lack the requisite skills in the first place.

Acceptance-Based Behavior Therapy

The last approach in this section, which once again has an integrative flavor, is a mindfulness/acceptance-based behavior approach for GAD (Orsillo et al., 2004; Orsillo, Roemer, & Barlow, 2003; Roemer & Orsillo, 2002, 2005, 2007; Roemer, Salters-Pedneault & Orsillo, 2006; Roemer, Salters, Raffa, & Orsillo, 2005). The approach incorporates elements of CBT (Borkovec, 1999; Borkovec, Alcaine, & Behar, 2004), acceptance and commitment therapy (Hayes, Strosahl, & Wilson, 1999; Hayes, Wilson, Gifford, Follette, & Strosahl, 1996), mindfulness CBT (Segal, Williams, & Teasdale, 2002), and dialectical behavior therapy (DBT) (Linehan, 1993, 1994).

The core concept of this model is that the most striking form of avoidance in GAD is experiential (Roemer et al., 2005). In other words, worrying about multiple future events functions to decrease internal distress and somatic activity in the short run, and helps the GAD sufferer avoid unpleasant internal experiences. In addition, worry is verbal and linguistic in nature (Borkovec & Inz, 1990), which is repetitive and further increases avoidance. GAD is also characterized by behavioral restriction. The restrictive element in GAD limits behavioral action into stereotypical patterns, and does not lend itself to effective problem-solving (Borkovec, Hazlett-Stevens, & Diaz, 1999). Behavioral restriction leads to worrying and catastrophizing, which form a reciprocally negative relationship, preventing the moving forward with one's desired goals or facing feared outcomes. GAD sufferers, unlike depressed patients, are not inactive, but are invariably engaged in restless, negative, and nervous activity that leads to a restricted life space.

Some other noteworthy conceptual themes of this approach and its overlap with GAD (Orsillo et al., 2004) are the following: worry is future-focused, worry and GAD are characterized by rigid habitual responding, worry serves an experientially avoidant function, and may inhibit action in valued directions.

To counteract the above limits that worry and experiential avoidance place on GAD patients, various acceptance-based treatments (Hayes et al., 1999) have been used to decrease strategies, aimed at avoiding private events (i.e., thoughts, feelings, memories, bodily sensations) and reduce patients' literal responses to their own thoughts. This also assists them in their ability to stay committed to behavior change, based on their values. Acceptance is one component where the individual is "experientially open" to the reality of the present moment. This allows for a focusing on valued directions, with the aim of taking action in valued areas of life (relationships, health, self-growth, and well-being). Mindfulness also plays a central role, in that it keeps the focus on the present moment, and can be incorporated into various relaxation techniques, such as progressive muscle relaxation and diaphragmatic breathing (Borkovec & Ruscio, 2001). Ideally, mindful focus can facilitate an alternative and more adaptive and flexible way of responding (Borkovec et al., 1999). Another technique used for GAD in this approach is to increase goal-directed action. "Goal directed action is likely to improve adjustment more broadly than simple symptom reduction" (Roemer & Orsillo, 2002, p. 62).

Given that GAD is a disorder marked by habitual and stuck patterns of responding across multiple domains (i.e., cognitive, somatic, behavioral) (Borkovec, 1994), this current approach being discussed "targets habitual responding and encourages mindfulness, acceptance of internal experiences, and mindful action as a replacement for the habitual restrictions in action that accompany worry" (Roemer & Orsillo, 2002, p. 63).

The basic phases of treatment in this protocol are (1) psychoeducation, (2) mindfulness, early cue detection, and monitoring, (3) relaxation/mindfulness techniques, and (4) mindful action. The scope of techniques used are evolving with more research, as is a more defined treatment approach (to be discussed under the empirical evidence part of this section) for this acceptance-based behavior therapy (ABBT) for GAD. However, summarizing to this point, this psychosocial treatment for GAD has been informed by integrations from CBT, acceptance and commitment therapy, mindful-based CBT and dialectical behavior therapy approaches. Yet, an acceptance-based behavioral approach has some unique features that differentiate it from standard CBT. Some of the key differences are that, in this approach, contextual factors are more primary; there is a more forgiving nonjudgmental attitude to experience; therapy is not aimed at worry being simply reduced and controlled, but internal and external experience, however painful and unpleasant, are faced in the present moment. In this way, actions are identified that GAD sufferers can value in order to live a "life worth living" (Orsillo et al., 2004).

The empirical evidence to support this approach continues to grow, and there have been several studies to date worthy of further exploration. In an 8-week group intervention, a mindfulness/meditative-based approach was used (Kabat-Zinn et al., 1992), where there was a clinically significant reduction in anxiety and depression in individuals meeting the criteria for GAD and panic. Therapeutic gains were maintained for 3 years (Miller, Fletcher, & Kabat-Zinn, 1995). A more recent uncontrolled 10-week session pilot study (Orsillo et al., 2003), using a similar version of the protocol presented earlier (Roemer & Orsillo, 2002), where four chronically anxious individuals first presented at a prestigious anxiety disorders clinic at Boston University, resulted in two of three individuals demonstrating marked reductions in symptoms, one showed modest improvements, and the fourth exhibited no significant improvement. There was 75% responder status and 80% high end-state functioning. The most significant result of the study and "perhaps more interesting than the demonstrated symptomatic reduction were the substantial changes made by all four group members" (Roemer & Orsillo, 2002, p. 66). The patients underwent noticeably positive changes in broader domains of functioning, for example, in vocational and relational areas, over the course of treatment. It was duly noted that the values and acceptance components of the treatment were patient rated as highly beneficial. Even though all the patients made significant life changes, it is still important to keep in mind that they continued to experience moderate levels of distress due to GAD and interference as a result of the illness at posttreatment.

There have been even more recent developments and refinement made to this approach within the past couple of years. These are worthy areas of investigation. In a publication by Roemer and Orsillo (2005), an overview of the model and treatment was presented, aimed at promoting experiential acceptance, which could ideally counter negative reactions that GAD sufferers have to their own internal experience. In combining an acceptance piece with behavioral change, the goal is to inculcate mindfulness training to promote experiential acceptance. The treatment protocol for the open trial consisted of an individual format consisting of 16 sessions; the first four sessions are orientation to the model, lasting 90 min in length, and the next 12 sessions are 60 min in length. The final two sessions are bi-weekly and each session begins with a mindfulness exercise. In addition, the first sessions include psychoeducation, experiential exercises, metaphors, and self-monitoring between sessions. Beginning in the second session, mindfulness and acceptance-based strategies are implemented. Throughout the therapy, choosing an authentic life is stressed for each individual, but especially in the later sessions, the focus shifts on behavioral action and the pursuit of desired values. Outside of sessions, mindfulness practices are encouraged. A case study by Roemer et al. (2006) replicated their

ABBT approach and demonstrated its effectiveness for one individual, lending more weight to this treatment for GAD.

In the actual open trial, minus a control group, by Roemer and Orsillo (2007), where the sample was 16, 5 were treated by the lead authors and 11 by graduate and postgraduate students. Several assessment measures, including the ADIS-IV-L, PSWQ, DASS, QOLI, AAQ (all mentioned in the assessment chapter of this text), plus the Affective Control Scale (Williams, Chambless, & Ahrens, 1997), were given at pre-, post-, and 3-month follow-up. The results were a reduction in clinician ratings of severity of GAD and decreased self-report measures of anxiety, worry and depressive symptoms from posttreatment for all 16 patients. In addition, there were decreases of other diagnoses, increase in quality of life, less experiential avoidance and fear of emotional responses, and large effects at 3-month follow-up. Many handouts, self-monitoring logs, assignments, experiential exercises, and discussions were included in this treatment to achieve such promising results.

Acceptance-based behavior therapy, in the most refined model discussed in the open trial, continued to make use of Borkovec's CBT for GAD, acceptance and commitment therapy, mindfulness-based cognitive therapy (MBCT), and dialectical behavior therapy. What has been added to the approach, in furthering the mindfulness training component, has been mindfulness-based stress reduction (Kabat-Zinn, 1990, 1994). According to Roemer and Orsillo (2007, p. 73), "training in the skill of mindfulness (i.e., paying attention, on purpose, in the present moment in a nonevaluative and expanded way to both internal and external sensations; (Kabat-Zinn, 1990; Segal et al., 2002) may help to break this habitual anxious cycle of worry."

Some encouraging news for ABBT for GAD is a recent randomized control trial that was conducted by Roemer, Orsillo, and Salters-Pedneault (2008). Thirty-one patients with DSM-IV GAD were assigned to immediate ($n = 15$) or delayed treatment ($n = 16$), and received an adapted treatment protocol of ABBT (Roemer & Orsillo, 2007). The patients were seen for four 90-min sessions, and then twelve 60-min sessions on an individual basis (the last two sessions were every other week). Clinical outcomes were measured by several highly reliable and valid instruments. The findings were that on both clinician-rated and self-reported GAD symptomatology, there were statistically significant reductions at posttreatment. These gains were maintained at 3- and 9-month follow-up. Aside from decreases in GAD symptoms, depressive ones were also reduced as a result of treatment. In addition, 78% of patients no longer met diagnostic criteria for GAD, and 77% achieved high end-state functioning at posttreatment. These gains were maintained percentage-wise over time, or in some cases, actually increased at follow-up. Given that the goal of ABBT is to decrease experiential avoidance and increase mindfulness, these also took place in this study. The higher than average end-state functioning and the other positive findings have now given considerable empirical weight to this approach. A comparison of ABBT to an active treatment in a trial, according to the authors, is also underway. One humble note by the coauthor of the above study – "I wouldn't call it tried and true yet – the RCT only shows that its better than no treatment – we need more data to ensure that it is efficacious beyond nonspecific factors, although I think our trial is promising" (Roemer, e-mail communication, 2008). This clinician would agree with this assessment.

One other note of interest – MBCT (Evans et al., 2008), derived from mindful-ness-based stress reduction (MBSR) (Kabat-Zinn, 1990; Kabat-Zinn et al., 1992), was tested in a group setting of 11 patients with GAD and found to lead to reductions in anxiety and depressive symptoms (from baseline to the end of treatment). The conclusion from this is that group MBCT may have potentially beneficial treatment efficacy for decreasing symptoms in patients with GAD. Randomized-controlled trials are clearly needed. In summary, ABBT has produced, to date, some encouraging results and offers the clinician one more option in maximizing clinical outcomes, while improving quality of life for those who suffer from GAD.

Conclusion

In this chapter a plethora of psychosocial treatments were broached in some detail, to give the clinician, who either treats this population or has an interest in doing so, some viable choices to add to their clinical armamentarium. It is still hard to refute the assertion that CBT remains the best-studied, most evidence-based and commonly used approach in the treatment of GAD. Alford and Beck (1997) suggest that CBT is multidimensional, has integrative power, and is the approach that best meets the criteria of psychotherapy integration. Up until more recently, this may have been true with little debate, as it was the only approach "proven" effective and tolerable for chronically worried and anxious patients.

The word "proven" has begun to take on multiple meanings. The psychotherapy landscape is changing, and even though some of the treatments in this chapter, according to the empirically inclined, require more data in the form of randomized-controlled trials to prove their worth or more extensive empirical evidence (with integrative therapy, emotion regulation therapy moving in that direction), others such as Wolfe's integrative model and supportive–expressive psychodynamic therapy may never achieve that evidence-based status. The latter may still be of value to those with GAD.

The argument above is subject to its own set of criticisms, and the clinician who adopts such a view would be well advised to avail himself or herself as much as possible of the "tried and tested" approaches as a first line treatment in GAD. According to the evidence-based premise, CBT (including Dugas's intolerance of uncertainty approach), ABBT, and metacognitive therapy appear to be first line psychosocial treatments for GAD, given that they have completed successful RCTs.

In addition, one could argue that, based on a "common factors approach", which may at first glance smack in the face of empirical evidence and logic, a clinician also becomes morally obligated to find out, in parallel fashion, what the person with GAD wants, needs, and expects from his or her treatment. This should be done routinely, no matter what the treatment of choice. In this way, a clinician is both better prepared to use what has worked before with GAD patients and is flexible enough to be able to draw from deeper resources (such as clinical experience, the therapeutic relationship, and patient preference).

The ultimate goal should be the welfare of the patients with GAD and the best clinical outcomes across broad measures of functioning, not absolute allegiance to either one's own theory or practice approach, however alluring and intoxicating this may be.

Chapter 5
Pharmacotherapy of Generalized Anxiety Disorder

This chapter title is somewhat of a misnomer, as it implies that what is being discussed here is simply the pharmacopeia for the treatment of GAD. Even though a revolution has taken place in the pharmacologic management of GAD, there has been growing research on the genetics and neurobiological correlates of the disorder. This information gives the clinician a more comprehensive theoretical understanding of GAD and the nature vs. nurture debate. For several years, some have felt that GAD was primarily a psychological disorder and should be treated by psychotherapy (Preston & Johnson, 2004). A more sophisticated and broader view is emerging, and factors in the reality that, for most psychiatric conditions (including GAD), the answer is not a simple either psychology or biology response. In most cases, a combination of both influences contributes to the symptomatology, pathogenesis, and management of many different emotional maladies (Nutt, Rickels, & Stein, 2002).

The initial part of this publication has focused extensively on various conceptual models and psychosocial treatments aimed at maximizing treatment outcomes in GAD. However, without looking more closely at the biomedical contributions to this disorder, it would become increasingly apparent that a serious disservice is taking place when it comes to GAD sufferers. Even after all the empirical research on the medical model is presented on GAD, there will always remain a few select diehards, as occurs in all human endeavors, who remain myopically committed to the psychosocial approach, while others, without question, will continue to favor the biological one. Once again, this is often at the detriment of the individual needs of the patient and relies on the exclusive authority (often dogmatism) of the researcher and clinician.

Genetics

Genetic studies suggest a moderate degree of inheritability for generalized anxiety disorder (GAD) (Shulz et al. 2005). Prevalence rates for GAD range from 20% (Noyes, Clarkson, Crowe, Yates, & McChesney, 1987) to 22% (Skre,

M.E. Portman, *Generalized Anxiety Disorder Across the Lifespan*,
DOI: 10.1007/978-0-387-89243-6_5, © Springer Science + Business Media, LLC 2009

Onstad, Edvardsen, Torgersen, & Kringlen, 1994) for individuals who have a first-degree relative with GAD, compared with 4% in the control sample (Noyes et al., 1987). Twin studies show that 21% of monozygotic twins are concordant with GAD, compared with 13% for dizygotic ones (Andrews, Stewart, Allen, & Henderson, 1990). Scherrer et al. (2000) examined 3,362 male twin pairs for a minimum of 1-month duration (lifetime prevalence of 12.3%), and estimated inheritability at 38%. It was also found that there was no evidence for the effect of a shared environment on risk for GAD. Two other findings from this study are worthy of mention: (1) the inheritability of GAD is slightly lower than panic, and (2) heritability of GAD is the same as that observed for MDD, as they are both marked by chronic dysphoria. Another finding related to GAD and panic disorder showed that GAD patients more frequently had first-degree relatives with GAD, and panic disorder patients were more likely to have had first-degree relatives with panic disorder (Noyes et al., 1992).

Other studies of twins suggest a shared genetic propensity to both GAD and MDD (Noyes, 2001). Genetic studies seem to strongly imply that GAD and MDD share a common genetic basis, and that the environment affects their manifestation (Kendler, Neale, Kessler, Heath, & Eaves, 1992a). Kendler (1996) has gone so far as to say that GAD and MDD can, for all intensive purposes, be considered basically the same disorder, using replicated data from subsequent interviews in his samples. This assertion was also based on later data from two samples of Swedish twin studies (Kendler, Gardner, Gatz, & Pedersen, 2007; Roy, Neale, Pedersen, Mathe, & Kendler, 1995). The statement by Kendler that GAD and MDD are virtually the same disorder, was in response to older claims that GAD did not exist as a valid syndrome. This lends further support to the notion that it is the non-genetic factors that differentiate the two disorders (Hettema, e-mail communication, 2008). This seems to be confirmed in a later study by Kessler et al. (2008), where they concluded that GAD and MDD are not the same disorder, based on the difference in risk factors. The most recent review of the relationship between GAD and MDD was recently published by Hettema (2008). This article will clearly, as the author asserts, shape the direction in the future *DSM-V* to a more refined understanding of these two disorders' connection. There seems to be, based on growing research, some obvious areas of similarity between the conditions and also marked differences.

Some have argued that it is not genetic factors specifically, but heritability – a general biological vulnerability to anxiety and other factors – which synergizes, creating the right conditions for the emergence of GAD (Barlow, 2002; Kendler, 1996; Kendler et al., 1995). In other words, there is an interplay of biological (physiological), psychological (information processing), and environmental (interpersonal functioning) (Cassidy, 1995; Cassidy & Shaver, 1995) components that converge, creating a confluence of dimensions that directs the composite influences that shape the formation of GAD into a distinct disorder.

In returning to the more traditional twin studies, GAD is moderately regulated by genetic factors, accounting for 30% of the variance due to inheritability (Kendler et al., 1995; Kendler, Neale, Kessler, Heath, & Eaves, 1992b). Additionally, heritable traits such as neuroticism, negative affectivity, and anxiety can account for 30–50% of the influence and may also play a role in the development of anxiety disorders (Brown, Chorpita, & Barlow, 1998; Clark, Watson, & Mineka, 1994; Trull & Sher, 1994; Zinbarg & Barlow, 1996). Akiskal (1998) and colleagues (Akiskal et al., 2005) feel that personality traits start early in life and lead to an anxious temperament, a precursor for GAD.

In a meta-analysis of family and twin studies, family members were six times more likely than others to have GAD (Hettema, Neale, & Kendler, 2001). This clearly demonstrates a moderate familial aggregation. In addition, in the twin studies, 32% of variance in liability to GAD was attributable to additive factors, including the environment. Hettema, Prescott, and Kendler (2004) found, in a study of 8,000 twins of male–male, female–female, and male–female combinations, that GAD and the personality trait of neuroticism are very strongly and heavily linked by genetic factors. The correlation was .80 between neuroticism and general anxiety. These findings argue that genetic factors underlying the trait of neuroticism are nearly indistinguishable from those that influence liability to GAD, while environmental risk factors, on the other hand, are only modestly correlated between neuroticism and GAD. Another intriguing result is that the rates of genetic correlation between neuroticism and GAD are similar or greater in men, suggesting no statistical power to confirm that neuroticism and GAD can be explained by a greater sharing of genetic risk factors in women (in spite of women suffering from the disorder, according to most research, in a 2:1 ratio to men). No specific genetic loci have been identified and replicated in independent samples (Merikangas & Low, 2005).

The bottom line is that GAD is inheritable, but the estimates are rather imprecise (Hettema, personal e-mail communication, 2007). Yet, genetics are important factors in understanding GAD and should not be dismissed out of hand.

Neurobiology

Several neurotransmitters have been implicated in anxiety states, and there seems to be a dynamic interaction among several of these different systems (Shulz et al., 2005). More particularly, the GABA (γ-aminobutyric acid) neuronal system may play a significant role in GAD. Benzodiazepines, in the way of abnormalities in the GABA receptor site, have been reported to be helpful in anxiety disorders such as GAD (Tiihonen et al., 1997). In animal studies GABA-A receptor dysfunction may contribute in the development of GAD (Crestani et al., 1999). Patients with GAD show a decrease in peripheral benzodiazepine receptors and reductions in pBR messenger ribonucleic acid (Rocca et al., 1998). In addition, clinical studies demonstrate that this class of medications is effective in treating GAD (Rickels, Case, Schweizer, Garcia-Espana, & Fridman, 1991). Nutt et al. (2001) found that, even though the GABA-A receptor complex is affected by a cluster of genes in chromosome of the subunits 5, there is no evidence of any chromosomal abnormality specifically associated with GAD.

Another neurotransmitter, norepinephrine, has shown inconclusive and inconsistent findings when it comes to GAD. One study found elevated plasma levels of norepinephrine and decreased A2-adrenergic function in GAD patients (Sevy, Papadimitriou, Surmount, Goldman, & Mendlewicz, 1989). Norepinephrine activity is elevated in GAD, causing receptor downregulation, while other studies have not been able to replicate these findings (Matthew, Ho, Francis, Taylor, & Weinman, 1982; Munjack et al., 1990). A response to clonidine (an A2 adrenergic agonist) has been seen in patients with GAD, suggesting a decrease in A2 adrenergic receptor sensitivity, as seen in MDD (Abelson et al., 1991).

In regard to serotonin, both overactivity and underactivity of the serotonergic system has been hypothesized in the pathogenesis of GAD (Jetty, Charney, & Goddard, 2001; Nutt et al., 2001). When it comes to the hypothalamic–pituitary–adrenal axis, cortisol, the primary hormone implicated in stress, has been shown to be elevated in GAD patients (Tafet et al., 2001). In another study by Tafet, Toister-Achituv, and Shinitzky (2001), exogenous cortisol induced an increase in the serotonin transporter gene. The serotonin transporter gene, located on chromosome 17q – polymorphism of the second intron of the gene – was seen in higher rates in 39 patients with GAD (Ohara et al., 1999).

In summary, there have been both serotenergic and noradrenergic abnormalities in patients with GAD (Nutt et al., 2001). Gabanergic dysregulation also appears to play a role in GAD. However, due to the mixed findings and paucity of data in this area, further research is necessary to tease out the neurobiological correlates of GAD and other anxiety spectrum disorders.

One final caveat – the pathobiology for GAD is still in a state of change and constantly evolving, in spite of more recent evidence that the neurobiology of GAD indicates a role for neurophysiologic (Davis, 2006) and neurochemical (Matthew, Price, & Charney, 2008) processes, derived from data found in animal studies. However, these conclusions are speculative at present.

Medications Used for Generalized Anxiety Disorder

There are several medication classes that have been used effectively in the treatment of GAD. The multiplicity of pharmaceutical agents target different neurotransmitter systems, has unique side effect profiles, and requires individualized dosing schedules, dependent on the patient's needs and presenting symptoms. This revolution in pharmacotherapy for GAD has accelerated greatly over the last 5–10 years. Academic psychiatrists and psychopharmacologists have been collecting a plethora of empirical data from multiple research centers to determine which psychotropic agents can ameliorate the chronic, all too often, debilitating cognitive and somatic symptoms of GAD.

In looking at the data more globally before starting a more comprehensive review of the pharmacologic options for GAD, Yonkers, Dyck, Warshaw, & Keller

(2000), in a 5-year national follow-up, found a 38% remission rate for those taking medications, and comorbidity was reduced by 50%. Granted that the research used *DSM-III-R* criteria for GAD, another study (Pollack, 2002), in a noncomplicated GAD sample within a 6-month period, found that adequate pharmacotherapy led to remission rates of 70%. However, relapse was quite high at 6–12 months after discontinuation of medications. Hales, Hilty, and Wise (1997) found a relapse rate of 25% within a month of discontinuing, and 60–80% within a 1-year period.

For many years the benzodiazepines (i.e., valium, alprazolam, clonazepam, ativan, and others) have been the "gold standard" (Nutt et al., 2001, p. 65) and treatment of choice (Doble, Martin, & Nutt, 2003; Uhlenhuth, Balter, Ban, & Yang, 1999) in decreasing the symptoms of anxiety and tension in a rapid way for chronically anxious patients. According to Shader and Greenblatt (1993), they are the most studied class of medications, and effective treatments for GAD. Even though benzodiazepines continue to have their place as a legitimate pharmacological option for GAD, nonresponders to antidepressants, and those with unfavorable reactions, a paradigm shift has taken place, arguing for the use of selective serotonin reuptake inhibitors (SSRIs) and venlafaxine – a selective norepinephrine reuptake inhibitor (SNRI) – as first line treatments for this population (Davidson, 2001; Lydiard, 2000; Pollack, 2001). Several reasons for this shift have been offered, including a broader spectrum efficacy of antidepressants, less risk of developing dependence and withdrawal, a relatively benign side effect profile, and the greater potential to prevent or treat emergent depressive symptoms that often co-occur with GAD (Ballenger et al., 2001; Culpepper, 2002; Gorman, 2002). However, in order to present a balanced and even-handed picture of the wide-ranging psychiatric medications available at this point for treating GAD, this publication will cover the different psychotropic agents and the empirical data that support their clinical use.

Benzodiazepines have been reserved for shorter term use, as adjuncts to antidepressants and, in a minority of cases, for long-term maintenance in more chronic and complicated profiles (Pollack, 2001; Davidson, 2001; Schweizer, 1995). They are generally well tolerated but can cause sedation, decreased concentration, and decreased psychomotor function. These side effects normally occur early in treatment, and are transient in nature, and patients gradually tolerate the side effects without losing the benefits of the anxiolytic one (Ballenger, 1999).

In a multicenter, double-blind, randomized trial using 121 outpatients with GAD, Figueira (1995) demonstrated the efficacy of alprazolam extended release at 2 mg/day, a benzodiazepine, with this disorder. Mumford, Evans, Fleishaker, and Griffiths (1995) confirmed this finding and added that the extended release version of alprazolam caused less potential for abuse than the immediate release type. In two other studies, Moller, Volz, Riemann, and Stoll (2001) and Rickels et al. (2002), using *DSM-IV* criteria for GAD and conducting a fixed-dose, double-blind study, with 2 mg/day and 1.5 mg/day respectively, found alprazolam to be superior to placebo, and effective in the short-term treatment of GAD.

Additionally, the Harvard/Brown Anxiety Research Program (Salzman, Goldenberg, Bruce, & Keller, 2001) studied prescription rates in the early to mid-1990s and found more monotherapy with benzodiazepines for GAD than with SSRIs alone or in combination. If anything, there is a more recent trend towards using SSRIs/SNRIs alone, as mentioned earlier, combining SSRIs with benzos (Lydiard & Monnier, 2004; Ninan, 2002) and less monotherapy with benzos alone. However, confirming studies have not been many, even at this point, for combination medication strategies in this population.

Overall, "several randomized, controlled trials of benzos have demonstrated acute clinical efficacy in reducing GAD symptom severity. The long-term efficacy of benzos is less robust" (Pollock & Kuo, 2004, p. 5). Yet there still remains, more today than in the past, an inherent prejudice against prescribing benzos for longer term maintenance in chronically anxious patients (Preston & Johnson, 2004). Few controlled studies support the long-term use of these medications in GAD, yet given the chronicity of this disorder, many patients may need these drugs for years (Connor & Davidson, 1998). This is certainly depriving patients, especially those with more somatic clinical presentations, of the relief necessary to decrease functional impairment in key social and vocational areas, and ultimately improve their quality of life.

Benzodiazepines continue to play an important role in the amelioration of symptoms with a certain subset of GAD sufferers (Nutt, 2005; Rynn & Brawman-Mintzer, 2004). An excellent and humane article by Hoehn-Saric (2007) on the pharmacotherapy of GAD and its somatic treatments discusses the need to consider the uniqueness of each patient and how treatment plans have to be tailored to meet each patient's specific needs. Hoehn-Saric concludes that a minority of patients need continuous pharmacologic treatment, including benzodiazepines. He writes, "it would be short-sighted and insensitive to deny such patients medications that could improve their quality of life" (Hoehn-Saric, 2007, p. 36). In summary, there needs to be a more balanced view and use of the benzodiazepines in the treatment of GAD (Williams & McBride, 1998).

Buspirone, an azapirone, and the first nonbenzodiazepine to receive the Food and Drug Administration (FDA) approval for GAD, has marshaled some evidence to support its effectiveness in treating GAD. Using *DSM-III* data (Enkelman, 1991; Laakman et al., 1998; Olajide & Lader, 1987; Pecknold et al., 1989) and *DSM-III-R* criteria, Pollack, Worthington, Manfro, Otto, & Zucker (1997) found that 15 mg/day of buspirone was equally effective as diazepam, and superior to placebo in the treatment of GAD. In another study, Davidson, DuPont, Hedges, and Haskins (1999) compared buspirone (30 mg/day) with venlafaxine (150mg/day) against placebo, finding both drug treatment groups outperforming the placebo. Yet, venlafaxine exhibited an earlier onset of therapeutic benefit. In addition, venlafaxine showed advantages over buspirone on the Hamilton Depression Scale anxiety subscore (Hamilton, 1960). Lader and Scotto (1998) found, in a study drawn from six primary care settings comparing buspirone (30 mg/day) with hydroxyzine (37.5 mg/day) vs. placebo, that buspirone was not significantly different than placebo. Hydroxyzine was superior to buspirone and placebo. Rickels et al. (1982) found buspirone to be effective in the treatment of GAD; "however recent studies are more equivocal about buspirone's efficacy in GAD and the symptoms of its common comorbid conditions" (Pollock & Kuo, 2004, p. 5).

In a comprehensive meta-analytic review of the literature regarding efficacy of drug treatments for GAD, drawn from databases, hand searches, secondary sources, the Internet, contacting researchers and pharmaceutical companies, the results of 48 studies were integrated comparing benzodiazepines with buspirone (Mitte, Noack, Steel, & Hautzinger, 2005). The conclusion of the results demonstrated that benzodiazepines and buspirone were equally effective in the short-term treatment of GAD patients. In terms of reduction of symptoms, there were no significant differences, yet compliance was higher for benzodiazepines than for buspirone.

The data appear inconsistent, as some studies confirm buspirone's efficacy for GAD, while other studies see it as having limited utility and versatility as a first line medication option for this disorder (Ballenger, 1999; Gitlin, 1996). Arana, Rosenbaum and Hyman (2000) have argued that it has a narrowness in terms of its anxiolytic effect; clinicians often use subtherapeutic doses and it appears not to be useful when GAD presents with comorbid depressive symtomatology (Bakish, 1999; Lydiard & Monnier, 2004). This tends to make it a second line treatment in cases of potentially uncomplicated GAD. In particular, it may prove a viable alternative to benzodiazepines for those individuals with GAD and a substance abuse history.

The bulk of the research dollars and human investment of time (on the part of biologically minded academic researchers in the field of psychiatry and psychopharmacology) has been devoted to testing the efficacy of antidepressants and other novel agents with this clinical population. In addition, large pharmaceutical companies often provide the back drop, in many cases, for these psychotropic agents to be researched and tested in order to benefit the chronically anxious patient. The FDA, a licensing board of no small renown, which grants their approval to a large number of these medications, provides the sine qua non to market these same agents worldwide for the particular purpose of addressing the clinical needs of millions of GAD sufferers.

The question then remains – are we actually offering the much needed symptom relief patients with GAD require, or are we in many cases indiscriminately marketing and prescribing medications to medicate away common feelings of worry and anxiety so pervasive in our culture? There are those social critics (Dworkin, 2006) who feel strongly that primary care physicians have created an epidemic, producing a large class of patients who are now artificially happy, but no closer to the goal of achieving authentic and enduring well-being than they were before starting these medications. Some sophisticated voices have argued that psychiatric maladies are not always about "twisted neurons" (McHugh, 1999), but deeper life concerns that require a lessening of the distance between the idealized world we all desire to a greater or lesser degree and the world of reality that we face every day. Other less discriminating voices are more vociferous in their call for a demedicalization of mental illness and the use of the *DSM*, plus abandoning drug therapy as a means to combat human suffering (Breggin, 1994, Breggin & Cohen, 2000; Healy, 1999, 2004; Szasz, 1984).

Proponents of the medical model have also made their voices heard (Andreasen, 1984; Andreasen & Black, 2001; Nutt & Ballenger, 2003; Nutt et al., 2001; Stein, 2004; Stein & Hollander, 2002; Stein, Lerer, & Stahl, 2005), and attempt to use evidence-based research in support of their claims, rather than more subjective appeals by their opponents, who rely on limited objective support for antimedication diatribes.

On the basis of many years of clinical experience and serious research efforts delving into the pros and cons of medication use for GAD patients, I have quelled my initial skepticism. Over the years, an increasingly vital role that a select group of medications can play in enhancing the lives of chronically worried and anxious patients has been observed. There is no need to hide my own bias on this matter. These agents are not a panacea, but offer symptomatic relief for many with GAD. GAD patients tend not to be on the loud or vocal side about their misery and discontent. Given that they often suffer in silence for many years before seeking help, this is a large victory – when relief is palpable and calms their internal disquietude.

Allgulander (2007), a prominent psychiatrist and leading expert on GAD, challenges the more passive attitude of GAD sufferers. He argues quite cogently, that patients with GAD have a skeptical attitude towards anxiolytics. This is due, in large part, to their readings about these medications on Web sites, which often make claims, as discussed above, that distort and confound the truth. The attitude that GAD patients bring to the prescribing psychiatrist and/or physician is of critical importance to understand, and can offset the potential of viewing these patients as demanding or difficult.

These ideological rivalries, in the final analysis, often bear little fruit. However, some dissention in the ranks of those motivated by a genuine concern for the welfare of GAD patients (rather than knee jerk visceral attacks on medication use as a whole for psychiatric disorders) can aid in promoting a much needed corrective to potential excess. Dissemination of accurate information regarding both the risks and benefits of medication can be done with greater discrimination. This can pave the way to more individualized pharmacologic management of patients with GAD and the judicious use of various pharmaceutical options available to medical providers directly involved in treating these individuals. This is especially critical given that "the importance of optimizing treatment for GAD is underscored by evidence that GAD is associated with significant morbidity, chronicity and poor long term prognosis" (Lydiard & Monnier 2004, p. 351). Having said this, the empirical data surrounding the cornucopia of the most commonly used medications (and newer ones being investigated) for this disorder can now be further explored within a larger social and moral context.

Venlafaxine, a selective norepinephrine reuptake inhibitor, has been the most widely studied antidepressant for GAD and the first to be given FDA approval. In a 6-month trial, Gelenberg et al. (2000), using the HAM-A, found that 69% of those treated with venlafaxine exhibited a clinical response, compared with 42% for placebo. Remission rates were higher for the drug-treated group. Overall, the authors, based on their research, concluded that venlafaxine improved anxiety across all measures. In a 6-month fixed-dose trial by Allgulander, Hackett, and Salinas (2001), there was a 52% response rate for venlafaxine-XR-treated subjects. The doses used were 37.5, 75, and 150 mg/day. At 8 weeks, the 75/150-mg/day dosing were superior to placebo on all measures. The 37.5-mg/day dose was only better on the Hamilton anxiety subscale. At 24 weeks there was greater efficacy maintained at all doses, and with higher doses even greater improved social functioning. Rickels, Pollack, Sheehan, and Haskins (2000), in a double-blind, study using a placebo as a control group, treated 300 nondepressed GAD outpatients with 75, 150, and 225 mg/day of venlafaxine. Improvements in symptoms began as early as the first week. The most clinically significant findings occurred in the group receiving 225 mg/day and persisted through the 8 weeks of treatment. The medication was generally well tolerated and reduced both somatic and psychic symptoms. Guitierrez, Stimmel, and Aiso (2003) confirmed, in a clinical research update, both the short-term and long-term effectiveness of venlafaxine in treating GAD.

A more recent clinical trial (Meoni, Hackett, & Lader, 2004), using a pooled analysis from five short-term (8 weeks), double-blind, multicenter, placebo-controlled studies, measuring venlafaxine XR efficacy on somatic and psychic symptoms with 1,841 patients with DSM-IV GAD criteria, confirmed previous outcome measures. The results demonstrated a decrease in both psychic and somatic symptoms, beginning from 1–2 weeks of treatment. In psychic symptoms there was a 58% response rate vs. 38% for placebo at week 8. By week 24, the response rate increased to 66% for the venlafaxine-treated group vs. 35% for placebo. In regard to somatic symptoms at week 8, there was a 56% response rate for the drug-treated group and 43% for placebo. At week 24, the rates were 67% for venlafaxine-treated patients vs. 47% for placebo. Venlafaxine reduced at a similar rate of >50% for both psychic and somatic symptoms, whereas the placebo group had a greater effect on just somatic symptoms (>40% rate). Overall there was a greater improvement in psychic symptoms over somatic ones when venlafaxine was compared with placebo. In an 8-week, double-blind, placebo-controlled study of Greek outpatients with GAD using a flexible-dose of venlafaxine XR (75–150 mg/day) vs. placebo, 62.5% achieved remission on venlafaxine XR vs. 9.1% of those on placebo (Nimatoudis et al., 2004).

A post hoc analysis of pooled data from five placebo-controlled, double-blind, randomized studies in nondepressed GAD patients treated with venlafaxine XR vs. placebo, was carried out by Stahl, Ahmed, and Handiquet (2007) to determine the temporal response of psychic and somatic symptoms. It was concluded that venlafaxine XR was beneficial in reducing both types of symptoms, and the longer periods on medication led to greater additional improvements in these symptoms. Maintenance on the medication may be a more prudent choice in partial responders earlier in their treatment, than switching to another class of medication in a premature manner, according to the authors of this analysis. Finally, venlafaxine is generally well tolerated and effective in the short- and long-term treatment of GAD.

There have been several multicenter, placebo-controlled studies testing the effectiveness of paroxetine, the first SSRI approved for the treatment of GAD. Pollack et al. (2001), using a flexible-dose of paroxetine, ranging from 20 to 50 mg/day, demonstrated a 50% reduction on the HAM-A (Hamilton, 1959) ratings, and a greater response rate than placebo. In addition, this clinical trial used 324 patients meeting the criteria for GAD and was done over an 8-week period. There was a 72.4% response rate for the drug-treated group and 42.5% remission rate for those who completed the study. There were also high placebo rates of 26.3% in terms of clinical response, and a 55.6% rate for those who completed the study. Remission rates were not measured for the placebo group. Another short-term study of 8 weeks duration supported the effectiveness of 20–50 mg/day of paroxetine in the treatment of GAD (Rickels et al., 2003). Bellew, McCafferty, Iyengar, and Zaninelli (2000) further confirmed the efficacy of paroxetine for

GAD and, once again, found a reduction in HAM-A scores. Paroxetine (20 mg/day) showed superior effects, compared with imipramine (75 mg/day) and 2-chlordes-methyldiazepan (4.2 mg/day). Sheehan, Harnett-Sheehan, and Raj (1996) confirmed, using the Sheehan Disability Scale (SDS; Sheehan, (1983)), decreased impairment on paroxetine as early as week 1. Both responders and remitters showed a lessening of symptoms.

Stocchi et al. (2003), in a sample of 559 patients with GAD, observed, after 8 weeks in a single-blind trial using 20–50 mg/day of paroxetine, greater remission rates over time and increased relapse with placebo. There was a 73% remission after 6 months on paroxetine in this study, demonstrating that the longer course of treatment proved important. Continuing paroxetine in this same sample for 24 weeks led to an 11% relapse in the drug-treated group and 41% in the placebo. This is considered the only placebo-controlled relapse prevention study of this medication.

Finally, in a review of the paroxetine clinical trials database, where 3 short-term studies lasting 8 weeks, and a longer 6-month relapse prevention study were evaluated (Rickels, Rynn, Iyengar, & Duff, 2006), it was found that this medication was effective and safe in the short- and long-term treatment of GAD. Paroxetine also allowed a sizeable number of patients with GAD to achieve remission and prevent relapse.

Another SSRI, sertraline, has been investigated with somewhat less frequency, but has proven to have a positive effect on outcomes for GAD sufferers. Allgulander et al. (2004), in a large sample of *DSM-IV* criteria GAD subjects using a flexible-dose of 50–150 mg/day vs. placebo, revealed that, in a 12-week treatment trial, sertraline produced superiority in quality of life and subject satisfaction, compared with placebo. In addition, the study examined the effects of sertraline on both psychic and somatic symptoms in a randomly assigned sample of 378 patients with GAD. Patients had scores of ≥18 on the HAM-A to meet diagnostic criteria, and exhibited a decrease of 7.7 points for taking sertraline, while having a 5.2 point reduction for those on placebo. Some additional results revealed, at the end of 12 weeks, 6.7 point reduction for psychic symptoms and 5.0 point reduction for somatic ones. Remission rates were 31% on sertraline and 37% for completers of the study. There was an 18% remission for placebo and 23% for completers on placebo. Generally, the medication was well tolerated, with comparable rates of discontinuation due to side effects at 8% for those taking sertraline and 10% on placebo. Finally, the anxiolytic effect was active by week 4, and the drug continued to be effective through week 12 across all primary and secondary measures.

One of the most recent clinical trials (Dahl et al., 2005) to date using sertraline was aimed at determining the efficacy of this antidepressant on both psychic and somatic symptoms. In a 12-week, double-blind, placebo-controlled, flexible-dose study (50–150 mg/day), with 184 *DSM-IV* outpatients assigned to the drug treatment group and 184 to placebo, the results were clinically significant in terms of reductions on psychic and somatic symptoms across both primary and secondary measures. Similar levels of reductions in symptoms were found at week 12 using the HAM-A on the psychic factor (59.3%) and the somatic factor (53.6%). In addition, quality of life was rated as improved by the GAD subjects, as measured by the Quality of Life, Enjoyment, and Satisfaction Questionnaire (Q-LES-Q; Endicott et al., 1993).

One interesting footnote is that, in contrast to the *DSM-IV*, with its focus on "worry" (a psychic symptom), somatic symptoms of anxiety among GAD outpatients in these investigations were a prominent component of their overall clinical presentations, in spite of the samples being selected based on high levels of psychic anxiety. The magnitude of these findings is impressive, given that they were conducted at 21 investigational sites in Australia, Canada, Denmark, Norway, and Sweden. Rating scales were the HAM-A, investigator-rated Clinical Global Impression, Severity and Improvement scales (CGI-S and CGI-I; Guy, 1976), the Montgomery and Asberg Depression Rating Scale (MADRS; Montgomery & Asberg, 1979) for secondary depressive symptoms, and finally the Q-LES-Q.

In the most recent double-blind, placebo-controlled, randomized, flexible-dose 10-week study (Brawman-Mintzer, Knapp, Rynn, Carter, & Rickels, 2006), 117 outpatients with DSM-IV GAD were treated with sertraline vs. 174 that completed placebo. Findings were generally consistent with those of Allgulander et al. (2004) study. Differences between groups were smaller in this trial, and there were higher placebo rates. Response rates were 59.2% on sertraline vs. 48.2% on placebo. Sertraline proved effective in the treatment of GAD in this study.

In a rare study (Ball, Kuhn, Wall, Shekhar, & Goddard, 2005), comparative in nature, where paroxetine and sertraline were evaluated, measuring the effectiveness of one drug against the other, 55 patients with DSM-IV GAD criteria in a parallel group, double-blind, flexible-dose study, were randomly assigned to receive either paroxetine or sertraline for 8 weeks. Several measures were used to assess the outcomes, which included mean changes in Hamilton Rating Scales for Anxiety, the Clinical Global Impression Scale (responder/remission rates), the Indiana University GA Measurement Scales (Ball, Lightfoot, Goddard, & Shekhar, 2003), self-report ratings of anxiety, quality of life outcomes, and tolerability assessed using systematic assessment for both treatment emergent events and symptoms. The results proved virtually identical, with both drug treatment groups showing significant decreases in mean Hamilton scores: 57% ± 28% with paroxetine vs. 56% ± 28% with sertraline. There was no significant difference found between medication groups for either response or remission rates. The tolerability was similar in terms of side effects. In summary, they were equally effective and well tolerated for the treatment of GAD.

The newest antidepressant medication (with anxiolytic properties in the arsenal for treating GAD) is escitalopram, an SSRI, which now has FDA approval for this disorder. In a multicenter study of patients with DSM-IV GAD, Davidson, Bose, Korotzer, and Zheng (2004) found that 10–20 mg/day of escitalopram was superior to placebo in reducing HAM-A scores. The lower dose of 10 mg/day was effective for most patients with GAD. In this double-blind, placebo-controlled study, using a flexible-dose of escitalopram, response rates at week 8 was 68% for escitalopram and 41% for placebo. The GAD patients were 18 or older, met *DSM-IV* criteria, and had a baseline HAM-A greater or equal to 18. For the first 4 weeks the subjects were on 10 mg/day of escitalopram, then a flexible dose of 10–20 mg/day or placebo. On the HAM-A, the mean change from baseline was −11.3% for escitalopram and −7.4% for placebo. There was a significant improvement as early as week 1, and the total score on the HAM-A was significantly reduced on the psychic anxiety scale. Somatic symptoms were also improved, even though it was not reported in the research (Davidson, e-mail communication, 2004). Finally, it was revealed that the anxiolytic effect, especially that which targeted somatic symptoms, seemed to respond to 10 mg/day. The higher dose of 20 mg/day was generally not needed in this GAD sample.

Baldwin, Huusom, and Maehlum (2004) revealed that escitalopram is effective at 5 mg/day, and more so on 10–20 mg/day than paroxetine, but is better tolerated by individuals who present with GAD. This was based on a "medium term treatment" trial in a randomized, double-blind, placebo-controlled, parallel group, fixed-dose, 12-week study ($n = 681$) using doses of 5, 10, and 20 mg/day of escitalopram compared with placebo, and paroxetine (20 mg/day). The higher doses of escitalopram were superior to paroxetine and placebo on both the HAM-A psychic anxiety (10 mg/day, week 4 onwards; 20 mg/day, week 10) and somatic anxiety factors (week 12).

Baldwin and Nair (2005), in a follow-up comprehensive review article, summarize the current evidence-base for the pharmacological treatment of GAD. In a pooled analysis of three positive, double-blind controlled studies with 856 patients (421 received escitalopram, 419 received placebo) meeting *DSM-IV* diagnostic criteria for GAD, it was found that escitalopram had prominent anxiolytic properties for GAD. The findings of three studies have been published separately (Davidson et al., 2004; Goodman, Bose, & Wang, 2005; Stein, Anderson Frus, & Goodman, 2005), yet they have produced similar results. The trial designs for all three studies were also virtually identical, and they have been subject to pooled analysis in the cited publications.

Overall, the conclusion of the pooled analyses indicate that escitalopram, at a dose of 10 mg/day, is superior to placebo from week 1 until the dose is optionally increased to 20 mg/day at week 4 or 6. The superiority of escitalopram to placebo continued with the 10-mg/day dose until the end of the study. Escitalopram was superior on all primary and secondary measures as determined from baseline to week 8 on HAM-A scores. Response rates were 47.5% with drug treatment vs. 28.6% on placebo. Those very much improved were 52.0% on escitalopram and 37.0% on placebo. In terms of remission, 26.4% reported this on escitalopram, while 14.1% did on placebo. The above studies lasted only 8 weeks and are considered "acute treatment" trials. Stein (2005) pooled the data from these studies and found escitalopram to be efficacious for GAD on a range of anxiety and depressive measures, and demonstrated significant improvement in quality of life. In the end it was concluded that this medication has broad spectrum efficacy for GAD. These findings were confirmed by other investigators (Goodman et al., 2005).

The "long term treatment" trials for GAD using escitalopram have been investigated in two studies. The first one was an open-label, flexible-dose (10–20 mg/day) extension study, in patients who previously had completed double-blind, acute treatment (Davidson et al., 2004). The second study was a randomized, double-blind, flexible-dose comparison of escitalopram (10–20 mg/day) and paroxetine (20–50 mg/day) (Bielski, Bose, Nil, & Chang, 2004). In the first study, those patients who had participated in one of the three double-blind, placebo-controlled, "acute treatment" trials could now enter a 24-week, open-label extension trial (Davidson, Bose, & Wang, 2005), receiving escitalopram at a fixed-dose (10 mg/day) for the first 4 weeks, then a flexible-dose (10–20 mg/day) until the end of the study. The majority of patients were responders (76.1%), and there was a gradual reduction of HAM-A scores over 24 weeks. In the second investigation of escitalopram, patients underwent 1 week of single-blind, placebo treatment, followed by 24 weeks of double-blind treatment with escitalopram or paroxetine, and a final 2-week down titration period. There were 123 patients (escitalopram, $n = 61$; paroxetine, $n = 62$) who underwent double-blind treatment. HAM-A scores reduced for both drug-treated groups, yet there was not a significant difference (albeit a numerical one) for the escitalopram-treated group (mean dose of 14.4 mg/day) over paroxetine-treated (mean dose of 29.9 mg/day) at 8 and 24 weeks of treatment (65% vs. 55.7% and 78.3% vs. 62.3%, respectively). One important note – escitalopram was better tolerated in this study than paroxetine.

In several clinical reviews, escitalopram demonstrated effectiveness in the treatment of GAD. Sylvester (2003) found, after reviewing three 8-week studies, that treatment with escitalopram led to significant remission rates for GAD. The rates of remission were similar to those witnessed after 5-year follow-up with CBT treatment. Finn (2004) concluded, based on a poster presentation by Davidson (sponsored by the National Institute of Mental Health (NIMH)), that in an open label study, 85% of completers rated anxiety and tension as mild or not present on the HAM-A. In addition, anxiety scores continuously improved over a 24-week period in patients taking escitalopram for GAD.

Finally, a unique study, conducted in 59 centers in eight countries, had investigated the effects of escitalopram in the prevention of relapse in GAD patients who had responded to acute treatment. In a study by Allgulander, Florea, and Huusom (2006), the efficacy and tolerability of escitalopram in the prevention of relapse was explored. Of the initial 491 adult patients with a diagnosis of GAD, 375 of them responded to initial 12-week treatment and were then randomly assigned to 24–76 weeks of double-blind treatment with escitalopram (20 mg/day) ($n = 187$) or placebo ($n = 181$). The results of the analysis demonstrated that the risk of relapse was four times greater for placebo (56%) vs. escitalopram-treated patients (19%) at the end of treatment. In conclusion, the investigation found that escitalopram was effective at 20 mg/day in preventing relapse and well tolerated in the long-term treatment of GAD.

In an important study by Allgulander et al. (2007), the impact of escitalopram on health-related quality of life (HRQoL) was assessed, as well as the effect of relapse on HRQoL on work productivity. This was conducted alongside a double-blind, placebo-controlled, relapse prevention clinical trial (Allgulander et al., 2005). At baseline, GAD patients revealed significantly impaired quality of life vs. the general population in a 12-week open trial treatment period. There were significant improvements in HRQoL on all dimensions of the SF-36 (Brazier, Roberts, & Deverill, 2002; McHorney, Ware, Lu, & Sherbourne, 1994). After randomization, relapsed patients exhibited significantly lower quality of life than did nonrelapsed patients. It was concluded that short-term treatment with escitalopram reverses functional and daily living impairments. In addition, GAD relapse is associated with deleterious effects on HRQoL and work productivity.

Escitalopram has become the "hot medication" in the acute, medium, and long-term treatment and relapse prevention of GAD. It has demonstrated, in clinical trials, relatively higher treatment outcomes than the other SSRIs/venlafaxine with fewer side effects. One important note is that only the above-mentioned study has investigated relapse prevention on escitalopram. Additionally, there were no relapse rates measured for patients in this study who discontinued escitalopram entirely after staying on the 10-mg/day dose long term. More investigations of this type, with empirical studies that include the other antidepressants, need to be conducted in order to replicate the above findings. The challenges raised are critical, suggesting fertile ground for ongoing research and important areas of future inquiry. However, even with the caveats in mind, these are nonetheless encouraging results.

Another medication, called duloxetine hydrochloride, a dual reuptake inhibitor of serotonin and norepinephrine (SNRI), has been shown effective for GAD in three placebo-controlled trials. Rynn et al. (2008) examined the efficacy, safety, and tolerability of duloxetine. In a 10-week, double-blind, progressive-titration, flexible-dose trial using 60–120 mg/day of duloxetine, it was found that in the drug-treated sample ($n = 168$) vs. placebo ($n = 159$) there was greater improvement in HAM-A scores. In addition, there was a higher response rate and greater global functioning in work, society, family, and home. In this study, duloxetine was effective, well tolerated, and a safe treatment for GAD. In a similar study, that was a 9-week, multicenter, randomized, double-blind, fixed-dose, placebo-controlled, parallel group design, Koponen, et al. (2007) compared 60 mg/day duloxetine ($n = 168$), 120 mg/day duloxetine ($n = 170$), or placebo ($n = 175$). Both doses of the duloxetine resulted in improvements in anxiety symptom severity – both psychic and somatic symptoms, greater functional improvement and greater response, remission and maintenance of treatment gains. In the last placebo-controlled trial (Hartford et al., 2007), a multicenter, randomized, double-blind, flexible-dose, placebo-controlled and active-controlled group (venlafaxine extended release, 75–225 mg/day), duloxetine (60–120 mg/day, $n = 162$) was compared with venlafaxine ($n = 164$) or placebo ($n = 161$). Both duloxetine and venlafaxine showed the greatest improvements with the HAM-A. They were both effective treatments for GAD, especially for worry, anxious mood, and tension. They were also beneficial in the improvement of role functioning.

In a pooled data set from all completed duloxetine trials by Allgulander et al. (2007), the aim was to show the most likely clinical outcomes associated with this medication in the treatment of GAD. The conclusion, from over 1,100 patients, demonstrated that duloxetine was effective in reducing anxiety severity and increasing patient's global role functioning. Remission occurred in one third of patients and both psychic and somatic symptoms were helped. In a study by Endicott et al. (2007), the goal was to examine the efficacy of duloxetine treatment for improving functioning in clinical outcomes for GAD patients in three independent clinical trials. Duloxetine reduced role functioning disabilities associated with GAD and enhanced the patient's quality of life and well-being in all three clinical studies. In other words, patients with GAD were better able to carry out their roles and responsibilities, and this resulted in increased enjoyment, greater engagement with the positive attributes of well-being – satisfaction with life, physical health, and self-fulfillment.

In the most recently published study, duloxetine (Davidson et al., 2008), dosed at 60–120 mg/day, was evaluated in a double-blind, placebo-controlled trial with 405 patients ($n = 204$ for duloxetine-treated vs. $n = 201$ for placebo-treated) suffering from *DMS-IV-TR*-defined GAD to determine its effectiveness at relapse prevention. After 26 weeks in the double-blind continuation phase, which followed a more acute open label phase of patients with GAD who were treatment responders, it was concluded that 13.7% of duloxetine-treated patients relapsed, compared with 41.8% in placebo-treated patients. These results were based on several outcome measures. Even though most of the past research on duloxetine has been in acute clinical trials, this relapse prevention study demonstrated the efficacy of longer term maintenance gains over time. These are encouraging findings.

Another class of agents, more rarely used in the treatment of GAD, has been the tricyclics. In a well-cited study by Kahn et al. (1986), imipramine, a tricyclic, was proven to decrease tension and improve mood. In another study (Rickels, Downing, Schweizer, & Hassman, 1993), imipramine was compared with trazadone, valium and placebo. Imipramine exhibited a 73% improvement in symptoms, 69% for trazadone, 66% for valium, and 47% for placebo. Rocca, Fonzo, Scotta, Zanalda, and Ravizza (1997), in one clinical trial using *DSM-IV* criteria for GAD patients during an 8-week uncontrolled comparative study, found a two third response rate for imipramine, valium, and paroxetine. Imipramine had the most side effects, and valium was the most effective for somatic symptom control. The tricyclics, on the whole, tend to have limited use in GAD because of their side effect profile of constipation, dry mouth, blurred vision, weight gain, and cardiovascular incidences.

Pregabalin is the first anxiolytic to be introduced, in more than 10 years, that works via a novel mechanism of action (Montgomery, 2006). It is a structural analogue of γ-aminobutyric acid (GABA), one of the key inhibitory neurotransmitters in the brain (Bandelow, Wedekind & Leon, 2007). However, it is not active at GABA receptors, nor does it acutely alter upgrade or degradation (Frampton & Foster, 2006). Pregabalin's anxiolytic effect in GAD has been demonstrated in seven acute randomized, double-blind, placebo-controlled trials of 4–8-week duration, and in one 6-month relapse prevention study, at doses ranging from 150–600 mg/day using twice or thrice daily dosing (Owen, 2007). The studies break down into six acute treatment ones (Feltner et al., 2003; Montgomery, Tobias, Zornberg, Kasper, & Pande, 2006; Pande et al., 2003; Pohl, Feltner, Fieve, & Pande, 2005; Rickels et al., 2005). One acute study failed (Pande, Crockatt, Feltner, Liu-Dumaw, & Werth, 2000). Another study was an 8-week study for elderly patients with GAD (Montgomery, Chatamra, Pauer, Whalen & Baldinetti, 2008). There was also a 6-month adult relapse prevention study (Feltner et al., 2008). With the exception of the elderly study, the trials relied on a fixed-dose design of 150–600 mg/day.

The specific studies on pregabalin, mentioned above, in the treatment of GAD, require further examination to flush out more clearly the effectiveness of this medication.

In the study by Pande et al. (2003), this double-blind, randomly assigned, controlled trial consisted of 276 patients, given either 150 mg/day (50 mg t.i.d.) or 600 mg/day of pregabalin (200 mg t.i.d.), 6 mg/day (2 mg t.i.d.) lorazepam, or placebo. The results suggested that all active treatment groups from baseline to endpoint were more effective than placebo as measured on the HAM-A. However, even though 150 and 600 mg/day of pregabalin demonstrated clinical equivalence, lorazepam was seemingly more effective than the lower dose of pregabalin. On the psychic and somatic components of the Hamilton anxiety subscales, 600 mg/day pregabalin and lorazepam reduced scores on the psychic subscale vs. placebo. On the somatic subscale, all three drug-treated groups significantly reduced these scores, compared with placebo. Pregabalin was effective in the treatment of GAD, but the higher dose of 600 mg/day was more effective than the lower dose. In a similar randomized, double-blind, placebo-controlled, fixed-dose, multicenter study by Feltner et al. (2003), with identical drug-treated groups and dosing schedules (with a sample of 271), they found 600 mg/day of pregabalin to be the most effective treated group over placebo for GAD. Lorazepam (6 mg/day) was also more effective than placebo. In regard to psychic and somatic symptoms, 600 mg/day of pregabalin exhibited significantly superior improvement on both these anxiety subscales over placebo. Lorazepam demonstrated significantly superior improvement only on the somatic subscale, but not on the psychic one over placebo. Pregabalin was confirmed as effective in the treatment of GAD.

Rickels et al. (2005) conducted a 4-week, multicenter, double-blind, placebo-controlled trial of pregabalin and alprazalom, with a total of 696 patients, who were screened for the study. The treatment groups consisted of 300, 450, 600 mg/day of pregabalin, 1.5 mg/day of alprazalom, and placebo. At endpoint, all drug-treated groups showed greater efficacy vs. placebo. In addition, all the groups demonstrated significance over placebo on all secondary measures, including the CGI-I, the HAM-A psychic/somatic factors, HAM-A (anxiety/worry and tension items), and the HAM-D. The exception to this was on the somatic anxiety factor for 450 mg/day of pregabalin and 1.5 mg/day of alprazalom. Finally, the greatest responders were those individuals taking 300 mg/day and 600 mg/day of pregabalin. Once again, pregabalin was effective in the treatment of GAD.

In a study by Pohl et al. (2005), the efficacy of pregabalin in the treatment of GAD was examined in a 6-week, double-blind, placebo-controlled comparison of b.i.d. (twice a day) vs. t.i.d. (thrice a day) dosing. The treatment groups were pregabalin (200 mg/day (b.i.d.), 400 mg/day (b.i.d.), 450 mg/day (t.i.d.)) compared with placebo. Comparisons between b.i.d. vs. t.i.d. dosing showed no differences on the HAM-A change scores at end point. All the doses were significantly more effective on psychic and somatic anxiety factor scores than placebo. Once again, pregabalin was an effective treatment for GAD and dosing twice or three times per day had no effect on clinical outcomes.

The efficacy and safety of pregabalin in the treatment of GAD were tested in a 6-week, multicenter, randomized, double-blind, placebo-controlled comparison of pregabalin and venlafaxine (Montgomery et al., 2006). A total of 621 outpatients with GAD were randomly assigned to pregabalin (400 or 600 mg/day), venlafaxine

(75 mg/day), or placebo. All the treatment groups were superior compared with placebo, as measured by changes on the HAM-A. The 400 mg/day pregabalin dose appeared to be superior on all primary and secondary measures. This dose was the most effective on the somatic subscale score. Pregabalin, on both doses, were comparable on the psychic subscale score. Both doses of pregabalin and venlafaxine improved depressive symptoms on the HAM-D total score at end point. Pregabalin also began to show effectiveness by week 1, similar to the other studies. Venlafaxine began to exhibit therapeutic effectiveness as early as week 2. Pregabalin was rapidly effective for the treatment of GAD, had less withdrawal discontinuation than venlafaxine, and was helpful with both psychic and somatic symptoms.

The efficacy of pregabalin in GAD for elderly patients was demonstrated in a double-blind, placebo-controlled, parallel-group trial ($n = 272$; mean age, 72 years) (Montgomery et al., 2008). Pregabalin was flexibly dosed from 150–600 mg/day from weeks 2–6 following a 1-week dose escalation to 150 mg/day. Pregabalin proved superior to placebo in the HAM-A total score – on both psychic and somatic factors. The mean maximal dose tolerated in this elderly population was 270 ± 145 mg/day. Pregabalin was effective and well tolerated in this elderly GAD population.

Feltner et al. (2008), in an 8-week multicenter, randomized, placebo-controlled, double-blind study, evaluated the efficacy of pregabalin in preventing relapse of GAD. This was done after a response to short-term treatment. In a sample of patients with GAD, 168 were randomized to receive 450 mg/day of pregabalin, and 170 to placebo for 6 months. The time to relapse was the primary barometer of efficacy in this study. In the placebo group, 50% had relapsed by day 23, while 42% of pregabalin-treated had relapsed at end point. Attrition was high, which the authors attributed, in part to the length of this study being long term. The conclusion of the study confirmed that pregabalin is effective in preventing relapse in patients with GAD at a fixed-dose of 450 mg/day. One drawback of the study was its premature termination – the FDA requested additional data on some preliminary toxicology findings in mice, even though there were no such risks found in human subjects. It is difficult to say for sure the reasons behind the non-FDA approval of pregabalin for GAD, in spite of strong evidence for its efficacy with this clinical population.

According to Frampton and Foster (2006), pregabalin is the ideal anxiolytic. It has rapid onset like the benzodiazepines, increased efficacy in treating somatic symptoms and secondary insomnia, a safety profile similar to the SSRIs/SNRIs. It also has decreased acute risk of CNS impairment without long-term concerns over dependence or withdrawal. Montgomery (2006, p. 2151), a leading authority on this medication writes, "in conclusion, pregabalin is the most promising new addition to the anxiolytic armamentarium in quite some time." Time will only tell what lies in store for pregabalin in the future treatment of GAD.

Studies have confirmed that tiagabine, a gaba reuptake inhibitor, is effective in the treatment of GAD. Rosenthal (2003), in a 10-week, randomized, open label trial with paroxetine as a positive control, concluded that this novel anxiolytic decreased anxiety and depressive symptoms, and improved quality of sleep and overall functioning. Schaller, Thomas, and Rawlings (2004) found tiagabine effective in low dose acute anxiety treatment. Tiagabine was, in general, well tolerated. In a more recent study (Pollack et al., 2005) the goal was to evaluate the efficacy and tolerability of tiagabine in adults with GAD. An 8-week, randomized, double-blind, multicenter, placebo-controlled study was conducted, where tiagabine was initiated at 4 mg/day and flexibly dosed to 16 mg/day. The sample consisted of 134 drug-treated patients with GAD, while 132 were given placebo. The results found that in the tiagabine group there were reduced symptoms of anxiety, an early onset of the therapeutic effect and no associations with changes in sexual functioning or depressive symptomatology. The most recent research on tiagabine (Pollack, Tiller, Xie, & Trivedi, 2008), citing results accumulated from three randomized, double-blind, placebo-controlled, parallel group studies, found that this medication was not effective with adult patients with GAD. Based on the overall empirical findings, the data appear mixed on the efficacy of tiagabine in GAD. Yet, the most current research just cited disconfirms the earlier, and more favorable, outcomes for this medication.

Hydroxyzine, an antagonist of histamine receptors, showed efficacy and safety in three double-blind studies over placebo with GAD patients. The first study by Darcis, Ferreri, Burtin, and Deram (1995), which was a 4-week, double-blind, placebo-controlled investigation, took place with 110 patients suffering from GAD. The results showed significant efficacy of hydroxyzine over placebo at a daily dose of 50 mg/day. Another 4-week, double-blind, controlled-study (Lader & Scotto, 1998) compared the efficacy of hydroxyzine (50 mg/day) vs. buspirone (20 mg/day) and placebo. Hydroxyzine proved superior to placebo on the HAM-A; while both hydroxyzine and buspirone fared better on CGI and HAD ratings. There was an idiosyncratic dosing of buspirone in this study. In the most recent study, examining hydroxyzine in this population (Llorca et al., 2002), a 3-month, multicenter, double-blind, placebo-controlled, randomized trial compared hydroxyzine (50 mg/day) vs. bromazepam (6 mg/day). This included, in total, a 2-week, single-blind randomized treatment, then 12 weeks of double-blind, randomized treatment, followed by 4 weeks of single-blind, run-out placebo. Hydroxyzine was more effective than placebo, yet there was no statistical difference between hydroxyzine and bromazepam. This medication showed both efficacy and safety in the treatment of GAD and appears to be a viable alternative to benzodiazepines in this population. The results of this study were consistent with the research of Ferreri and Hantouche (1998), which found hydroxyzine more effective for psychic symptomatology. Barlow (1988) confirmed that hydroxyzine acts more specifically on the psychic component of anxiety (which could limit its effect with GAD patients who have marked somatic tension), and has no rebound anxiety, no dependency, and no withdrawal symptoms. It also appears to confer long-term treatment benefits.

In summary, there are many psychotropic agents available for the treatment of GAD. The effectiveness of many of these medications have been empirically supported and given approval by the FDA. Others await further research efforts to achieve confirmation. The question is less about their effectiveness, but more to do with the degree of effectiveness, and whether pharmacotherapy for GAD can sustain remission after the drug has been discontinued with acute, medium, and longer-term use.

For short-term acute anxiety, benzodiazepines are often the first line of defense, especially when there is primarily somatic symptomatology. Buspirone, imipramine, and other antidepressants have also been used and proven effective for acute treatment as well (Baldwin & Nair, 2005; Baldwin & Polkinghorn, 2005). Yet, it seems more reasonable, based on the data, that for acute, medium, long-term maintenance treatment and relapse prevention (i.e., paroxetine, escitalopram, duloxetine), antidepressants are the favored psychotropics of choice for GAD (SSRIs and venlafaxine). Duloxetine, an antidepressant with neurotransmitter effects similar to those of venlafaxine, may also prove a viable option with GAD patients. Hydroxyzine, in milder and less somatic cases of GAD, may also be an effective treatment. However, the data are still somewhat limited for hydroxyzine. Beta blockers are rarely used for GAD, but can be helpful for peripheral noradrenaline-mediated symptoms. Thus far there has been no empirical data to support the use of antipsychotics as monotherapy for GAD sufferers (El-Khayat & Baldwin, 1998). Nonetheless, the use of atypical antipsychotics as monotherapy and adjuncts will be discussed under treatment-resistant GAD later in this publication. Finally, mood stabilizers such as valproate have not even been considered for the treatment of GAD, yet a study by Aliyev and Aliyev (2008) may suggest otherwise, and will be broached in a subsequent chapter.

"Given that GAD confers a level of functional impairment comparable to major depression" (Lydiard & Monnier, 2004, p. 354), early intervention, consisting of educational efforts and aggressive treatment, should be a significant public health priority. Even when properly identified, GAD tends to persist over time, making the need for creative, flexible, and individualized evidence-based pharmacologic approaches all the more necessary for those suffering from this all too common treatment refractory condition (Pollack et al., 2007).

Conclusion

In this chapter the focus shifted from the psychological to the biological correlates of GAD. Clearly, research on both the genetic and neurobiological underpinnings have come up with empirical findings that GAD is modestly inheritable, and several different neurotransmitters seem implicated in the disorder. The life of the mind with all its complexity has made the area of genetic influences and neurobiology in "psychiatric maladies" seem, at first glance, fuzzier and more speculative than in other seemingly better defined medical areas. Some leading psychiatrists in America (McHugh, 2005, 2008; McHugh & Slavney, 1998) have attempted to make the field of psychiatry more empirical in nature, defying the doomsayers and those who continue to view the medical side of mental illness as an illusion and reductionistic.

Attempts have been made in this chapter to present evidence-based research to support the reality that, not unlike cognitive, emotional, and interpersonal mediators of psychopathology in GAD, there are strong indicators of biomedical ones. A plethora of medications (most notably antidepressants) have ushered in a new paradigm shift for GAD. Many newer psychotropic agents with better tolerability and safety profiles are now available to bring symptom relief to those who, in the past, would have unfortunately endured their illness, rather than at present, be able to seek a modicum of solace in a pill.

The critics still abound, arguing that financial incentives from large pharmaceutical companies and payoffs to academic psychiatrists make honest empirical research an impossible endeavor. My own clinical experience and discussions with experts on the pharmacological treatment of GAD suggest otherwise, as many GAD patients do well on medications, and the prescribing physicians seem genuinely interested in their patients' long-term welfare.

Even though for every patient there is a different road to recovery, dismissing medications because of entrepreneurial bias or gain, the fact that biological mechanisms of change in GAD remain not fully understood, and psychosocial interventions work better, producing more sustained improvement, compromises the significant benefits highlighted in this chapter. Once again, the maxim that "one size does not fit all" applies as clinical judgment, empirical research, the therapeutic relationship, and patient preference, are all factors as to whether one GAD sufferer will decide to view their illness as being purely due to the effects of their environment and/or a result of their genetic endowment. The outcome of this host of factors, listed above, can often contribute to an individual patient's openness to starting a medication regimen, and potentially enhance their future responsiveness to pharmacotherapeutic intervention.

Chapter 6
Special Populations

Thus far in this publication the focus has been on the study and treatment of young and middle-aged adults with GAD. In my research and practice as a clinician, this has also been my area of specialization. However, this can create a myopic perspective of the condition (Beck & Averill, 2004). This neglect, until more recently, of pediatric, older adults, and culturally diverse patients (see next chapter) with GAD has created a serious clinical vacuum. The expansion of ensuing research efforts into these more marginalized clinical groups can open up new vistas as to how GAD manifests itself across the life span, while shedding light on the assessment, diagnosis, and treatment of these individuals.

In this chapter, the emphasis will be primarily on the psychosocial and pharmacological treatment of GAD in children, adolescents, and elderly patients. However, in order to give a wider and clearer view, it is imperative to first discuss in some detail the clinical presentation, assessment, and diagnostic parameters of both pediatric and older adult GAD. In addition, the fact that "GAD not only occurs across all ages but also is underdiagnosed at all developmental stages" (Rynn & Franklin, 2002, p. 155) creates even more of an imperative to journey in a strong and methodologically sound direction towards more rigorously unearthing the dynamics and unresolved mysteries still behind GAD.

Children and Adolescents

Pediatric anxiety in children dates back to the late nineteenth century (Albano, Chorpita, & Barlow, 2003). Generalized anxiety disorder (GAD) is clearly the most prevalent psychiatric disorder of childhood (Bernstein, Borchardt, & Perwien, 1996). Prevalence rates, based on strict diagnostic criteria, range from 2 to 4% (Anderson, Williams, McGee, & Silva, 1987; Bowen, Offord, & Boyle, 1990), and in child psychiatry clinics they tend to be around 10–14% (Beitchman, Wekerle, & Hood, 1987; Silverman & Nelles, 1988). Some have argued that there are lower rates of GAD in children and adolescents, compared with adults (Muller, 2001). In addition, according to Wittchen, Nelson, and Lochner (1998), GAD is rare in children and adolescents.

M.E. Portman, *Generalized Anxiety Disorder Across the Lifespan*,
DOI: 10.1007/978-0-387-89243-6_6, © Springer Science+Business Media, LLC 2009

Epidemiological studies suggest otherwise – GAD (referred to in this earlier research as overanxious disorder (OAD)) is one of the most common diagnoses (Feehan, McGee, Raja, & Williams, 1994; Lewinsohn, Hops, Roberts, Seeley, & Andrews, 1993; McGee, Feehan, Williams, & Partridge, 1990) among childhood anxiety disorders. OAD was dropped from the *DSM-IV* (American Psychiatric Association [APA], 1994) and became GAD. This assignation of "GAD" in children is a relatively new one (Beidel & Turner, 2005).

Fisher, Tobkes, Kotcher, and Masia-Warner (2006) argue that GAD typically presents in midchildhood and often follows the onset of another anxiety disorder. Average age of onset was found by Last, Strauss, and Francis (1987) to be between 10.8 and 13.4 years of age. In addition, Last, Hersen, Kazdin, Finkelstein, and Strauss (1987) found that children aged 9–13 were equally affected by GAD based on gender. However, in adolescence, it was found that an increased number of girls were diagnosed with GAD, compared with boys (Beidel & Turner, 2005; Kendall, 1994). The authors also add that the diagnosis of any anxiety disorder, rather than just symptoms of anxiety, including GAD, requires marked distress or impairment in the child's functioning. There is also a slow, insidious onset (Brown, Barlow & Liebowitz, 1994; Rapee, 1985, 1991) and a generally chronic course. However, parallel to the adult population, GAD in younger patients often goes undetected and untreated. If it is left untreated, the disorder results in significant deleterious impact on life tasks, such as academic, vocational (Connolly & Bernstein, 2007), and interpersonal, leading to major individual and societal costs. Given the seriousness of anxiety disorders such as GAD in children and adolescents, sound assessment and diagnosis, followed by the implementation of evidence-based supported treatments, are critical to improve outcomes in this population (Fisher et al., 2006).

One of the other "vexing issues in psychopathology research is the quest to establish the reliability and validity of diagnostic categories when these are applied to children and adolescents, and GAD has been 'the leader of the pack' when it comes to stumping clinical scientists" (Albano & Hack, 2004, p. 383). Overall, in spite of these barriers, empirical research has supported the clinical utility of GAD's diagnostic reliability and validity in children and adolescents (Flannery-Schroeder, 2004). More will be said about this in the section on assessment and diagnosis.

One final note to consider at this point, Vasey and Daleiden (1994, p. 185) write, "While the theoretical and empirical literature concerning worry has grown large ... surprisingly little of it concerns worry among children and adolescents." Cartwright-Hatton (2006), in writing a decade later, makes the case that, despite growing empirical evidence to support the existence of worry in children and adolescents, the theoretical understanding of this phenomenon has not advanced much with the ensuing passage of time. Few studies (whether psychological or biological) have been aimed at determining the etiology in GAD with children and adolescents (Beidel & Turner, 2005; Flannery-Schroeder, 2004). Nonetheless, the clinical phenomenology of GAD in younger patients has been explored with increasing specificity, and its unique clinical presentation does set it apart from chronically worried and anxious adults, middle-aged adults, and older adults.

Clinical Presentation

Children with the diagnosis of GAD have been described as "little adults," "hypermature," and giving off the "illusion of maturity" (Kendall, Krain, & Treadwell, 1999; Strauss, 1990). They often keep their distress internalized, making it difficult to be noticed by parents and caregivers (Rynn & Franklin, 2002). These experts have also found that their symptoms, when manifest in an internal manner, may not be overtly disruptive, in spite of marked suffering. In addition, this suffering may be experienced in physical ways, such as through stomach aches, insomnia, dry mouth, headaches, temper tantrums, and heart palpitations. More will be said about this later.

In terms of personality correlates related to GAD in children, the following ones have been found – being perfectionists, seeking excessive approval and reassurance, overly conforming, self-conscious, negative-self image, and high rates of somatic complaints (Beidel, Christ, & Long, 1991; Masi, Mucci, Favilla, Romano, & Poli, 1999). Anxious children have been described by parents and teachers as lacking social skills, withdrawn, and lonely (Strauss, Lease, Kazdin, Dulcan, & Last, 1989). They have also been found to be less liked by peers and have trouble making friends (Strauss, Lahey, Frick, Fram, & Hynd, 1988). Children with GAD are often viewed as well behaved, eager to please, perfectionistic, and overly mature (Ehrenreich & Gross, 2001).

Vasey (1993) described childhood worry as anticipatory, catastrophic, and self-referential. Cognitions of children with GAD are in the question of "what if," and numerous cognitive distortions take place (Albano & Hack, 2004). Negative self-talk is the most predominant distortion of thought (Howard & Kendall, 1996). Children with GAD reported, on average, 5.74 worries that span an average of 4.82 areas (Weems, Silverman, & La Greca, 2000). The most common areas of worry are health, school, disasters, personal harm, and future events. The most intense worries are war, personal harm, disasters, school, and family. The most frequent worries are friends, classmates, school, health, and performance. The researchers Beidel and Turner (2005) collated these worries and found that older children (aged 12–16) revealed more worries about performance, little things, and appearance than did younger children (aged 6–8). In sum, these academics found that children with GAD, especially older ones, had the highest number of worries and the most intense ones. Vasey and Daleiden (1994) seemed to confirm this finding, in that 8–12-year-olds had a greater variety and complexity of worries than 5–6-year-olds. The older children were also better able to extrapolate on the negative outcomes of their worries. It was also found (Albano & Hack, 2004) that, as a rule, younger children report more diffuse symptoms and complaints, whereas older children and adolescents reveal worries and fears that center on not meeting some inappropriate standard or goal. In GAD the bar is often set too high.

In two Italian studies with children and adolescents suffering from GAD (Masi et al., 1999, 2004), cognitive complaints were the predominant ones with feelings of restlessness (98–100%), apprehensive expectation (94–95%), need for reassurance (83–86%), and negative self-image (74–90%) being the most common. Physical complaints were the next most frequently occurring symptoms (72–75%). Interestingly enough, in the Italian studies, GAD was defined more broadly, and 25–27% of the sample received the diagnosis of GAD without endorsing any physical complaints being present. In terms of the symptom profile of GAD, excessive worry, subjective anxiety, and somatic symptoms are the main characteristics of the diagnosis.

Somatic complaints are common in GAD (Eisen & Engler, 1995) and tend to be diffuse (Kendall et al., 1991). Tracey, Chorpita, Douban, and Barlow (1997) reported complaints such as restlessness (74%) being the most frequently endorsed physical symptom in a childhood GAD sample, followed by irritability (68%), concentration difficulties (61%), sleep disturbance (58%), easily fatigued (52%), headaches (36%), muscle tension (29%), and stomach aches (29%). Muscle tension was the most endorsed by children and parents in a sample by Kendall and Warman (1996). Many children first present to their pediatrician because of bodily complaints.

Other associated problems can range from nail biting, skin picking, affective lability (Albano et al., 2003), to escalating avoidance and social anxiety (Chansky & Kendall, 1997). Comorbidity can run high in pediatric GAD and contributes to increased functional impairment (Masi, Favilla, Mucci, & Millepiedi, 2000), especially when depression co-occurs with GAD. Depression is a commonly occurring comorbid diagnosis, and complicates the clinical presentation in large part by increasing the child's impairment and distress (Albano & Hack, 2004). GAD is highly comorbid with other anxiety disorders as well, such as separation anxiety disorder and social anxiety disorder (Rynn & Franklin, 2002). Teasing out these comorbid conditions to ensure an accurate diagnosis of GAD can assist in treatment planning, and becomes critical during the assessment process.

Assessment and Diagnosis

Assessment in GAD for younger patients should include multiple methods, using various informants in a variety of contexts (Morris, Hirshfeld-Becker, Hennin, & Storch, 2004). Assessment is critical and serves the purpose of guiding the development of treatment planning, better defining symptoms and behaviors for selective interventions, and helping to stay focused on goals for the duration of treatment (Albano & Hack, 2004). The main approach to assessment is multimethod and multi-informational (March & Albano, 2002). According to the most revised practice parameters set for the treatment of childhood anxiety disorders (Connolly & Bernstein, 2007), it is essential, in the assessment process, to differentiate normal vs. pathological worry. Various recommendations are offered and a good summary can be found in Kaplan (2007). The ultimate goal is to use evidence-based treatments, which can be accomplished via a comprehensive assessment process that includes asking precise screening questions, using a formal evaluation to determine which anxiety disorder is present, using a multimodal treatment approach, and considering severity and the degree of impairment. Psychotherapy should then be considered (i.e. CBT), including parent, child, family interventions and SSRIs (plus other medications), which need to be kept in mind during the process.

In addition, during assessment, an awareness of several issues are important: (1) be aware of normal developmental childhood fears (Gullone & King, 1993), (2) be sensitive to cultural and gender issues (Dong, Yank, & Ollendick, 1994; Fonseca, Yule, & Erol, 1994; King, Gullone, & Ollendick, 1992), (3) be mindful of cognitive differences between children and adults – children may struggle with difficulty answering highly complex emotion-related questions (Schniering, Hudson, & Rapee, 2000), and (4) do a complete and detailed medical workup with extensive laboratory investigations.

Beidel and Turner (2005) stress the need for diagnostic interviewing, self-report measures, and behavioral assessment. The assessment usually, according to these leaders in the field, begins with a diagnostic interview with both child and parent. In addition, they argue that behavioral observation is often the first indicator that is detectable by others that an anxiety disorder is present. Therefore, these overt behavioral expressions are central data in the assessment process.

In terms of specific assessment protocols for GAD, experts in the field confirm that semi-structured and structured interviews are critical instruments in the diagnosing of GAD. In regard to diagnostic interviews, Albano and Hack (2004) argue that these interviews do the following – establish the presence or absence of symptoms, determine the level of impairment and duration of the disorder, and exclude alternative diagnoses. However, one caveat needs to be clear – all of the instruments to date, except for the Anxiety Disorders Interview Schedule for *DSM-IV* child/parent version (ADIS-IV-C/P; Silverman & Albano, 1996) and the Penn State Worry Questionnaire, the children's adaptation (PSWQ-C; Chorpita, Tracey, Brown, Collica, & Barlow, 1997), are not GAD-specific. The ADIS-IV-C/P (most notably the GAD category) has good psychometric properties (Silverman, Saavedra, & Pina, 2001).

The most commonly used diagnostic structured instrument includes the following.

Anxiety Disorders Interview Schedule for Children/Parent Revised (ADIS-C/P; Silverman & Albano, 1996)

This is a clinician-structured interview used to identify the principal diagnosis. It also determines the most severe current distress and/or impairment. There is a 0–8 distress/impairment severity scale. The ADIS-IV is based on the *DSM-IV* criteria. The anxiety section was expanded and there is screening for all the other anxiety disorders. Each diagnostic section has a series of screening questions, and positive responses lead to a more in-depth evaluation of that particular area. There is good–excellent test–retest reliability in the ADIS-IV-C/P (Silverman et al., 2001), and moderate to high interrater reliability (Rapee, Barrett, Dadds, & Evans, 1994; Silverman & Nelles, 1988). There is a child/parent version, but children and parents are interviewed separately. It consists of two semi-structured interview schedules, one designed to interview the child and the second for the child's parent, which is more extensive in nature.

Self-report measures, as defined by Beidel and Stanley (1992), help (a) in the ability to describe the self as anxious from a cognitive perspective, (b) to determine whether terms such as fear, anxiety, and worry have the same meaning for children and adolescents as they do for adults, and (c) to assess whether the child can differentiate based on *b*.

The self-report inventories that have proven the most commonly used for children are the following.

The Multidimensional Anxiety Scale for Children (MASC; March, Parker, Sullivan, Stallings, & Connors, 1997)

This scale assesses a range of anxiety symptoms. There is a calculation of a total score, and scores on various subscales (physical symptoms, harm avoidance, social anxiety, separation, and panic). It is a 39-item, 4-point Likert, self-report rating scale for use in children and adolescents aged 8–17. The normative data are extensive; it has excellent reliability and a broad range of validity data. For example, 3-week test–retest reliability for this scale is 0.79 in clinical samples (March et al., 1997) and 0.88 in school-based samples (March & Sullivan, 1999).

Screen for Child Anxiety and Related Emotional Disorders (SCARED; Birmaher et al., 1997, 1999)

This screen is designed to assess *DSM-IV* symptoms of anxiety in youth. It has both a parent and a child version. The initial screen (Birmaher et al., 1997) is an 85-item questionnaire that yields five factors (somatic/panic, general anxiety, separation anxiety, social phobia, and school phobia). There is a total score and one for each of the five factors. In a replication study (Birmaher et al., 1999), a 41-item questionnaire was administered to a new sample. This reduced version of the SCARED yielded the same five items as the original screen. They both have good psychometric properties in clinical and community samples, and appear to be sensitive to the effects of treatment (RUPP Anxiety Study Group, 2001). The psychometric properties are consistent for African American, European, and American samples (Boyd, Ginsburg, Lambert, Cooley, & Campbell, 2003).

Children's Manifest Anxiety Scale – Revised (RCMAS; Reynolds & Richmond, 1979)

The scale consists of 37 true/false items (28 anxiety and 9 Lie scale items) that assess a variety of anxiety symptoms. It also assesses three factors: physiological arousal, worry/oversensitivity, and concentration. It focuses on children's anxious complaints that mirror *DSM-IV* diagnostic categories. Strauss (1988) found good psychometric properties and national normative data.

Penn State Worry Questionnaire – Children's Adaptation (PSWQ-C; Chorpita et al., 1997, Pestle, Chorpita, & Schiffman, in press)

This is the most specific self-report measure of the cognitive component of GAD and worry (see Appendix B). It is the children's adaptation of the adult PSWQ discussed in an earlier chapter. There are 14-items, and children rate on a 4-point Likert Scale. It has good internal consistency, is unifactorial, and has favorable reliability and validity (Chorpita et al., 1997). Another publication on the psychometric properties of the PSWQ-C (Pestle, Chorpita, & Schiffman, in press) has not yet been published, but should offer some fresh information about the children's version of this questionnaire. There is also a parent version (PSWQ-P, see Appendix B), but there is little or no data on it at this point (Pestle, e-mail communication, 2008).

Assessment of pediatric anxiety has been complicated by changing diagnostic criteria of OAD to GAD, a dearth of research, and yet-growing recognition of the importance of exploring, in more detail, childhood anxiety (Flannery-Schroeder, 2004). Prior to 1994 there were numerous problems with the old GAD diagnostic category (Beidel & Turner, 2005), which included limited reliability, overdiagnosis, inappropriateness of the specific criteria, lack of distinction from other anxiety disorders, uncertain relation to adult disorders, and lack of external validity (Werry, 1991).

In looking at the progression of GAD over the years to its present form, there has not been the same parallel attention to research on childhood worry, compared to adults. In the *DSM-II* (APA, 1968) it was considered an overanxious reaction, under "phobic neuroses," and tied to psychoanalytic theory. In *DSM-III* (APA, 1980) and *DSM-III-R* (APA, 1987), the diagnosis was called overanxious disorder (OAD), and considered atheoretical with empirically derived categories. It was not until *DSM-IV* (APA, 1994) that GAD became empirically validated (Tracey et al., 1997). Finally, in the *DSM-IV-TR* (APA, 2000), persistent worry about multiple life domains, activities, and events became the defining criteria of GAD (the same as in adults).

Connolly and Bernstein (2007) expanded the clinical picture of this disorder in a highly descriptive way to capture its essence for both researchers and clinicians. They stated that, in children and adolescents, GAD is chronic, and is defined by excessive worry about a number of different areas such as school, work, interpersonal relationships, family, health and safety, world events, natural disasters, and includes at least one somatic symptom (rather than the three required to meet adult GAD). Difficulty controlling the worry is also a requirement to meet the diagnostic criteria.

Now that GAD has established itself as an independent, legitimate, and disabling diagnosis in children and adolescents, the need to examine the psychosocial treatments available will now be explored in detail at this point.

Psychosocial Treatments

A few important considerations to mention are in order before looking closely at the psychosocial treatments for GAD in children and adolescents. First, to date, CBT is considered the optimal psychological treatment of choice for pediatric anxiety disorders in randomized-controlled trials (Arnold et al., 2003; Flannery-Schroeder & Kendall, 2000; Kendall et al., 1997). Second, there are no specific evidence-based CBT treatments that have been solely tailored for GAD in childhood and adolescence (Beidel & Turner, 2005). This does not mean, in the studies described here regarding younger GAD patients, that there were not, in many cases, a sizeable number of the research samples meeting the diagnostic criteria for this disorder. Therefore, GAD in children was being evaluated to determine the effectiveness of CBT with this population. However, given that GAD is considered often comorbid with other childhood anxiety disorders (Silva, Gallagher, & Minani, 2006), researchers decided to use mostly mixed samples of the commonly occurring childhood anxiety disorders in their empirically based designs (Fisher et al., 2006). I, for one, believe that some of the studies could just as easily have investigated whether CBT had a therapeutically positive outcome on only GAD patients, without including mixed samples. Finally, some of the earlier research was done with young patients with OAD, the precursor diagnosis to GAD. Even with these caveats, it is still possible to determine whether CBT had a positive effect on the overall sample or not in these clinical trials. An excellent review of a CBT protocol for anxiety disorders in children and its theoretical underpinnings can be found in Gosch, Flannery-Schroeder, Mauro, and Compton (2006) for the interested clinician.

The first study on record (Kane & Kendall, 1989) did in fact use a manualized CBT approach, called the Coping Cat Program, with four children with OAD. The treatment consisted of 16–20 individualized sessions, consisting of four components: (1) increase awareness of somatic and cognitive reactions to anxiety, (2) define cognitions in anxiety-provoking situations, (3) develop a coping plan (challenging self-talk, determining which adaptive coping activities might prove beneficial), and (4) self-evaluation/self-reinforcement plus behavioral training (modeling, shaping, exposure, relaxation techniques, and role playing). This was a single case design that proved effective for all four children.

The first controlled trial (Kendall, 1994) consisted of participants aged 9–13 (suffering from separation anxiety disorder, OAD, avoidant disorder), randomized to the Coping Cat Program or a wait-list control. There were significant improvements at the end of treatment on self-report measures of coping skills, negative cognitions, anxiety, and depression. In the treatment group, 64% no longer met diagnostic criteria at posttreatment and this was maintained at 3.35 years (Kendall & Southam-Gerow, 1996). There were similar ratings of improvement by collaterals, and behavioral observation was part of the treatment protocol. In a replication study (Kendall et al., 1997) of the above one, the CBT group had a 53% improvement and no longer met the diagnostic criteria, whereas the wait-list control group, by contrast, showed a 6% improvement. In a 7.4-year follow-up (Kendall, Safford, Flannery-Schroeder, & Webb, 2004) of the Kendall et al. (1996) study, 90.3% of the children and adolescents no longer met the diagnostic criteria of the primary diagnosis. However, 50% of the original sample did receive added treatment, which calls into question the long-term efficacy of this approach.

In another study using Kendall's CBT protocol plus family intervention, Barrett, Dadds, and Rapee (1996) used a sample of 79 children with varying diagnoses, including SAD, OAD, and SP, who were randomly assigned to one of two treatment groups, CBT or CBT plus family vs. a wait-list control. The CBT treatment group was individual therapy. The CBT and CBT plus family both demonstrated superior results over a wait-list control. However, the combination treatment sample of 84% did not meet diagnostic criteria, and was superior to the 57% for CBT alone at posttreatment. In a follow-up study, Barrett, Duffy, Dadds, and Rapee (2001) concluded that 81% of children with OAD/GAD did not have this diagnosis 6 years later. However, there were no differences between the treatment modalities at that point. In a slightly different format, using a group modality (Barrett, 1998) where the sample size was 60 (of which 30 had GAD), group CBT and group CBT plus family were superior to wait-list control. Group CBT plus family were superior at 70.7%, no longer meeting diagnostic criteria, vs. 55.9% in the group CBT. This was maintained at 12-month follow-up. In this study, specificity for GAD is not known. Other studies of a similar nature have produced disparate results. Mendlowitz et al. (1999) found a benefit to parental inclusion, whereas Nauta, Scholing, Emmelkamp, and Minderaa (2003) found no clinical benefit from parental involvement. In another CBT treatment, that combined CBT interventions plus family skills and an additional component focused on establishing friends, called the FRIENDS program (Shortt, Barrett, & Fox, 2001), 69% of those with OAD/GAD had no diagnosis at posttreatment, vs. 6% on the wait-list control. Results were maintained 1 year later.

In a study by Cobham, Dadds, and Spence (1998), the influence of parental anxiety on the outcome of family treatment was explored, comparing child CBT vs. CBT plus family (parent anxiety management). In the case of nonanxious parents, there was no enhancement to the treatment outcome (81% in CBT and 80% in combined treatment were free of their diagnosis). Where the parents were anxious, especially with girls, the combined treatment was superior, in the children being less likely to have an anxiety diagnosis. However, the initial improvement was not maintained at 1-year follow-up. This seems to suggest that there is an immediate benefit to parental anxiety in children's outcomes, but not in the long term.

In a study by Eisen and Silverman (1993), using *DSM-III-R* OAD diagnostic criteria in a multiple baseline design, there were six sessions of cognitive therapy plus six sessions of relaxation therapy plus six sessions of combination treatment. The greatest improvement was seen in the combination treatment. Significant improvement took place from pre- to posttreatment, and it was maintained at 6 months. The interventions matched the child's particular symptom profile, and greatest responses were individualized. Eisen and Silverman (1998), in a multiple baseline design study with a sample size of four with anxiety disorders, who received ten individual sessions with prescriptive randomized treatments – cognitive treatment for cognitive symptoms, somatic treatments for physical treatments or non-prescriptive (treatment not matched to the target symptoms), found that prescriptive treatments were more effective than the non-prescriptive ones. Once again, Silverman et al. (1999), in a randomly controlled trial, compared the utility of group CBT (GBCT) vs. a wait-list control. The anxiety disorders in this study included SP, OAD, and GAD. The protocol was 12 weeks of graded exposure, parent–child contingency management, and cognitive self-control training. The GCBT treated group had 64% no longer meeting diagnostic criteria, vs. 13% for a wait-list control at posttreatment. Maintenance of gains was reported at 3-, 6-, and 12-month follow-up.

In an adapted version of the Silverman CBT treatment, Ginsburg and Drake (2002) applied the treatment to a school setting. The sample size was 12 African American children with a variety of different anxiety and mood disturbances. CBT was compared to an attention support group, and found superior at 75% no longer meeting criteria, compared to 20% for the non-CBT-treated group. Anxiety was significantly decreased on self-report measures.

Flannery-Schroeder and Kendall (2000), in a study measuring the difference between individual and group CBT, found that 73% who received individual treatment no longer met diagnostic criteria, vs. 50% of the group-treated sample. Yet, on self-reported measures of anxious distress, only the children in the individual CBT format demonstrated significant improvement. This study appeared to favor the individual treatment over the group one.

Manassis et al. (2002) compared a group to individual CBT format with children suffering from various anxiety disorders. The sample size was 78 (ages 8–12), and 60.2% had a diagnosis of GAD. Both the group and individual format had a parental component. They also led to maternal reports of decreased anxiety in the treated groups. There were no treatment differences based on the intervention modality on several measures, except that clinician ratings indicated superiority of the individual-treated group. Once again, this seemed to favor individual treatment vs. a group format. Interestingly enough, the mother's actual scores of the child's anxiety were still elevated, yet the father's ratings of the child's anxiety, and the child's self-reported ratings were not affected in either direction by treatment.

A recent study (Kendall, Hudson, Gosch, Flannery-Schroeder, & Suveg, 2008) compared several different groups and an active control group, including individual (child) cognitive–behavioral therapy (ICBT), family cognitive–behavioral therapy (FCBT), and a family-based education/support/attention (FESA), serving as an active control group. The sample size was 161 youths, aged 7–14, with diagnoses of separation anxiety disorder, social phobia, or GAD. There were treatment gains in all the treatment groups. FCBT and ICBT were superior to FESA in reducing the primary anxiety disorder. ICBT was superior to FCBT and FESA on reports by teachers of the children's anxiety. Gains in treatment lasted for a year follow-up. FCBT was superior to ICBT when both parents suffered from an anxiety disorder.

In another group CBT study, Rapee (2000) randomized 96 participants (aged 7–16) with various anxiety disorders to either GCBT or a wait-list control group. There were nine sessions over 11 weeks. Parents were trained in child management skills. The improvement rate was 88.3%, based on unbiased clinician rating and maintained at 1-year follow-up.

In a study designed to target adolescents with GAD, separation anxiety, and SAD, Siqueland, Rynn, and Diamond (2005) compared CBT vs. CBT plus attachment family-based therapy. There was equal efficacy in both groups at post-treatment and 6–9-month follow-up. CBT produced 67% posttreatment diagnosis-free outcomes, compared to 40% in the other treated group. The results increased to 100% for CBT alone and 80% at follow-up. There was no wait-list control group in this study.

Thus far, on the basis of the studies presented, CBT is efficacious in treating pediatric anxiety. Is it due to specific treatment ingredients or common therapeutic factors (Wampold, 2001)? In sum, individual CBT treatment seems favorable over group formats, in spite of being less cost efficient. The addition of a family component to CBT has produced some mixed results, while reducing parental anxiety during treatment has short-lived effects on children's therapeutic outcomes (Fisher et al., 2006).

Several reviews and more recent meta-analyses have been done to look more closely at the data in this area. In-Albon and Schneider (2007) found, on the basis of a 24-study meta-analysis, that CBT is effective in the treatment of childhood anxiety disorders. Recovery rates for individual CBT was 72.1% vs. 66.0% for group CBT (some had a family component mixed in). The effect size for child-focused treatment was 0.53 vs. 0.63 for family-focused. Earlier studies favored individual treatment, while recent results seem to suggest equal efficacy between individual and group CBT modalities (Barrett, 1998; Muris, Mayer, Bartfelds, Tierney, & Bogie, 2001). There were also no differences found between child alone and children/parent treatments. Overall, the effect size for CBT was 0.86, which is quite high. No differences were found between various treatment modalities (individual, group, child-focused, family-focused), and gains were maintained for up to 2 years. The authors cogently argue that RCT studies need to focus on specific anxiety disorders (including GAD). Non-CBT studies are also lacking to make meaningful comparisons.

An earlier review by Compton et al. (2004) confirmed the above findings, that CBT is the treatment of choice for children and adolescents with anxiety and depressive disorders. CBT produces effect sizes in the medium–large range. Twenty-one RCTs were investigated in this review. Cartwright-Hatton, Roberts, Chitsabesan,

Fothergill, and Harrington (2004) reviewed the effectiveness of CBT as a treatment for childhood and adolescent anxiety disorders. In ten randomized controlled trials of young children, younger than 19 years of age (excluding PTSD, phobia or OCD), remission rates were 50.5% in the CBT group and 34% in the control group. In summary, CBT was efficacious in the treatment of youth as young as age 6. The results only demonstrated outcomes up to posttreatment.

Having explored a broad sampling of psychosocial treatments, we now turn to pharmacotherapy for youth with anxiety disorders, including GAD. The fact that some younger patients do not respond to psychological interventions, for various reasons (more often because of comorbidity, which creates increased severity and functional impairment, and CBT not being accessible or beneficial) (Fisher et al., 2006), makes the need to consider and incorporate these medication options into individualized treatment planning more pressing.

Pharmacological Treatments

There are, unlike in the literature on psychosocial treatments for pediatric anxiety disorders, pharmaceutical agents that have been specifically evaluated for only GAD in this population. Several different classes have been investigated, but antidepressants (SSRIs) are the treatment of choice for children and adolescents with GAD (Beidel & Turner, 2005).

The first study to explore the use of benzodiazepines in OAD (avoidant disorder also included) was by Simeon and Ferguson (1987). In this open-label trial, 58% showed moderate improvement by week 4, and this gain was maintained in a 4-week drug-free period. OAD was not examined separately in this study. In a subsequent placebo-controlled study by Simeon et al. (1992), 30 youths with a mean age of 12.6 years (21 had OAD and 9 had avoidant disorder) were studied, and similar results found improvement in the drug-treated group over placebo at 4 weeks, but not at posttreatment follow-up. In summary, benzodiazepines have been investigated for pediatric anxiety, but mostly in small open-label trials (Reinblatt & Riddle, 2007). Benzodiazepines are used as a last resort for youths (Kratochvil, Kutcher, Reiter, & March, 1999), but may prove helpful with anxiety disorders that have marked somatic symptoms accompanied by functional impairment, or may be used adjunctively with antidepressants in the short term (Rynn & Franklin, 2002).

Buspirone is not a first line treatment for anxious youth. There has been some improvement noted in two open-label trials (Kutcher, Reiter, Gardner, & Klein, 1992; Simeon, Knott, Dubois, & Wiggins, 1994). However, the improvement has not been replicated in any RCTs (Connolly & Bernstein, 2007).

In regard to antidepressants, Birmaher et al. (1994), in a retrospective study, evaluated the efficacy of fluoxetine (mean dose, 25.7 mg) in 21 children and adolescents, aged 11–17. They carried different anxiety disorder diagnoses (OAD, avoidant disorder, social phobia). There was an 81% improvement at 6–8 weeks, as measured by chart review of nurses and patients' mothers. In another open trial by Fairbanks et al. (1997), children having various anxiety disorders (aged 9–18 years) who were nonresponsive to psychotherapy were administered fluoxetine. Improvement was apparent at 6–9 weeks, and lower doses were used when there was less comorbidity. The sample size was 16, and the data were not analyzed for specific diagnoses. Yet, 81% demonstrated a moderate–marked improvement, albeit 62.5% still met diagnostic criteria for an anxiety disorder at posttreatment. In another study by Birmaher et al. (2003), consisting of a 12-week trial, 74 patients with GAD, separation anxiety, and social phobia were randomized to fluoxetine or a matching placebo. In this case 61% showed much or very much improvement vs. 35% for placebo, based on treating clinician's ratings. In the case of GAD, 67% improved over 36% for placebo. Further more, children with GAD treated with fluoxetine did not exhibit improvements in functioning over placebo. In other words, symptom relief of anxiety occurred with treatment, but not necessarily enhanced functioning. Unfortunately, 50% of the children were still symptomatic at posttreatment.

In a study by Clark et al. (2005), fluoxetine was once again studied – this time for longer term treatment in various childhood anxiety disorders (GAD, SAD, SP). Both children and adolescents (7–17 years of age) were evaluated in open treatment of 1 year after they completed a randomized, controlled trial comparing fluoxetine ($n = 42$) vs. placebo ($n = 10$). The medication group was found to be clinically effective for maintenance treatment in this clinical population.

Rynn, Siqueland, and Rickels (2001) evaluated a different SSRI called sertraline vs. placebo with 22 children and adolescents (aged 5–17) in a 9-week, double-blind treatment phase with pediatric GAD. They were randomly assigned, in groups of four, to the drug-treated group or placebo. The maximum dose given was 50 mg/day. On the HAM-A total score, psychic/somatic factors and Clinical Global Impression Scale (CGI), there was a significant improvement on sertraline from week 4 to the end of the study. Sertraline was found to be a safe and effective treatment for pediatric GAD at 50 mg/day.

In a large, multicenter, controlled trial (Rupp Anxiety Study Group, 2001), known as the RUPP Anxiety Trial, patients (aged 6–17 years) with separation anxiety, social anxiety, and GAD were randomized over 8 weeks to fluvoxamine or placebo. Both groups also received supportive therapy. The drug-treated group proved superior, with 76% improvement, based on clinician rating, vs. 29% for placebo. There was no additional improvement beyond week 6. GAD response was better than for social phobia. Overall, 94% of those patients with an initial response maintained their improvement (RUPP, 2002). This was a large, well-controlled study.

A study with venlafaxine, a SNRI (Kahn & Henderson, 2000), with 156 patients, compared venlafaxine with placebo and found 64% much improved–very improved in the medication group, and 40% in the placebo. This was based on the CGI-I. Rynn, Riddle, Yeung, and Kunz (2007), in a much more recent study, evaluated whether venlafaxine was efficacious, safe, and tolerable in the treatment of pediatric GAD. The study consisted of two randomized, double-blind, placebo-controlled trials that were conducted at 59 different sites in 2000 and 2001. The patients were 6–17 years of age, and met diagnostic criteria for DSM-IV GAD. A flexible dose was given to 157 participants, and 163 received a placebo for 8 weeks. In Study 1, the venlafaxine-XR-treated group exhibited statistically significant improvements across primary and secondary outcome measures. In Study 2, there were significant improvements on some secondary outcome measures, but not on the primary outcome measure. Response rate was 69% on venlafaxine and 48% on placebo. There were also decreased impairment and severity scores on venlafaxine. It is safe to say that this medication is seemingly effective and well tolerated for short-term treatment of pediatric GAD (in spite of some mixed results in the studies). Side effects are similar to those of the SSRIs, and there is a need for periodic blood pressure monitoring at higher doses while patients are on this medication.

One caveat is important to consider – Rynn, the lead researcher on the venlafaxine study, and a prominent psychiatrist, writes, "If cognitive-behavioral therapy is available and patients can access it, it is reasonable to take that approach first" (as cited in Leonard, 2007, p. 6). Finally, Rynn adds that clinicians need multiple treatment options to address pediatric GAD effectively in younger patients (especially those that have failed first line pharmacological and psychological treatments).

In an evidence-based medicine review of pharmacotherapy for anxiety disorders in children and adolescents (Compton, Kratochvil, & March, 2007), RCTs were included to determine the optimal treatment for pediatric anxiety. The RCTs supported SSRIs as first line treatment, and concluded that there were mixed result with SNRIs such as venlafaxine. In terms of risks and the relatively recent "black box warnings" affixed to these medications for youths with anxiety disorders, the evidence demonstrated a 4% vs. 2% risk (antidepressant over placebo, respectively) (Hammad, 2004). There was a modest increase in relative risk for an adverse event such as suicide. No completed suicides have occurred, and the risks and benefits always need to be considered when embarking on any treatment protocol. The authors concluded that multimodal treatment is the rule in treating pediatric anxiety. This translates into evaluating many factors, before pharmacotherapy and/or psychotherapy are started, with clinically anxious youth.

Reinblatt and Riddle (2007), in a review of the pharmacological management of childhood anxiety disorders, make a case based on the research that, in regard to pediatric GAD, SSRIs are effective treatments and venlafaxine may be effective if a trial on an SSRI fails. The side effect profile for SSRIs are generally benign, but can include (as in adults) GI distress, insomnia, activation vs. bipolarity (Walkup & Labellarte, 2001), and sexual dysfunction (especially concerning adolescents) (Scharko, 2004).

In conclusion, pharmacological approaches for the treatment of pediatric anxiety, including GAD, have expanded greatly over the years. This has made it possible to help many more afflicted young people suffering from the debilitating impact of GAD. One important note – an important research project is underway, called the Child and Adolescent Multimodal Study (CAMS trial), which is comparing several treatment modalities – medication alone (sertraline), CBT alone, combination treatment (CBT and sertraline), and pill placebo. This randomized controlled trial includes 488 youth (aged 7–17) with GAD, separation anxiety, and social phobia (Albano, e-mail communication, 2007). The study is funded by the National Institute of Mental Health, and will have important implications for the treatment of childhood anxiety disorders. Now we turn to GAD in the elderly and the dynamics behind this particular group of sufferers.

Older Adults

Aging in itself can be a source of increased worry and distress for many older adults. The idea alone of getting older may be accompanied by anxiety-ridden thoughts and feelings, compounded by loss of health, issues of financial security, changes in relationships, and decline in one's mental faculties (Dada, Sethi, & Grossberg, 2001). Even though some older adults may not recall their past episodes of worry, on account of a lifetime of developing wisdom, effective coping strategies, or even a healthier perspective on life (Wetherell, 2006), this does not mean that GAD is nonexistent in this population. In fact, close to 15% of the elderly are self-described worriers (Wisocki, 1994). GAD is the most common anxiety disorder among adults over the age of 60 (de Beurs et al., 1999; Diefenbach, Stanley, & Beck, 2001; Jones, Ames, Jeffries, Scarinci, & Brantley, 2001; Wittchen et al., 2002). The prevalence rates range in older adult with GAD from 0.71 to 7.8% (Beekman et al., 1998; Flint, 1994, 1999). Blazer, George and Hughes (1991), on the basis of epidemiological research, further suggest that the prevalence of GAD in the elderly is lower than in younger clinical age groups. Scogin (1998) argues that GAD is alive and well in the elderly, and the epidemiological studies underestimate prevalence rates. Flint (1994) found that pure versions of GAD are less common, and older adults often present with and report a mixture of anxiety and depressive symptoms. This seems to imply that fewer older adults may meet the diagnostic criteria for GAD, in spite of prominent and noticeable anxiety symptoms (Beck & Averill, 2004). The verdict appears to be in question about the prevalence of GAD in the elderly.

It may also be worth noting that GAD in the elderly creates a special opportunity to better differentiate and explore the nature of normal vs. pathological worry and anxiety in later life, while expanding our conceptual understanding of this disorder as a whole (Beck & Averill, 2004). In many ways, research on young adults has served for several years as a gateway and base upon which to extrapolate areas of convergence and divergence between the two clinical groups. The inferences on older adults have been primarily derived using the empirical data drawn from younger GAD sufferers (Stanley, 2002). One of the inherent problems in this methodology is that older adults with GAD display their own unique manifestations of the disorder. With that in mind, we can now turn to these clinical presentations.

Clinical Presentation

In terms of worry content with older adults, health issues and maintenance of their independence are more pressing worries than work-related ones (Doucet, Ladouceur, Freeston, & Dugas, 1998). The most common topic of concern is health (Wisocki, Handen, & Morse, 1986). They also worry about decline in functioning, falls, incontinence, poor health of loved ones, becoming victimized, and being a burden to others (Kogan & Edelstein, 2004). According to Diefenbach et al. (2001), not unlike in younger adults with the disorder, it is the uncontrollability and frequency, not just the content, that differentiate GAD patients from normals. Montorio, Nuevo, Marquez, Izal, and Losada (2003) seem to confirm this, by arguing that older adult patients with GAD worry "more" about all topics (family, personal health being the most prevalent), and minor matters compared to normal older adults and those with subsyndromal anxiety. The worry of older adults is marked by anxiety, distress, and negative affect (Wisocki et al., 1986). However, the worry is not as closely related to depression as it is in younger adults (Wisocki, 1994). The majority of older adults with GAD do not suffer with concomitant depression (Beekman et al., 2000).

Quality of life is also impaired and comparable to that found in major depression (Wetherell et al., 2004). A study by Wetherell et al. (2004) also found, in a sample of 75 treatment-seeking, older patients with GAD, that 39 of them had comorbid diagnoses and reported worse health-related quality of life. One caveat – it was not the comorbidity per se that led to decrements in quality of life, but the presence of GAD. GAD and symptoms of anxiety and depression are correlated to impairment across all areas of quality of life. The most prominent area affected by GAD in relation to quality of life in the elderly was found to be role functioning limitations (decrease in activities, not being able to focus on activities, less feelings of accomplishment).

In addition, worry is less future-oriented in older adults than that found in younger adults (Powers, Wisocki, & Whitbourne, 1992). Others have found few age-related distinctions, and suggest that the phenomenology of GAD seems to be similar in older and younger adults (Beck, Stanley, & Zebb, 1996; Mohlman, 2004).

Other findings in this population worth noting are that older adults are reluctant to seek treatment for anxiety (Blazer et al., 1991), and when they do it is more often at their PCP (Barlow, Lerner, & Esler, 1996). Those who do seek treatment are inclined to discontinue their treatment in a premature manner (Gould et al., 2004). Somatic symptoms in older adults with GAD are often more frequently reported with their anxiety (Beck et al., 2004). The distinction in the disorder's presentation in the elderly may be due to disparate phenomenology that can be a result of generational differences in one's willingness to express, in overt ways, their emotional experience. Others argue that emotional states may be experienced with less intensity and frequency in older adults than in younger adults (Kogan, Edelstein, & McKee, 2000).

In terms of onset of symptoms, Le Roux, Gatz, and Wetherell (2005) examined the differences between early onset (before age 50) and late onset symptoms (after age 50) of 67 patients with GAD in a psychotherapy study. They found that, with early onset (57% reported), there was a greater risk of comorbidity, increased psychotropic use, and increased severity of worry relative to somatic symptoms (anxious and depressive). In later onset (43% reported), there was more functional impairment because of actual problems (physical ones), not physical disability. In other words, in the later onset cases there was "role disability." There was also more benzodiazepine use in the later onset cases. Interestingly enough, many older patients with GAD reported an earlier onset in childhood and adolescence. Yet, 50% still did develop the disorder in later life.

In looking at the course of persistent anxiety in the elderly, Schuurmans et al. (2005), 6 years after baseline, found that 23% of 62 patients in the sample met the criteria for an anxiety disorder, and 47% suffered from subclinical anxiety (partial remission). The use of benzodiazepines was high at 43%, while antidepressant use was 7%. The use of mental health-care facilities was 14%, which was low for persistent anxiety. The study started with 112 patients over the age of 55 years and was called the Longitudinal Aging Study Amsterdam. In summary, 69% of the total sample continued to suffer from either subsyndromal or full-blown anxiety at the 6-year follow-up. Even with this rather unfavorable outcome, percentages for full remission were on the high side (31%). This is in contrast to results with younger adults, where full remission ranged over 5–10 years from 12–31% (Angst & Vollrath, 1991).

Assessment and Diagnosis

Assessment in elderly patients has generally followed the same pattern as that for younger adult patients with GAD. However, there have been more recent advances in the assessment of anxiety in the elderly, and intimations that the elderly experience anxiety differently than younger adults (Beck & Stanley, 2001). These authors add that, in older adults with anxiety, there are age-related physical and mental changes, generational differences in identifying and labeling mood states, and a shifting nature in their current concerns. This is congruent with the theme of this publication; that GAD across the life span seems to manifest itself in diverse ways depending on the age cohort.

One instrument that has proven to be uniquely targeted for the elderly patient with GAD is the following.

The Worry Scale for Older Adults (WS; Wisocki, 1988)

This 35-item self-report measure was designed to examine the nature and severity of worry in older adults (see Appendix A). It assesses worry about finances, health, and social functioning. Each item lists a potential topic of worry and, on a Likert-like scale, the how much of the time spent worrying responses (frequency) range from "never" to "much of the time" (for example, more than twice a day). This scale can be administered in 5–10 min, with 0 for "never," 1 for "rarely," etc. The scores are summed to give total scores. Subscales are totaled by calculating, by summary, items in each subscale (finances, 1–5; health, 6–22; social conditions, 23–35). The possible total score ranges from 0 to 140, and higher scores are reflective of more frequent worry. The psychometric properties have been acceptable (Stanley, Beck, & Zebb, 1996; Stanley, Novy, Bourland, Beck, & Averill, 2001). A revised/ expanded 88-item version of this scale has been validated in the elderly (Hunt, Wisocki, & Yanko, 2003; Wisocki, 1994). It includes six dimensions: finances, health, social/interpersonal, person concerns (crime, psychological difficulties, family concerns, and world issues). There are other additional items on the revised scale that have been summarized in Wetherell (2006). The Cronbach alpha for the revised Worry Scale in the elderly is 0.97 for total score and ranges from 0.88 to 0.95 on the subscales.

Other self-report instruments that have proved useful in the assessment of the elderly are the Penn State Worry Questionnaire (Meyer, Miller, Metzger, & Borkovec, 1990). It has been validated in older adults vs. normal controls, and an 8-item version of this assessment tool appeared to be psychometrically comparable to the original one with elderly GAD patients (Hopko et al., 2003). There is also the State-Trait Anxiety Inventory (Spielberger, 1983), Hopkins Symptom Checklist (Derogatis, Lipman, Rickels, Uhlenhuth, & Covi, 1973), Zung Self-Rating Anxiety Scale (Zung, 1971), Beck Anxiety Inventory (Beck & Steer, 1990), Padua Inventory (Sanavio, 1988), and the Fear Questionnaire (Marks & Matthews, 1979).

Several more structured diagnostic interviews can also be used in the elderly, including the following: Anxiety Disorders Interview Schedule – updated for *DSM-IV* (Brown et al., 1994); the Structured Clinical Interview – updated for *DSM-IV* (First, Spitzer, Gibbon, & Williams, 1997); and the Hamilton Anxiety Scale (Hamilton, 1959). These tend to be more time-consuming and less cost-efficient, and may prove to be more cumbersome to administer with an elderly population.

In establishing an accurate diagnosis of GAD in the elderly patient, the assessment instruments used above form only part of the evaluative process. Needless to say, a thorough history of the patient, their family, caregivers, a mental status examination, and complete physical are standard practice (Flint, 2005). In addition, unexplained physical symptoms, such as fatigue, aches and pains, GI distress, sleep disturbance, and concurrent medical disorders, need to be teased out by the PCP, with whom they normally have their first contact (Flint, 1994; Wittchen et al., 2002).

Wetherell, Le Roux, and Gatz (2003) found that a sleep disturbance was the best discriminator with older adults who have GAD from those with subsyndromal anxiety symptoms vs. normal controls. On the basis of *DSM-IV*, the criteria to meet diagnostic threshold for GAD in older adults is the same as in younger adults (APA, 2000). This includes frequency, excessiveness, number of topics of worry, perceived difficulty controlling worry, restlessness, fatigue, irritability, muscle tension, and sleep disturbance (Wetherell et al., 2003), which in turn distinguishes older adults with GAD from those without the disorder.

Comorbid diagnoses, whether they are other mental disorders and/or physical conditions, also need to be ruled out to confirm GAD in older adults. For example, GAD and depression have concurrence rates ranging from 11 to 55% (Lenze & Mulsant 2005; Wittchen et al., 2001). However, when GAD and MDD co-occur in the elderly, which is less common than in younger GAD patients, there is still a significantly greater impairment in functioning (Zimmerman & Chelminski, 2003). The presence of muscle tension is more characteristic of GAD than MDD (Joorman & Stober, 1999), as is an increased positive affect (Kessler et al., 1999), increased autonomic suppression, and different genetic and environmental determinants (Wittchen et al., 2001). Symptoms of panic disorder, phobic disorders, plus use of prescribed and non-prescribed medications (caffeine, illicit substances) should also be assessed (Flint, 2005) in making the diagnosis of GAD. Aggressive and assaultive behaviors can, in the elderly patient, often be a signal of anxiety (Fisher & Noll, 1996). GAD plus cognitive disorders is an even more complex issue (Beck & Averill, 2004). Thus, differential diagnosis is an inherent challenge with older adult patients with GAD.

The elderly are more likely than younger patients with GAD to have more medical illnesses, given the nature of being older. This can have a deleterious effect on health-care utilization (Katon et al., 1990), emergency room usage, (Diefenbach et al., 2003; Diefenbach, Robinson, Tolin, & Blank, 2004), quality of care received (de Beurs et al., 1999), and severity of medical problems (Sherbourne, Wells, & Sturm, 1997). There was an increased likelihood of receiving a diagnosis of GAD as a linear function of the number of medical illnesses present at the time (Mohlman & Price, 2006). In addition, differentiating GAD vs. normal aging and subsyndromal anxious adults is also important for diagnostic purposes and has been studied by researchers (Montorio et al., 2003; Wetherell et al., 2003). Findings were consistent with greatest frequency and severity of worry in relation to social and interpersonal matters, finances, minor matters, own health, muscle tension combined with the additional endorsement of 5 of 6 associated symptoms in older adults with GAD. This worry was, by its nature, beyond the individual's control and contributed to loss of autonomy and, combined with associated GAD symptoms, did indeed interfere with daily functioning.

Having discussed some of the key issues and challenges surrounding GAD in later life, the discussion can now turn to what a clinician can do to assist these patients in decreasing their symptoms and improving global functioning. For that, psychosocial treatment and pharmacological ones become areas of exploration and options in the clinician's therapeutic arsenal.

Psychosocial Treatments

Cognitive behavioral treatment has been the best studied approach in older GAD patients. It includes psychoeducation, recognition of anxiety symptoms, relaxation training, cognitive restructuring, imaginal/in vivo exposure to worrisome thoughts, and situations with prevention of nonadaptive behaviors. There has been a growth in research on the disorder over the past several years, with a subset of these studies devoted to psychosocial treatment of late-life anxiety (Mohlman, 2004). Several investigative groups have designed CBT protocols to determine its efficacy in this population (Beck & Averill, 2004).

The first randomized controlled trial of group CBT vs. supportive therapy (ST) used *DSM-III-R* diagnostic criteria for GAD and had a sample size of $n = 48$; the patients were 55 years and older, and community dwelling (Stanley, Beck, & Glasco, 1996). The treatment consisted of 14 ninety-minute sessions of CBT vs. ST. They were both equally effective in reducing worry, anxiety, and depressive symptoms. The gains were maintained at 6-month follow-up. There were more treatment responders on 3 of 4 outcome measures in the ST group.

In a follow-up study, Stanley et al. (2003), with a sample of 85 community-dwelling older adults aged 60 and older, where 64 had a primary diagnosis of GAD and 21 had co-occurring GAD, found that when group CBT was compared to a minimal contact control group (MCC) over 13 fifty-minute sessions, there was a decrease in GAD severity in the CBT group. There were significant improvements in worry, anxiety, depression, and quality of life, resulting from CBT relative to MCC. Gains were maintained in the CBT group for up to a year for most patients. At posttreatment, the scores in the CBT group did not demonstrate a return to normative functioning. Both groups showed a decrease on the Beck Depression Inventory (BDI; Beck & Steer, 1987). Responders in the CBT group were at 45% compared to 8% in the MCC.

In a CBT-flexible protocol (Gorenstein, Papp, & Kleber, 1999), participants following acute treatment attended monthly individual booster sessions for 6 months. CBT was enhanced with learning and memory aids (ECBT) vs. a wait-list control in 15 adults, aged 60–79. There was a 75% response rate in the ECBT group, compared to 14% response in the WL group. The ECBT participants demonstrated significant improvements from baseline on two self-report measures (rates of posttreatment GAD, GAD severity ratings). Overall, ECBT showed improvement on more measures and yielded larger effect sizes than CBT (when both were compared against WL). However, standard CBT and ECBT were not directly compared in this study.

In a pilot study, Mohlman and Gorman (2005), on the basis of Gorenstein et al. (1999), examined the role of executive functioning in individual CBT with anxious adults pretreatment and posttreatment. A sample of 32 patients with GAD, where 10 were intact (average–better scores on executive tasks), 5 were improved (low average–moderate scores), and 7 were significantly impaired (low average–borderline), were compared to a wait-list. The aim of the study was to determine executive dysfunction on CBT clinical outcomes. The findings found that 50% of the intact, 67% of the improved, and none of the impaired or WL met responder criteria at the end of treatment. The CBT group followed an enhanced format with reminder telephone calls, feedback, and at-home practice assignments. The findings demonstrated that some degree of executive dysfunction does not impede the therapeutic effects of CBT on late-life GAD. The study needs replication, but is an important one given the age of the sample.

Wetherell, Gatz, and Craske (2003), in a sample of 75 (with a mean age of 67 and a primary diagnosis of GAD), compared group CBT ("worry reduction class" to reduce stigma) to a discussion group vs. a wait-list. The discussion group was similar to group CBT but did not focus on the learning of new skills. The protocol was 12 ninety-minute weekly sessions administered in groups of 4–6 participants. The findings demonstrated that both the CBT and discussion group, for those who attended at least seven sessions, exhibited improvements in reducing anxiety, worry, and to a lesser degree, depression relative to WL. In these treated groups one third were responders, and gains were maintained at 1-month follow-up. CBT had a larger effect size than discussion at posttreatment and 6-month follow-up.

A study by Barrowclough et al. (2001), consisting of 8–12 sessions of individual CBT vs. ST, where the mean age of the sample was 72 (19% of the 55 participants had GAD), over a 16-week period, treated in their homes, found that 71% in the individual CBT group were responders and fared better on several measures, compared to 39% response rate for the ST group.

In a pilot research program, Stanley et al. (2003) initiated an individualized CBT protocol in primary care to address the needs of older adults with GAD. In this small randomized clinical trial, CBT–GAD/PC (i.e., a version of CBT for GAD in primary care) was compared to usual care (UC), with a sample of 12 older medical patients with GAD. The protocol consisted of eight sessions, plus two more sessions if the patient was in crisis or in need of more time to learn novel coping skills. There were significant improvements in the CBT group on measures of worry and depression relative to the UC one. Some benefits were gained in the UC-treated group (similar to other studies: Stanley et al., 2003; Wetherell et al., 2003). There was flexibility in this study to accommodate individual needs. In addition, pneumonic aids and homework forms were simplified and incorporated into the CBT. These are promising preliminary results.

Mohlman et al. (2003), in two pilot investigations, compared individually administered CBT vs. WL. In the first study, a sample size of 27 patients with GAD were randomized to standard CBT or a waiting list. There were no significant differences between the groups on any outcome measure. Effect sizes averaged 0.43 for both groups. In Study 2, an enhanced form of individual CBT was compared to a WL with 15 patients with GAD. The enhanced group CBT implemented additional attention to at-home practice assignments, reminder telephone calls, and weekly review of concepts and interventions. The results demonstrated that enhanced CBT was superior to WL on two outcome measures. There were fewer patients who met criteria for GAD posttreatment. Effect sizes in the enhanced CBT group averaged 0.81. The response rate to the enhanced group reached 75%. This compares to 40% for standard CBT and 9–14% for a WL. Gains were maintained in the enhanced group for up to 6 months. Enhanced CBT was not directly compared to standard CBT. These results are encouraging, and seem to suggest that enhanced CBT offers various added strategies to offset the cognitive changes that take place with aging. This in turn seems to maximize clinical outcomes.

A promising case series, which is a CBT approach rooted in an intolerance of uncertainty conceptual model (Ladouceur, Leger, Dugas, & Freeston, 2004), with a sample size of eight GAD patients, examined this intervention in 14 weekly individual sessions of CBT. The results found that 7 of 8 patients no longer met criteria after treatment. Gains were maintained at 6- and 12-month follow-ups. The mean effect size was 1.67. There is a need to compare this with an active alternative treatment group and/or a wait-list in a RCT.

Gorenstein et al. (2005) compared CBT plus medication management (MM), vs. MM alone in a sample of 42 older adults (55% met criteria for GAD), who desired to terminate their antianxiety medication. They had been on medication for at least 8 weeks. The protocol was 13 individual 50-min sessions. The CBT plus MM group experienced significant improvements in decreasing phobic anxiety, obsessive–compulsive anxiety, somatization, and global severity of psychopathology measures. There were no differences in the groups on rates of taper or on worry, state and trait anxiety.

In a quantitative meta-analytic review of psychosocial treatments for a broad range of late-life anxiety disorders, Nordhus and Pallesen (2003) compared active interventions vs. active placebo vs. no-treatment groups. Seven of the fifteen studies compared CBT vs. active or passive control groups. The remainder of the studies were relaxation-based interventions (four studies), rational emotive therapy (one study), and personal construct therapy with control (one study). There was no appreciable difference between effect sizes – individual (0.54), group (0.44). Fisher and Durham (1999) found that individual formats out perform group ones for younger adults. The mean overall effect size was 0.55. This was noticeably lower than studies completed on younger adult patients (Gould et al., 2004).

In a more recent review of evidence-based treatments (EBTs) for GAD samples, or samples with other anxiety disorders and symptoms, Ayers, Sorrell, Thorp, and Wetherell (2007) looked at 17 studies, and found four types of EBTs to be efficacious in late-life anxiety. The four effective treatments are relaxation therapy, CBT, and, to a lesser extent, ST and cognitive therapy. CBT was found to have the most consistent support for GAD. In addition, EBTs are strong for GAD and should be standard clinical practice. The results of this review also found that psychosocial treatments were modestly efficacious, and that there is considerable room for improvement. Two other findings seem pertinent: group relaxation training was superior to group cognitive therapy, and individual cognitive therapy may be more effective because of its idiographic approach to assessment and treatment. In particular, relaxation training shows promise for older adults with anxiety. It is also low in cost, easy to deliver the intervention, and has proven to be efficacious. There is a need, based on this review, to look into combined treatments with medications and alternative psychosocial approaches other than (not in lieu of) conventional CBT, to enlarge the range of evidence-based options for the treatment of older adults.

Several themes and conclusions (albeit some may be more tentative than others) can be drawn from the research on psychosocial treatments for late-life GAD and anxiety disorders. Mohlman and Price (2006) concluded that there is not enough evidence to indicate the superiority of any one modality over another for late-life anxiety.

Group format, ST, CBT, and a discussion were better than no treatment (Stanley et al., 1996, 2003; Wetherell et al., 2003). Mohlman (2004) suggests that the group format, rather than the particular elements of any specific treatment condition, benefits across all therapies.

In regard to individual formats, CBT and, to a lesser extent, ST demonstrated efficacy (Ladouceur et al., 2004; Mohlman et al., 2003, 2005; Stanley et al., 2003). Once again, Mohlman (2004) found that the results from the individual studies have been mixed, with more modest effect sizes than those seen with younger GAD patients. Wetherell et al. (2003) argues that standard individual CBT may not be optimal for treating late-life GAD. Augmented CBT seems somewhat more effective than standard CBT (Gould et al., 2004; Mohlman et al., 2003). The most consistent predictor of change was adherence to homework after treatment and at 6-month follow-up (Wetherell et al., 2005), which lends further support to the potential advantage of using an augmented CBT protocol for this population. Overall, based on the collective research studies presented here, CBT appears less efficacious for late-life GAD, than for younger GAD patients.

A few final thoughts on this particular subject seem in order at this point. Wetherell, Sorrell, Thorp, and Patterson (2005) have concluded that, even though research continues to grow in the psychosocial treatment of late-life anxiety, the rationale behind the CALM Study (controlling anxiety on later-life medical patients) is that CBT protocols for anxiety in older adults appear to be less effective than in younger adults (confirming the above findings), and there does not appear to be significant evidence for the superiority of any one treatment over another for GAD and other diffuse forms of late-life anxiety. In addition, "most older adults remain symptomatic even after treatment with conventional CBT" (Wetherell et al., 2005, p. 75). A pilot investigation from the CALM Study produced some encouraging preliminary results for anxious older adults, and an RCT is underway, but not yet in press (Wetherell, e-mail communication, 2008).

Pharmacological Treatments

Research on the pharmacological treatment of late-life GAD has not been abundant in nature. There have been few controlled studies to date, even though medication in an early study was considered the first line treatment for late life anxiety (Blazer et al., 1991). However, in a paradoxical finding, it was found that many older adults do not prefer to take anxiolytics because of side effects (Wetherell et al., 2004). This makes the need to find medications with more tolerable profiles an option to psychotherapy for some older patients, especially in view of the fact that effect sizes are ~50% less in older adults with GAD, compared to younger patients with the same disorder (Wetherell et al., 2005).

Benzodiazepines are the most frequently prescribed psychotropics for late-life anxiety (Manela, Katona, & Livingston, 1996; Wetherell, Lenze, & Stanley, 2005). Prevalence rates range from 10% (Gleason et al., 1998) to 12% (Gray, Eggen, Blough, Buchner, & La Croix, 2003), reaching as high as 43% in one study for chronic anxiety (Schuurmans et al., 2005). Three RCTs examined the efficacy of these medications for older adults. Two of the studies focused on GAD (Bresolin et al., 1988; Frattola et al., 1992), and found that benzodiazepines are more effective than placebo. However, benzodiazepines are still not recommended for long-term treatment because of the potential for serious side effects, such as cognitive impairment, increased daytime sedation, unsteady gait, falls and hip fractures, and psychomotor impairment (Wetherell et al., 2005). If benzodiazepines are used, ones with short half lives, such as lorazepam (0.5–2.0 mg/day) and oxazepam, are preferred (Flint, 2005; Sheikh & Cassidy, 2000).

Buspirone has some efficacy in younger adult patients with GAD, in spite of mixed findings about its therapeutic effect and highly selective use. However, its role in elderly patients has been even more limited (Flint, 2005). Two prospective studies found that buspirone and oxazepam were better than placebo in older patients diagnosed with "anxiety state" or "anxiety neurosis" (Bohm et al., 1990; Koepke, Gold, Linden, Lion, & Rickels, 1982).

Antidepressants are the first line treatment choice in late-life GAD. In a study by Katz, Reynolds, Alexopoulous, and Hackett (2002), the safety and efficacy profile of an alternative treatment in older patients with GAD, based on having conducted a secondary analysis of five randomized, placebo-controlled trials of extended venlafaxine (venlafaxine ER) for adult patients with GAD, were evaluated. Ten percent of the patients were older than 60, with 5% being over 65. Results on the CGI-I demonstrated 66% of those 60 and older responded to venlafaxine, vs. 41% for placebo. Increasing age did not seem to influence response rates in either short-term or long-term treatments, which were comparable to younger patients (67% for venlafaxine vs. 44% for placebo). The conclusion was that venlafaxine ER is equally safe and efficacious in the treatment of older patients as it is in younger ones with GAD.

Lenze et al. (2005) examined the safety and efficacy of citalopram in an 8-week, randomized, placebo-controlled trial for late-life anxiety, with a sample of 34 patients (aged 60 and over), where 30 met the criteria of DSM-IV GAD. The total sample was either randomized to receive citalopram (an SSRI) or placebo. The assessment measures used were the HAM-A and the CGI. The findings demonstrated that 11 of 17 (65%) of the citalopram-treated group responded by 8 weeks, vs. 4 of 17 (24%) of the placebo-treated. This was considered the first prospective RCT to test the efficacy of an SSRI in the treatment of late-life anxiety. Citalopram was proven both safe and effective with this population. In regard to GAD, 10 of 15 (67%) responded, compared to 4 of 15 (27%) for placebo. This difference was a significant one. Sedation was the most prominent side effect.

In a longer term treatment study, consisting of a 32-week trial of citalopram, Blank et al. (2006) with 30 patients (27 of 30 had GAD) aged 60 and over, meeting *DSM-IV* criteria of an anxiety disorder, examined response, quality of life, and sleep outcomes. Several assessment measures were used in this study. The results are based on extending the Lenze et al. (2005) study. In terms of response rate, 18 of 30 (60%) patients were responders. There were also significant improvements in sleep and quality of life. The impact on somatic and psychic symptoms, based on the HAM-A, improved as well in a review study by Lenze et al. (2005) of 30 anxious patients (aged 60 and older) who participated in a 32-week trial of citalopram. However, a significant proportion still continued to have somatic symptoms, even across a long-term medication study.

The first study to investigate CBT vs. an SSRI was conducted by Schuurmans et al. (2006). A sample size of 84 patients, aged 60 years and older, with a primary diagnosis of GAD, PD, agoraphobia, or social phobia, were randomly assigned to one of three conditions. The treatment protocol consisted of 15 sessions of CBT, compared to pharmacotherapy with sertraline (eight 20-min sessions over 15 weeks with a maximum dose of 150 mg/day) vs. a wait-list control group. There were 52 completers in this study. In the CBT group there was a 44% response rate compared to 57% in the drug-treated group, and 11% for the placebo. In both the CBT and sertraline groups, there were significant improvements in anxiety, worry, and depressive symptoms at posttreatment and 3-month follow up. Yet, sertraline showed even more superior results on worry symptoms than CBT, as measured on the

Worry Domains Questionnaire (WDQ). Effect sizes for CBT were in the small–medium range at posttreatment (0.42) and 3-month follow-up (0.35), while the effect sizes for sertraline were in the large range at posttreatment (0.94) and 3-month follow-up (1.02). The wait-list had negligible effects at posttreatment (0.05). It appears from this study, that SSRI treatment was more effective than CBT. However, homework adherence in this study was a challenge; there were large attrition rates, and the follow-up period was on the short side. Yet the findings are still telling, and may point the way towards the use of SSRIs as the first line treatment in late-life anxiety.

A meta-analysis by Pinquart and Duberstein (2007) lends further support to the potential advantage of pharmacotherapy over psychotherapy with older adults who have anxiety disorders. Thirty-two studies of treatments focused on anxiety disorders ($n = 2,484$) in the elderly, who either received behavioral interventions or pharmacological ones. In comparing the two interventions, there was a stronger improvement found in those using pharmacotherapy over those receiving behavioral intervention ($d = 1.76$ vs. $d = 0.81$). However, when controlling for nonspecific change in the control group, the difference between groups in effect sizes tends to disappear, because effect sizes are greater in pill-placebo controls found in pharmacological studies vs. wait-list controls that occur in psychological ones. Having said that, the higher average treatment effects of pharmacotherapy compared to behavioral interventions suggests that drug treatment may be the preferred treatment of choice for late-life anxiety. Once again, patient preference and medical conditions can often influence the final treatment choice, in spite of empirical data that favor one modality over another.

On a final note – an NIMH-sponsored "study has been completed ($n = 177$, it is the largest to-date treatment study in late-life GAD). It used escitalopram vs. placebo, and you can get the specifics off the clinicaltrials.gov. Results look good but are unpublished at this point" (Lenze, e-mail communication, 2008).

Conclusion

In this chapter many studies were examined that attempted to explore the most optimal treatments for youth and older adults with GAD. In spite of there being no specific psychosocial treatment for pediatric GAD, it has been possible to extrapolate, from combined samples of children and adolescents with anxiety disorders (where GAD participants have been included), that CBT is an effective treatment for GAD, and should be considered the first line intervention. Pharmacotherapy has also been studied in youth with GAD, and SSRIs have proven effective with venlafaxine, producing more mixed results. When CBT fails to work, is not accessible, or the younger patient is distressed by the symptoms to the point of causing marked functional impairment, the use of medications should be considered as a viable treatment option. Black box warnings need to be taken seriously, as younger patients often have more difficulty expressing what they are feeling and that they may be experiencing significant side effects on medications. However, the risk has been overstated, depriving this population of the symptomatic relief that pharmaceutical agents can bring, with judicious use.

In regard to late-life GAD, there have been many specific psychosocial studies conducted with this population, but far less on the pharmacological side. The verdict on what works best seems to be the inverse of what is most effective with children. Standard CBT has proven to be less effective in this population, regardless of whether it was conducted in an individual or group format. Augmented CBT that includes mnemonics and adherence to homework assignments has appeared to produce more robust outcomes. Somehow, psychotherapy in this population that factors in age-related declines in memory and cognition has the potential to produce more significant results. Relaxation training, in a recent review of psychosocial EBTs for late-life anxiety (Ayers et al., 2007), was also recommended as an important treatment option to be implemented in this population. Yet, even with a paucity of pharmacological studies, pharmacotherapy in the form of certain SSRIs, appear to have the edge as the first line treatment in late-life GAD, based on the current evidence.

In conclusion, there is still, in both pediatric and late-life GAD, much more to learn about the pathogenesis and treatment options available in these "special populations," compared to young and middle-aged adults. Finally, conceptual models, including biomedical ones, have been better developed, thereby producing a much broader selection of psychological and pharmacological options to choose from, compared with those found in their much younger and older counterparts with the same disorder.

Chapter 7
Enigmas and Paradoxes

Generalized anxiety disorder is an enigmatic condition. Even with all the advances that have taken place in the development of conceptual models for GAD (especially with adult patients) and the plethora of empirical research, both from a psychosocial and pharmacotherapeutic standpoint, GAD still remains somewhat of a mystery. It is hard to pinpoint exactly why a mysterious aura surrounds this disorder, as various compelling explanations for GAD's diagnostic existence and treatments have been broached, and seemingly confirmed throughout this text.

To briefly summarize some of the ongoing concerns that mystify certain experts in the field; the disorder has undergone multiple diagnostic revisions over the years, creating, in the skeptic's mind, a lack of interrater reliability and independence for GAD. Some believe that it is more akin to a personality disorder than a symptom-based one. GAD sufferers do remain undertreated, even when they seek treatment, and it has been understudied, compared to the other anxiety disorders. Worry, a ubiquitous human experience, is one of the few persistent dilemmas of this disorder.

Metaphors, such as the "worried well" and the "invisible disorder", only continue to confound. Even though these terms are meant to characterize the essence of GAD, they often fall short in trying to capture the extent of pervasive suffering persons with GAD actually feel on a daily basis. This is the case, in spite of the fact (in fairness to those who use these terms as clinical descriptions) that there is a generally perceived sense, at this point in time, of the disorder's deeply painful and functionally impairing status.

It could be argued that GAD has come of age – on the one hand having been given greater legitimacy, while on the other, remaining full of unresolved paradoxes. Perhaps this is part of the attraction and mystique for me, and others who are interested in this clinical population, to more fully resolve the riddles behind GAD and, in turn, better help those who remain misunderstood.

Not unlike many other mental and physical maladies that humans face, an added challenge, lending further confusion to the understanding of GAD, is that topics such as prevention, the non-Western patient with GAD and anxiety, and treatment-resistant GAD have been critically neglected areas. The focus in health care, at least in the West, has been almost exclusively on tertiary care (providing treatment once

M.E. Portman, *Generalized Anxiety Disorder Across the Lifespan*,
DOI: 10.1007/978-0-387-89243-6_7, © Springer Science+Business Media, LLC 2009

the individual is already afflicted, rather than looking for ways to prevent it from occurring in the first place), studying Western homogenous samples of GAD patients in research studies, and directing interventions to those who are the most likely responders to uncomplicated first line treatments.

Unfortunately for persons with GAD, which can parallel life itself, easy solutions do not always conform and fall into neatly fixed categories. It then becomes a critical task to look outside the standard conventional box for unanswered questions that bear on GAD, and for that matter, life's ongoing enigmas and paradoxes.

Prevention

Roe-Sepowitz, Bedard, and Thyer (2005), on the basis of their research, have concluded that little attention has been paid to prevention of anxiety disorders. Their argument is that the anxiety disorders can be prevented, with access to treatment or prevention information in the early stages of the disorder (Leighton, 1987). It is the delay in treatment and shortage of information about anxiety disorders and their management that is the main contributor to the development of a diagnosable anxiety disorder. Craske and Zucker (2001) also suggest that, given that patients with anxiety disorders routinely camouflage their disorder in lieu of getting treatment, this leads them to subsequently becoming so distressed and functionally impaired by their symptoms, thereby further impeding efforts at prevention.

In a prevention workshop for college students (Seligman, Schulman, & DeRubeis, 1999), freshmen ($n = 231$) identified to be at risk for depression and anxiety were assigned to treatment or control groups during the course of a 3-year period. In the treatment group there were 16 hours of meetings over 8 weeks, plus the completion of homework assignments (led by a trainer/cotrainer). The intervention took place three times over 3 years. The modality was CBT-based with a broad repertoire. In the end, participants demonstrated fewer episodes of GAD and decreased anxiety symptoms, compared to the control group.

To date there are few, if any, evidence-based prevention models for adult anxiety disorders. Roe-Sepowitz et al. (2005) add that these types of models could help offset stigma, ignorance, social and financial costs, and functional impairment. What is also needed is more specialized training for clinicians during graduate school and beyond in evidence-based education in the area of primary prevention.

Tyrer and Baldwin (2006) confirmed that evidence for the effective prevention of GAD is scarce, and the focus, as I alluded to above, continues to be on tertiary care in patients with an established disorder. Brown, Elliot, Boardman, Ferns, and Morrison (2004) suggest that the growth of self-help and group psychoeducational community-based interventions for anxiety and depression may provide individuals with earlier help and prove beneficial. Thus far, this is yet to be determined in any systematic way, in spite of the pressing unmet need.

Cultural Considerations

In reviewing the subject of cultural effects on anxiety disorders, the general opinion is a mixed one (Kessler et al., 2005). What makes this subject difficult is that there has been a lack of research in this area. However, it could be argued that one's cultural attitudes towards mental health, language differences, and other factors would seem to have the potential to alter a person's experience of anxiety and the way it manifests itself to a clinician (Shulz et al., 2005). According to Leff (1994), the psychological mode of expressing distress and discomfort is an inherently Western phenomenon. For example, the somatizer/psychologizer ratio is higher in Spain compared with other countries (Garcia-Compayo, Sanz-Carrillo, Claraco, Arana, & Monton, 1997).

In an intriguing study by Hoge et al. (2006), subjects from diverse cultural backgrounds were evaluated, as they presented to mental health centers with the main complaint of anxiety. In this study, 23 subjects with GAD presented to a psychiatry department in an urban general hospital in Boston, MA, or 30 subjects with GAD went to a psychiatry department in Katmandu, Nepal. Those from Nepal were hypothesized to have higher rates of somatic focus than did their American counterparts with GAD. The sample consisted of male and female patients, aged 18–75, with DSM-IV GAD. Per the hypothesis, the Nepali patients had higher rates of somatic complaints than did the Americans with GAD. This research is consistent with previous findings – that those from Asian cultures exhibit more somatic symptoms of depression than those from Western cultures do. The authors think that one of the reasons is that stigma can lead to a minimizing of the expression of emotional distress and the favoring of somatic symptomatology.

Hsu (1999) argues that in Asia there is less of an emphasis on the mind/body dichotomy in traditional medicine, and therefore psychological distress to often manifests in somatic ways. Hsu and Folstein (1997) go so far as to say that somatic presentations may be the norm in most cultures, and Western psychologizers require explanation. Tseng (1973) makes the point that non-Westerners are also less prone to intense personal introspection of their affective states, and lack the semantic framework to conceptualize and express affect. "Cultural factors may also influence acceptable patterns of expression, leading to increased emotional discomfort in discussing emotional difficulties" (Hoge et al., 2006, p. 964). Clearly, health-care providers need to be mindful of these nuances in the clinical presentation and expression of emotional distress.

McLellarn and Rosenzweig (2004) believe that future studies need to explore more carefully the role of ethnicity, culture, and sociocultural variables in the prevalence, development, presentation, and treatment of GAD. They continue to observe that it is not the existence of anxiety or anxiety disorders in other cultures that is in debate, but rather the culture-specific expressions of disquietude, social reality, and symptomatic resolution that need greater attention.

Barlow (2002) suggests that, in all cultures, there are a subset of individuals who present as worried, apprehensive, fearful, and aroused, and make attributions related to their worries and arousal. In addition, he argues that prevalence rates are relatively consistent across cultures, in spite of different manifestations. For instance, in Lesotho (an African Nation), the prevalence of panic disorder and GAD are equal to or greater than rates in North America (Hollifield, Katon, Spain, & Pule, 1990). Once again, Barlow has found that somatic presentations are the most common expressions of emotional maladies in non-European countries.

In an interesting study, that may be an exception to this cultural norm, Bakhshani, Lashkaripour, and Sadjadi (2007) made use of a sample of 21 Iranian patients with GAD who were randomized to eight sessions of CBT ($n = 7$), antidepressant and benzodiazepine drugs ($n = 7$), or a control group ($n = 7$). The findings demonstrated that both short-term CBT (based on Clark (1990)) and pharmacotherapy were effective in reducing anxiety symptoms in this non-Western sample. However, CBT showed greater efficacy in changing dysfunctional assumptions and rules. This speaks to the fact that CBT, which often has as its focus the target symptom of worry (a psychic symptom), was beneficial in this population. The use of CBT in other countries, besides Iran, could shed further light on how patients in these non-Western nations clinically present and demonstrate, and that not all non-Westerners have a primary somatic focus to their GAD. These results also support the notion that CBT may be transportable and applied effectively in different cultures.

In summary, GAD would most likely look quite different, based on this brief but important discussion on cultural variation in the expression of psychopathology, across different non-Western vs. Western countries. Given this reality, patients, even in North America, present in heterogeneous ways dependent on multiple factors – the most salient being, in this publication, their age cohort.

One of those factors is gender differences. It has been established that women suffer from GAD in a ratio of 2:1, compared to men. Steiner et al. (2005) found that women and men with GAD, in a sample of 370 patients, had similar clinical presentations and responded equally well to sertraline (an SSRI), but that the onset of symptoms for women started earlier, and they reported an increased number of somatic symptoms. Another preliminary finding (Simon & Zalta et al. 2006) found a gender difference in the response to fluoxetine (another SSRI). In this post hoc analysis of women vs. men with GAD (particularly those with a later onset of GAD), women may have a poorer response to this medication. The study suggests, once again, that gender differences may play a role in pharmacotherapy response. Clearly, more research is needed in these areas to tease out both the more overt and subtle cultural differences, not only within, but between, countries and among divergent groups of patients with GAD.

Treatment-Resistant Generalized Anxiety Disorder

The most optimal means to manage treatment-resistant GAD is uncertain (Coplan, Tiffon, & Gorman, 1993; Rynn & Brawman-Mintzer, 2004). Fricchione (2004) discusses four possibilities: (1) increase current medication dose to 8 weeks, or an even longer trial (optimization), (2) combine psychotherapy and pharmacotherapy (data are lacking) (Foa, Franklin, & Moser, 2002), (3) consider comorbidity (Yonkers, Dyck, Warshaw, & Keller, 2000), and (4) combining medications (little empirical research) or augmenting with other agents (research is growing). Baldwin et al. (2005) found that there was no clear evidence to increase medication doses after an initial nonresponse. Pollack et al. (2007), in discussing treatment-resistant anxiety, argued that it has lagged behind similar studies of other conditions (Roy-Byrne & Cowley, 1998). In addition, he concluded that there is simply no consensus on treatment resistance.

Bandelow, Seidler-Brandler, Becker, Wedekind, and Ruther (2007), in a slightly different vein, looked at several acute treatments – comparing pharmacological and psychological ones for anxiety disorders. Their conclusion was that due to a lack of sufficient data, no final conclusions could be drawn for GAD regarding psychotherapy vs. pharmacotherapy. However, in this evaluation, where two of the studies were on GAD, CBT was superior over pharmacotherapy.

In one novel study (Pollack et al., 2008), where patients met the criteria for GAD and insomnia, they were given escitalopram for 10 weeks, and then randomized to receive either 3 mg of eszopiclone (a nonbenzodiazepine γ-aminobutyric acid receptor agonist) or placebo as an augmenting agent to the primary medication nightly for 8 weeks. For the final 2 weeks, eszopiclone was replaced with a single-blind placebo. The trial was a double-blind, randomized, placebo-controlled, parallel-group, add-on therapy 10-week study. The goal was to improve sleep quality, daytime functioning, and accelerate the anxiolytic response compared with the antidepressant alone in these patients with GAD and insomnia. Overall, the goal was achieved, as many features of sleep architecture improved, as did acceleration of the anxiolytic response and depression with the combined treatment.

In terms of augmentation in treatment-refractory GAD, Brawman-Mintzer, Knapp, and Niebert (2005), in a study of 40 patients who received an adequate dose of medication for 4 weeks, were either randomized to 5 weeks double-blind treatment with either placebo (16 of 20) or risperidone augmentation (15 of 19) (an atypical antipsychotic) at flexible doses (0.5–1.5 mg/day). The results demonstrated statistically significant improvements in the total HAM-A scale and on the subscale psychic anxiety factor. On the CGI-I 58% were much–very much improved (11 patients) vs. 35% in the placebo group (7 patients). The medication was generally well tolerated. Response rates were higher in the risperidone group, but did not reach clinical significance. The conclusion was that low-dose risperidone may be beneficial in the management of treatment-resistant GAD patients. Simon, Hoge et al., (2006), in a study using risperidone augmentation with patients having PD, SAD, or GAD, came up with similar findings. Risperidone was effective in reducing anxiety symptoms. The study was limited by the fact that there was no control group and it was an open-label trial.

In an open-label pilot study, using a different atypical antipsychotic called ziprasidone, monotherapy with this medication, using a flexible daily dose of 20–50 mg/day for 7 weeks, followed by a 3–7-day taper (Snyderman, Rynn, & Rickels, 2005), was tried with 13 patients meeting the criteria for GAD. The study found that on the HAM-A, remission rate was 36% and global improvement response was 54%. On the CGI-I, remission rate was 46% and global improvement response was 84%. All the patients in this study had failed at least one trial with buspirone, a benzodiazepine, or an SSRI. Even though this was a small sample size and an open-label pilot study, ziprasidone may be effective in treatment-resistant GAD.

In another augmentation study with aripiprazole (an atypical antipsychotic), Menza, Dobkin, and Marin (2007) conducted a 6 week, open-label trial pilot study to determine whether this medication would be effective and tolerable as an adjunct to nine patients (aged 18–64) with a GAD diagnosis. They had been previously treated with an antidepressant at a therapeutic dose for an adequate duration. Aripiprazole was added to the current medication regimen over a 6-week period. The dose was initiated at 10 mg/day, with adjustments as needed. There was one dropout from the study. On both primary outcomes there was significant improvement from baseline to endpoint. Of the total patients in the sample 8 of 9 were much–very much improved and 5 of 9 were responders (on the HAM-A). Secondary depressive symptomatology also exhibited improvements. The side effect profile was benign. In the most recent study to date (Hoge et al., 2008), which was an 8-week, open-label, prospective augmentation study, it was found that aripiprazole, once again, proved useful as an augmenting agent in patients with GAD or panic, who had a limited response to first line pharmacotherapy treatment. Overall, this medication may prove beneficial as an adjunctive agent in those who are not optimally responsive to antidepressants and have treatment-resistant GAD. Double-blind trials are still needed to confirm these findings.

An RCT for refractory GAD was conducted by Pollack et al. (2006), using a double-blind augmentation with olanzapine (another atypical antipsychotic) or placebo for patients still remaining symptomatic on fluoxetine. After 6 weeks (20 mg/day of fluoxetine), patients were either randomized to 6 weeks of olanzapine (mean dose, 8.7 ± 7.1 mg/day) or placebo augmentation. Fluoxetine-treated patients (24 of 46) were randomized to one group or another. Twelve patients were in the olanzapine-treated group vs. 12 in placebo (7 of 12 completed the olanzapine augmentation, 10 of 12 completed the placebo). Those patients receiving olanzapine were significantly more likely to be responders, suggesting that this medication has anxiolytic properties. Remission rate did not reach clinical significance. The major side effect was weight gain. In the final analysis, given that only a minority of patients with GAD experience sustained remission, the development of strategies to address this reality and the treatment-refractory nature of GAD are of serious clinical import.

In another augmentation study (Simon et al., 2008), the efficacy of quetiapine (another atypical antipsychotic) vs. placebo augmentation was examined. Patients with GAD were initially on paroxetine CR, flexibly dosed to a maximum of 62.5 mg/day. The GAD-refractory patients on paroxetine CR at 10 weeks were randomized to either quetiapine augmentation (flexibly dosed from 25–400 mg/day) or placebo. Those on the paroxetine CR ($n = 50$) showed a reduction on the HAM-A scores (40% achieved remission). There was minimal improvement in the quetiapine-augmentation-treated group. In other words, adding quetiapine to paroxetine CR conferred no therapeutic advantage.

In another study, currently in process (Cleveland Neuro-Sleep Research Institute), a multicenter, double-blind, randomized-withdrawal, parallel group, placebo-controlled, phase III trial tested the efficacy and safety of quetiapine (Seroquel SR) as monotherapy in maintenance treatment of GAD patients following an open-label stabilization period. The results are unpublished to date, as one of the lead researchers could not provide any further information, given that his role was limited to being an investigator during the research phase of the study (Woyshville, e-mail communication, 2008).

In an RCT (randomized, double-blind, placebo-controlled study) by Aliyev and Aliyev (2008), with a total of 80 men with DSM-IV GAD, patients were randomized to receive either valproate (depakine-chrono) ($n = 40$) for 6 weeks or placebo ($n = 40$). The GAD outpatients were aged between 18–65 years. The dose given was 500 mg thrice a day to the drug-treated group. The results found that 26 of 36 (72%) (6 patients in this group did not return, leaving the total sample at 36) depakine-chrono-treated group participants responded by week 6, vs. 4 of 38 (15%) placebo-treated patients. The drug-treated group was rated superior on the HAM-A scale. Valproate clinically and significantly improved anxiety symptoms over a 6-week period. The medication was both efficacious and well tolerated in this study. Dizziness and nausea are the most problematic side effects. It should be considered by the authors of the study as a useful new agent for GAD when other anti-GAD drugs have failed. Finally, determining how women respond to this novel GAD medication, and conducting a larger-scale study remain important areas of future inquiry.

In looking at treatment resistance in children and adolescents, residual symptoms are common (Reinblatt & Riddle, 2007). Clearly, the same suggestions made in the introduction of this section would apply to this clinical population. In one study, where participants had not responded to fluvoxamine after an 8-week phase, an open-label trial of fluoxetine (an SSRI) switch was done for up to 6 months, leading to a 71% response rate (Rupp, 2002). There have been no RCTs with youth regarding pharmacotherapy to address partial responders.

In regard to psychosocial interventions in treatment-resistant GAD, there are no studies at present that have addressed this challenge. Barlow (2001) recommends a full protocol of CBT (12–16 sessions), and when this fails, there is the need to consider alternative interventions, focus more on cognitions, increase exposure, try other empirically supported treatments and combine treatment modalities. In the case of adults and middle-aged adults, trying different psychological approaches, when one fails to work, would appear to be a plausible option. There are several evidence-based approaches now available, and others that have strong theoretical and empirical foundations to support their use. Others discussed in this text are more research-informed and process-oriented. They could also be tried when patients have a preference or the tried and tested do not seem to be producing the purported results.

In older adults, medication options and augmented CBT, based on the data, should be tried first, as multiple psychological approaches have not been tested with this population. Relaxation therapy and/or supportive counseling may also prove useful.

With children, CBT is the only psychosocial treatment approach that has been tested. When this approach fails, medication can be tried, or perhaps even a supportive–expressive approach (even though there is no data, as yet, that an unstructured modality with youth has any utility).

Gliatto (2000) suggests family involvement (role of support systems), possible Day Hospital Programs (structured), and drawing on community resources (Anxiety Disorders Association of America, National Institute of Mental Health, National Alliance for the Mentally Ill) as being of benefit with GAD patients. Other researchers have argued for the addition of a couples/marital intervention to standard CBT (Yoon & Zinbarg, 2007) – especially given the marked impairment in occupational, interpersonal, and social functioning in GAD. This may prove beneficial. Religious and spiritual connections, self-help (Hallowell, 2002; Lampe, 2004; Leahy, 2005), and exercise can also provide potential anchors and sources of consolation and viable outlets.

In the end, the choice of a psychosocial intervention, when first line treatments do not work in GAD across the life span, may end up being determined as much by clinical experience in doing what has worked in the past in similar cases, patient choice, and, if all else fails, trial and error, rather than any formulaic answers.

Conclusion

The topics discussed in this chapter have no easy solutions. The experts in the field have come to virtually no consensus on how to manage treatment-resistant GAD. Empirically supported prevention programs for GAD are nonexistent, and generalizing research findings regarding chronic worry and anxiety from a Western clinical population to a non-Western one is fraught with numerous challenges. However, even with this inherent gap in the literature, small steps have been made, and some select studies and ideas have been presented in this chapter to begin to start rectifying the above omission.

It is difficult enough to treat GAD in a Western homogeneous sample, let alone attempt to factor in the complexity of a foreign cultural surround. In regard to prevention, risk factors and protective factors need to be explored with greater depth and specificity. Once these factors are better isolated, data can be accumulated and programs set up to reach those most at risk to succumb to GAD. These neglected areas are difficult, not just for those who research and treat GAD, but for the other mental and physical maladies that plague human beings.

Given that GAD exacts a high individual and societal toll, the quest to prevent the emergence of the disorder, increase our sensitivities to those who suffer from this condition due to various cultural factors, and learn to better treat the seemingly untreatable reflects directly on our compassion and competence as health-care providers and humans. The stakes are high, yet the benefits immeasurable.

Chapter 8
Future Directions and Recommendations

In an attempt to avoid being parochial and accused of painting an uneven brush stroke while presenting GAD to clinicians of different persuasions, many broad and select themes have been the focus of this publication, and hence the title Generalized Anxiety Disorder across the Life Span: An Integrative Approach. Too much of the research to date has been geared towards the taking up of a position, and competing for academic dominance. Even though there is an increased tolerance for other mental health disciplines and their research efforts and clinical ambitions, compared to in the past, the training of specialists in their respective fields with a certain focus creates an almost inevitable potential for myopia.

Having said all that in regard to GAD, the subject of this publication, the central ideas in this text have not just been about life span development and integrative treatment. They have included a need for greater openness to different therapeutic options, and increased understanding among clinicians and researchers in properly managing this all too often intractable disorder. For example, the indiscriminate use of SSRIs is just as misguided as subjecting a patient with the disorder to 16 weeks of CBT, when there is no clear benefit. We need to look more closely at the patients' experiences themselves, in and out of the clinic, and check our own biases at the door. This does not mean that evidence-based research into the conceptual underpinnings or treatments for GAD should come to a halt. It simply implies that, with 50% response rates for GAD across the majority of psychosocial and pharmacological studies within almost all age groups (and even worse outcomes for older adults in standard CBT trials), there has been no clear victory for biology or psychology. Therefore, this demands, from those of us who care for these patients, increased ingenuity to maximize treatment outcomes in this clinical population. We need to scrutinize our motives more deeply and unify our efforts. Fricchione (2004) argues the point by summarizing that there are no formal guidelines from American or European professional societies for the management of GAD. This does not imply either a pessimistic or prophetic statement of doom and gloom for the millions of chronically worried and anxious patients worldwide. It only means that there is room for collective improvement.

M.E. Portman, *Generalized Anxiety Disorder Across the Lifespan*,
DOI: 10.1007/978-0-387-89243-6_8, © Springer Science+Business Media, LLC 2009

What will make a positive difference? There is no oracle providing an answer or panacea to this question. Some argue for a more multidimensional assessment, since current measures of response and remission remain inadequate for anxiety disorders (Bandelow, 2006). Others (Kessler & Brandenburg et al. 2005) suggest that a duration change for GAD could significantly influence the quantity of people diagnosed with GAD. In so doing, orphaned cases of GAD would be given more credibility and clinical significance (Rickels & Rynn, 2001). They also believe that severity of anxious symptomatology, not an emphasis on worry or duration, should be the most salient criteria in making the diagnosis of GAD. Maier et al., (2000) believe that the six month duration for GAD is too restrictive. Ruscio, Lane, Roy-Byrne, Stang, Stein, Wittchen and Kessler (2005) state that, by eliminating the excessiveness criteria for GAD, the lifetime prevalence rates of GAD would jump to 40%. The purpose being that this could highlight the need for future research into the optimal definition of generalized anxiety disorder. In addition, the defining criteria of excessiveness may only prove to be one form of GAD, but not the only one. The authors add that excessiveness of sadness is not a requirement of MDD.

The somatic focus of the disorder over time, with accompanying hyperarousal, has been replaced in current versions of *DSM* with the psychic phenomenon of worry as the cardinal symptom of GAD. Roth et al. (2008) feel strongly that broader GAD criteria should include those chronically anxious and hyperaroused patients, who are substantial in number and, at present, simply no longer meet diagnostic criteria. This clinical population, according to the authors, also exhibits much greater sympathetic activation. The placing of "Generalized Worry Disorder" and "Generalized Tension Disorder" into two unique categories, based on the above research, could also prove highly clarifying for GAD. Stein (2005), who was mentioned earlier in this text, even goes so far to say that GAD is in reality a "chronic tension disorder."

Allen, McHugh, & Barlow (2008) summarize recent advances in the development of A Unified Protocol for the Emotional Disorders (Barlow, Allen, & Choate, 2004; Moses & Barlow, 2006), where many patients had GAD at the Center for Anxiety and Related Disorders at Boston University. In this protocol a therapeutic shift is taking place in the way psychopathology is conceptualized and treated. The protocol consists of psychoeducation, antecedent cognitive reappraisal, prevention of emotional avoidance, and modifying of "emotion-driven behaviors." This is a more unified approach, based on new findings into the nature of emotion regulation. Its aim is to reconfigure the once dominant *DSM-IV* diagnostic categories with their specific manualized protocols per disorder into a more dimensionally based taxonomy, supplanting the current disorder-specific nomenclature (Brown & Barlow, 2005; Krueger, Markon, Patrick, & Iacono, 2005).

Instead of GAD and other particular diagnoses, there is a "general neurotic syndrome" (Andrews, 1990, 1996; Tyrer, 1989). This is an expression of various emotional disorders that manifest themselves in behaviorally variable ways in the context of this broader syndrome. In addition, Ehrenreich & Buzzella et al. (2007)

discuss the relevance of a life span developmental approach that makes use of emotion regulation concepts in treatment, and is applicable at all ages for intervention. The "tripartite model" (Barlow, 1988, 2000, 2002) forms the conceptual framework, and provides evidence for the interaction of three vulnerabilities, consisting of genetic contributions, a generalized psychological vulnerability (diminished sense of control), and early learning experiences. These seem to contribute to the development of certain anxiety disorders (Suarez, Bennett, Goldstein, & Barlow, 2009).

One other interesting aside – in Barlow (2008), GAD is left out of this volume for the first time after four editions. It is seemingly subsumed under the chapter heading called Emotional Disorders: A Unified Protocol (Allen et al., 2008). This tends to point the way, based on this deliberate omission in the text, towards approaching GAD conceptually and its treatment from a more integrative perspective.

The current status of this broadly focused emotion treatment approach has been reviewed in Ehrenreich et al. (2007). The protocol is ideally meant to be used with individual patients. The unified protocol was initially tested in three diagnostically heterogeneous groups. In more recent evaluations, the approach was examined in the individual treatment of six adults and three adolescents (Allen, Ehrenreich, & Barlow, 2005; Goldstein & Ehrenreich, 2005). The sample size of nine patients had a broad range of anxious and unipolar depressive disorders (including GAD). At completion of treatment, 5 of 6 adult patients reported a reduction of symptoms that no longer reached the clinical level. Several reported improvement in comorbidity. There was an 83% reduction in the primary diagnostic symptomatology to less than clinical levels.

In the adolescent sample, all three patients with their parents reported a reduction in the severity and impairment of primary diagnostic symptoms at posttreatment. At 6-month follow-up interview the gains were maintained and even further reductions in symptoms took place (Goldstein & Ehrenreich, 2005). Overall, this approach appears to be equal or even superior in both adults and adolescents to CBT for more homogenous diagnostic clinical populations (samples were small in this study).

The protocol may hold promise for "internalizing disorders" such as GAD, and represent an integrative, transdiagnostic emotion-driven model, which focuses more on etiological commonalities in the sequelae of symptoms and behaviors than disorders. This protocol has some kinship with the work of Harvey, Watkins, Mansell, and Shafran (2004).

In a highly original RCT by Westra, Arkowitz, and Dozois (2007), four sessions of motivational interviewing (MI) alone were evaluated to determine its effectiveness as a pretreatment for CBT in GAD vs. no pretreatment. Multiple assessment measures were used in this study. Sample size in the CBT group was 33, and in the MI plus CBT combination was 34. The augmentation of CBT plus MI offers highly promising effects on GAD, by increasing motivation (leading to changes in worry and stress), improving response rates to CBT, and increasing engagement with CBT. Other findings were also significant, in that MI alone has a positive impact on worry reduction and a moderate effect on worry severity. In other words, the data in the study indicate that MI works better for those with high severity. End-state functioning at posttreatment was 6.09 for MI plus CBT vs. 5.64 for CBT alone. Percentages of cases achieving very high end-state functioning at posttreatment was 85% for the combination-treated group of MI + CBT, and 65% for the CBT alone one. Those not meeting the diagnostic criteria for GAD were also lower at 1 year in the MI plus CBT group (57%), compared with CBT alone (79%). These preliminary results are most encouraging, and point the way towards using MI alone and in tandem with CBT to enhance clinical outcomes in GAD.

Another development that could impact GAD in a significant way is building on strengths, not focusing exclusively on pathology. Seligman (2002, p. 2) argues cogently that "we need to call for massive research in human strengths and virtues". This philosophy of therapeutic change, as it relates to GAD, could help make the lives of those suffering with the disorder psychologically and physically healthier by instilling hope (Snyder, Ilardi, Michael, & Cheavens, 2000). In addition, assisting them view life with a greater sense of agency and mastery (McHugh & Slavney, 1998), rather than as passive victims of genetics and habit, could prove empowering and self-determining.

The most significant contribution to emerge from the positive psychology movement (Fava, 1999) bearing on GAD, that has its roots in a strengths perspective, is a psychotherapeutic approach developed by a research team of mental health professionals at The University of Bologna. Their approach is called well-being therapy (WBT). They argue that, in contrast to the view endorsed by the *DSM*, well-being does not follow the removal of distress (Ruini & Fava, 2004). In other words, the mental health field in general has focused on health being equated with absence of illness, not the presence of wellness (Ryff, 1989; Ryff & Singer, 1996). This has changed somewhat with time, as quality of life measures, as discussed earlier, are being used more in clinical studies of GAD combined with the more conventional symptom reducing assessment instruments.

The two leading founders of WBT, Giovanni Fava and Chiara Ruini, incorporated the theoretical underpinnings of Ryff's (1989) cognitive multidimensional model of psychological well-being into their own approach. Well-being therapy is based on six constructs that do not simply bring the person out of negative functioning (i.e. removal of symptoms), but facilitate the progression towards restoration of the positive (i.e. wellness). These dimensions are as follows: (1) autonomy, (2) environmental mastery, (3) personal growth, (4) relations with others, (5) purpose in life, and (6) self-acceptance.

Autonomy comprises independence, self-determination, ability to resist outside social pressures, and possessing an internal locus of control. Environmental mastery consists of seizing environmental opportunities, being involved in vocational and familial activities, and having the competency in managing one's everyday affairs. Personal growth is about being open to new experiences, facing challenges and tasks, and the process of self-realization. Positive relations refer to having warm, trusting, affectionate, and intimate relationships with others, where the individual is capable of empathy and mutuality. Purpose in life is where a person has meaning in life, replete with goals, desires, and a sense of direction and purpose.

Self-acceptance is having positive cognitions towards the self, both the stellar and the imperfect qualities, while accepting one's total experience.

Before presenting the empirical evidence to support the efficacy of augmenting WBT with CBT in the treatment of GAD, it is important to explicate the specific applied interventions and how this type of therapy is similar and different from the standard CBT approach. One of the ironies about WBT is that both of the developers of the model are well trained in CBT and include components of it in their treatment package for GAD.

Well-being therapy, when used alone, proceeds in three distinct phases of treatment: (1) initial sessions, (2) intermediate sessions, and (3) final sessions. In the initial sessions, the chief concern is identifying episodes of well-being. Using a structured diary that emphasizes self-monitoring and observation (Emmelkamp, 1974), patients rate, on a scale of 0–100 (0 = absence of well-being, 100 = intense feelings of well-being), episodes of well-being. Needless to say, just as it can be difficult for individuals with a history of vulnerability, poor coping skills and low self-worth to identify strengths (McQuaide & Ehrenreich, 1997), so too individuals with low "hedonic book keeping" (Meehl, 1975) more often than not may have an incapacity to experience and report periods of well-being. They may bring a blank diary to these sessions (Ruini & Fava, 2004), revealing challenges in accessing any well-being episodes from their thoughts or feelings.

This initial phase of treatment usually lasts one to two sessions, depending on resistance and compliance with the goals of the interventions. During the intermediate sessions, patients are encouraged, once episodes of well-being are recognized, to attempt to identify ruptures in well-being. Instead of focusing on distress, individuals are encouraged to stay with the thoughts and feelings associated with well-being. Beck's model (1976) of challenging automatic thoughts and the subsequent cognitive distortions to facilitate well-being that may interrupt the process of enjoying pleasurable activities through graded behavioral assignments (Beck, Emery & Greenberg, 1985) is reinforced at this stage. This phase can last two to three sessions, and is largely dependent on each patient's motivation and strengths. In the final sessions, the therapist can monitor progress, introducing the specific constructs and dimensions outlined in Ryff's conceptual framework. The PWB – Psychological Well-Being Scales, an 84-item, self-rating inventory (Ryff, 1989) – can be used as an additional source of information and confirmation. The therapist then explains the contents of the constructs in greater detail and their application in promoting well-being. At this juncture in treatment, impairments related to the constructs and the realization of well-being can be elicited, as alternative ways of thinking and experiencing are explored using the dimensions with the patient.

Ultimately, WBT, in its pure form, is about eight sessions. However, there exists the potential of extending treatment to 12–16 sessions, if necessary, to meet the needs of a patient in assisting to further bring out the promotion of well-being. The therapy in a nutshell is a short-term, directive, structured, educational, and collaborative approach.

The similarities it shares with CBT are that both have a short-term, structured, directive, collaborative, and educational orientation. In addition, CBT and WBT often include scheduling of activities, assertiveness training, and problem-solving (Beck, Emery & Greenberg, 1985; Ellis & Becker, 1982). There is a search for impairments in thinking in CBT and impairments in well-being in WBT. However, in WBT, "it is only when such insights about these impairments in well-being dimensions are translated into behavioral terms that a significant improvement has been made" (Ruini & Fava, 2004, p. 164).

The main difference between WBT and CBT is that, in CBT, the focus is on psychological distress and its reduction through automatic cognitive control, whereas in WBT the goal is advancement of psychological well-being based on Ryff's constructs. According to Fava (2000), WBT is better conceptualized as a psychological approach within the broader spectrum of self-therapies. One last distinction is that WBT, unlike CBT, tends to keep its rationale and strategies at the outset more cryptic, which relies on the individual's progressive discovery of positive appraisals related to the self. In some ways, WBT, in contrast to CBT, has more subtlety in terms of its directiveness and structured focus.

In one study to date, Fava et al. (2005) empirically studied the potential effectiveness of WBT as an augmenting treatment to CBT for GAD. Twenty patients with DSM-IV GAD, without comorbidity, were randomly assigned to either eight sessions of CBT or the sequential administration of four sessions of CBT, followed by another four sessions of WBT. Assessment methods included the Anxiety and Depression Scales of Paykel's Clinical Interview for Depression (Paykel, 1985), Ryff's Psychological Well-Being Scales (Ryff, 1989), and Kellner's Symptom Questionnaire (Kellner, 1987). A 1-year follow-up was also implemented. The results demonstrated that there was a significant advantage to the CBT plus WBT sequential combination over CBT alone with both observer and self-rated methods at posttreatment. The gains were also maintained at 1-year follow-up. Finally, "all dimensions of psychological well-being significantly increased in the CBT–WBT combination" (Fava et al., 2005, p. 29).

A few limitations about this investigation have been addressed by the authors. The study is preliminary in nature. Sample size was small, and treatment was provided by only one psychiatrist with advanced training in CBT and anxiety disorders. Given these caveats, the need for a larger sample of patients to be tested, plus a study comparing CBT vs. WBT head on, is indicated. This might tell us more about the overall effectiveness of WBT for GAD and what is lacking in standard CBT. In the end, WBT is a potentially positive addition to the already existing treatments for GAD (even if it is an augmenting therapy to other, more evidence-based, approaches such as CBT).

Final Remarks

This publication has come full circle. The evolution of GAD from an historical perspective has been elucidated, as have the prevalence rates, costs, and burdens this disorder causes to the individual sufferer and the larger society. GAD continues to be enigmatic and paradoxical, in spite of renewed and growing interest and research that has helped better define the parameters of this elusive condition.

A comprehensive review of assessment instruments, diagnostic issues, conceptual models, and both psychosocial and pharmacological treatments across the life span were broached, further reinforcing the reality that GAD is still difficult to understand and treat with any modality. Two world-renowned authorities on GAD (Rynn & Brawman-Mintzer, 2004, p. 719) write that "although medications and psychotherapy have shown efficacy in treating GAD, at the end of treatment response rates are limited for both types of treatment with a large number of patients at the end of treatment still experiencing a significant amount of troubling symptoms."

The lacunae to find more effective treatments to maximize outcomes, and additionally to enhance the standard protocols, have led researchers and clinicians to develop and consider using more diverse and often integrative models to achieve the overarching purpose of helping optimize approaches to more effectively treat GAD. These newer approaches are not meant to replace standard treatments such as CBT or SSRIs, but to make a broader range of therapeutic options available.

Integration used here, in the broadest sense (not limited to integrative therapy), and its relation to GAD in the form of a more multimodal approach to treatment, is based, in part, on what has been discouraging and less than robust clinical outcomes for this disorder with standard single modality "one size fits all" treatments. In addition, GAD transcends a purely cognitive and biological model (Mennin, 2004; Wolfe, 2005). Hoehn-Saric (2005, p. 30), an erudite thinker, writes: "GAD is a heterogeneous disorder; patients differ in onset, type and intensity of worries, degree of hyperarousal and physical manifestations. Personality traits influence their behavioral response." He adds, "treatment of the GAD patient needs to be individualized" (p. 34).

Overall, an integrative approach is clearly indicated, bearing in mind that what is meant is a treatment perspective that matches the most appropriate, evidence-based, research-informed and humane modalities of care (whether they be psychosocial and/ or pharmacological), for the particular GAD sufferer. The guiding principle and lessons gained from this work is, "As in depressive illness, it is likely that outcomes in GAD will be improved through the use of efficacious and acceptable treatments in a concerted treatment manner" (Baldwin & Nair, 2005, p. 447; Baldwin & Thompson, 2003).

One final note to consider in the treatment of GAD is that evidence-based integration will only maximize treatment outcomes to the extent that the quality of the therapist–patient relationship is an authentic and sound one. "The strength of the therapeutic alliance is robustly related to treatment outcome" (Havens, 2004, p. 56; Orlinsky, Grawe, & Parks, 1994; Safran & Muran, 2000). Without this, it is not possible to establish the foundation on which all future psychotherapeutic and/or pharmacological processes can have a positive effect. In lieu of this fact, many scholars have turned their research and clinical attention to empirically supported treatments (Messer, 2001, 2002; Norcross, 2002), which highlight the fact that special focus needs to be placed on the therapeutic relationship. In addition, the most responsible way to approach treatment for GAD is to build on this, whether the final treatment is an evidence-based one or some other effective, but research-informed, mode of intervention (Messer, 2002).

In the end, those who suffer from GAD will not be sacrificed to inflexible, monolithically imposed treatment approaches, but will be collaborative partners in the process and outcome of, not just getting better, but rather in becoming well and improving the overall quality of their lives.

Appendix A

Assessment Tools for Adults and Older Adults

DASS				
Please read each statement and circle a number 0, 1, 2 or 3 that indicates how much the statement applied to you *over the past week*. There are no right or wrong answers. Do not spend too much time on any statement.				
The rating scale is as follows:				
0 Did not apply to me at all				
1 Applied to me to some degree, or some of the time				
2 Applied to me to a considerable degree, or a good part of the time				
3 Applied to me very much, or most of the time				

1	I found myself getting upset by quite trivial things	0	1	2	3
2	I was aware of dryness in my mouth	0	1	2	3
3	I couldn't seem to experience any positive feeling at all	0	1	2	3
4	I experienced breathing difficulty (e.g. excessively rapid breathing, breathlessness in the absence of physical exertion)	0	1	2	3
5	I just couldn't seem to get going	0	1	2	3
6	I tended to over-react to situations	0	1	2	3
7	I had a feeling of shakiness (e.g. legs going to give way)	0	1	2	3
8	I found it difficult to relax	0	1	2	3
9	I found myself in situations that make me so anxious I was most relieved when they ended	0	1	2	3
10	I felt that I had nothing to look forward to	0	1	2	3
11	I found myself getting upset rather easily	0	1	2	3
12	I felt that I was using a lot of nervous energy	0	1	2	3
13	I felt sad and depressed	0	1	2	3
14	I found myself getting impatient when I was delayed in any way (e.g. elevators, traffic lights, being kept waiting)	0	1	2	3
15	I had a feeling of faintness	0	1	2	3
16	I felt that I had lost interest in just about everything	0	1	2	3
17	I felt I wasn't worth much as a person	0	1	2	3
18	I felt that I was rather touchy	0	1	2	3

(continued)

(continued)

19	I perspired noticeably (e.g. hands sweaty) in the absence of high temperatures or physical exertion	0	1	2	3
20	I felt scared without any good reason	0	1	2	3
21	I felt that life wasn't worthwhile	0	1	2	3

Reminder of rating scale:
0 Did not apply to me at all
1 Applied to me to some degree, or some of the time
2 Applied to me to a considerable degree, or a good part of the time
3 Applied to me very much, or most of the time

22	I found it hard to wind down	0	1	2	3
23	I had difficulty in swallowing	0	1	2	3
24	I couldn't seem to get any enjoyment out of the things I did	0	1	2	3
25	I was aware of the action of my heart in the absence of physical exertion (e.g. sense of heart rate increase, heart missing a beat)	0	1	2	3
26	I felt down-hearted and blue	0	1	2	3
27	I found that I was very irritable	0	1	2	3
28	I felt I was close to panic	0	1	2	3
29	I found it hard to calm down after something upset me	0	1	2	3
30	I feared that I would be "thrown" by some trivial but unfamiliar task	0	1	2	3
31	I was unable to become enthusiastic about anything	0	1	2	3
32	I found it difficult to tolerate interruptions to what I was doing	0	1	2	3
33	I was in a state of nervous tension	0	1	2	3
34	I felt I was pretty worthless	0	1	2	3
35	I was intolerant of anything that kept me from getting on with what I was doing	0	1	2	3
36	I felt terrified	0	1	2	3
37	I could see nothing in the future to be hopeful about	0	1	2	3
38	I felt that life was meaningless	0	1	2	3
39	I found myself getting agitated	0	1	2	3
40	I was worried about situations in which I might panic and make a fool of myself	0	1	2	3
41	I experienced trembling (e.g. in the hands)	0	1	2	3
42	I found it difficult to work up the initiative to do things	0	1	2	3

PSWQ

Enter the number that best describes how typical or characteristic each item is of you, putting the number next to the item

1	2	3	4	5
Not at all typical		Somewhat typical		Very typical

_____	1	If I don't have enough time to do everything I don't worry about it.
_____	2	My worries overwhelm me.
_____	3	I don't tend to worry about things.
_____	4	Many situations make me worry.
_____	5	I know I shouldn't worry about things, but I just can't help it.
_____	6	When I am under pressure I worry a lot.
_____	7	I am always worrying about something.
_____	8	I find it easy to dismiss worrisome thoughts.
_____	9	As soon as I finish one task, I start to worry about everything else I have to do.
_____	10	I never worry about anything.
_____	11	When there is nothing more I can do about a concern, I don't worry about it any more.
_____	12	I've been a worrier all my life.
_____	13	I notice that I have been worrying about things.
_____	14	Once I start worrying, I can't stop.
_____	15	I worry all the time.
_____	16	I worry about projects until they are done.

Generalized Anxiety Disorder Questionnaire: IV (GADQ-IV)

1. Do you experience excessive worry? Yes _____ No _____
2. Is your worry excessive in intensity, frequency, or amount of distress it causes?
   Yes _____ No _____
3. Do you find it difficult to control your worry (or stop worrying) once it starts?
   Yes _____ No _____
4. Do you worry excessively or uncontrollably about *minor things* such as being late for an
   appointment, minor repairs, homework, etc? Yes _____ No _____
5. Please list the most frequent topics about which you worry excessively or uncontrollably:

   (a) _____   (d) _____

   (b) _____   (e) _____

   (c) _____   (f) _____

6. During the *last six months*, have you been bothered by excessive worries more days than not?
   Yes _____ No _____
7. During the past six months, have you often been bothered by any of the following symptoms?
   Place a check next to each symptom that you have had more days than not

   _____ restlessness or feeling keyed up or on edge   _____ Irritability

   _____ difficulty falling/staying asleep or restless/   _____ being easily
          unsatisfying sleep   fatigued

   _____ difficulty concentrating or mind going blank   _____ muscle tension

8. How much do worry and physical symptoms interfere with your life, work, social activities,
   family, etc.? Circle one *number*:

0	1	2	3	4	5	6	7	8

   None   Mild   Moderate   Severe   Very severe

9. How much are you bothered by worry and physical symptoms (how much distress does it
   cause you)? Circle one *number*:

0	1	2	3	4	5	6	7	8

   None   Mild   Moderate   Severe   Very severe
   Distress   Distress   Distress   Distress   Distress

SWLS

Below are five statements with which you may agree or disagree. Using the 1–7 scale below, indicate your agreement with each item by placing the appropriate number on the line preceding that item. Please be open and honest in your responding. The 7-point scale is as follows:

> 1 = strongly disagree
> 2 = disagree
> 3 = slightly disagree
> 4 = neither agree nor disagree
> 5 = slightly agree
> 6 = agree
> 7 = strongly agree

_____ 1. In most ways my life is close to my ideal.
_____ 2. The conditions of my life are excellent.
_____ 3. I am satisfied with my life.
_____ 4. So far I have gotten the important things I want in life.
_____ 5. If I could live my life over, I would change almost nothing.

Diener, E., Emmons, R. A., Larson, R. J., & Griffin, S. (1985). The satisfaction with life scale. *Journal of Personality Assessment, 49*(1), 71–75.

Worry scale for older adults (WS)

Instructions: Below is a list of problems that often concern many Americans. Please read each one carefully. After you have done so, please fill in one of the spaces to the right with a check that describes how much that problem worries you. Make only one check mark for each item.

THINGS THAT WORRY ME.....	Never	Rarely 1–2 times per month	Sometimes 1–2 times per week	Often 1–2 times per day	Much of the time More than 2 times a day
Finances					
1 That I'll lose my home					
2 That I won't be able to pay for the necessities of life (such as food, clothing, or medicine)					
3 That I won't be able to support myself independently					
4 that I won't be able to enjoy the "good things" in life (such as travel, recreation, entertainment)					
5 That I won't be able to help my children financially					
Health					
6 That my eyesight or hearing with get worse					
7 That I'll lose control of my bladder or kidneys					
8 That I won't be able to remember important things					
9 That I won't be able to get around by myself					
10 That I won't be able to enjoy my food					
11 That I'll have to be taken care of by my family					
12 That I'll have to be taken care of by strangers					

13	That I won't be able to take care of my spouse				
14	That I'll have to go to a nursing home or hospital				
15	That I won't be able to sleep at night				
16	That I may have a serious illness or accident				
17	That my spouse or close family member may have a serious illness or accident				
18	That I won't be able to enjoy sex				
19	That my reflexes will slow down				
20	That I won't be able to make decisions				
21	That I won't be able to drive a car				
22	That I'll have to use a mechanical aid (such as a hearing aid, bifocals, a cane)				

Social conditions

23	That I'll look "old"				
24	That people will think me unattractive				
25	That no one will want to be around me				
26	That no one will love me anymore				
27	That I'll be a burden to my loved ones				
28	That I won't be able to visit my family and friends				
29	That I may be attacked by muggers or robbers on the street				
30	That my home may be broken into and vandalized				

(continued)

(continued)

	Things that worry me.....	Never	Rarely 1–2 times per month	Sometimes 1–2 times per week	Often 1–2 times per day	Much of the time More than 2 times a day
31	That no one will come to my aid if I need it					
32	That my friends and family won't visit me					
33	That my friends and family will die					
34	That I'll get depressed					
35	That I'll have serious psychological problems					

Other worries

36						
37						
38						
39						
40						

Appendix B

Assessment Tools for Children and Adolescents

PSWQ-C

Directions. This form is about worrying. Worrying happens when you are scared about something and you think about it a lot. People sometimes worry about school, their family, their health, things coming up future, or other kids of things. For each sentence that you read, circle the answer that best tells how true that sentence is about you.

1.	My worries really bother me	Never true	Sometimes true	Most times true	Always true
2.	I don't really worry about things	Never true	Sometimes true	Most times true	Always true
3.	Many things make me worry	Never true	Sometimes true	Most times true	Always true
4.	I know I shouldn't worry about things, but I just can't help it	Never true	Sometimes true	Most times true	Always true
5.	When I am under pressure, I worry a lot	Never true	Sometimes true	Most times true	Always true
6.	I am always worrying about something	Never true	Sometimes true	Most times true	Always true
7.	I find it easy to stop worrying when I want	Never true	Sometimes true	Most times true	Always true
8.	When I finish one thing, I start to worry about everything else	Never true	Sometimes true	Most times true	Always true
9.	I never worry about anything	Never true	Sometimes true	Most times true	Always true
10.	I've been a worrier all my life	Never true	Sometimes true	Most times true	Always true
11.	I notice that I have been worrying about things	Never true	Sometimes true	Most times true	Always true
12.	Once I start worrying, I can't stop	Never true	Sometimes true	Most times true	Always true
13.	I worry all the time	Never true	Sometimes true	Most times true	Always true
14.	I worry about things until they are done	Never true	Sometimes true	Most times true	Always true

PSWQ-P

Directions. This form is about worrying. Worrying happens when you are scared about something and you think about it a lot. People sometimes worry about school, their family, their health, things coming up in the future, or other kinds of things. For each sentence you read, circle the answer that best tells how true that sentence is about your child.

1.	My child doesn't worry when s/he doesn't have enough time for everything	Never true	Sometimes true	Most times true	Always true
2.	My child's worries really bother him/her	Never true	Sometimes true	Most times true	Always true
3.	My child doesn't really worry about things	Never true	Sometimes true	Most times true	Always true
4.	Many things make my child worry	Never true	Sometimes true	Most times true	Always true
5.	My child knows s/he shouldn't worry about things, but just can't help it	Never true	Sometimes true	Most times true	Always true
6.	When my child is under pressure, s/he worries a lot	Never true	Sometimes true	Most times true	Always true
7.	My child is always worrying about something	Never true	Sometimes true	Most times true	Always true
8.	My child finds it easy to stop worrying when s/he wants	Never true	Sometimes true	Most times true	Always true
9.	When finishing one thing, my child starts to worry about everything else	Never true	Sometimes true	Most times true	Always true
10.	My child never worries about anything	Never true	Sometimes true	Most times true	Always true
11.	If there is nothing more s/he can do, my child doesn't worry about it	Never true	Sometimes true	Most times true	Always true
12.	My child has been a worrier all his/her life	Never true	Sometimes true	Most times true	Always true
13.	My child notices when s/he worries about things	Never true	Sometimes true	Most times true	Always true
14.	Once my child start worrying, s/he can't stop	Never true	Sometimes true	Most times true	Always true
15.	My child worries all the time	Never true	Sometimes true	Most times true	Always true
16.	My child worries about things until they are all done	Never true	Sometimes true	Most times true	Always true

Reprinted with permission from Bruce F. Chorpita, Ph.D.

References

Abelson, J. L., Glitz, D., Cameron, O. G., Lee, M. A., Bronzo, M., & Curtis, G. C. (1991). Blunted growth hormone response to clonidine inpatients with generalized anxiety disorder. *Archives of General Psychiatry, 48*(2), 157–162.

Akiskal, H. S. (1998). Toward a definition of generalized anxiety disorder as an anxious temperament type. *Acta Psychiatrica Scandinavica, 98*(Suppl. 393), 66–73.

Akiskal, H. S., Mendlowicz, M. V., Jean-Louis, G., Rapaport, M. H., Kelsoe, J. R., Gillin, J. C., & Smith, T. L. (2005). TEMPS-A: Validation of a short version of a self-rated instruments designed to measure variations in temperament. *Journal of Affective Disorders, 85*, 45–52.

Albano, A. M., Chorpita, B. F., & Barlow, D. H. (2003). Childhood anxiety disorders. In E. J. Marsh & R. A. Barkley (Eds.), *Child psychopathology* (2nd ed., pp. 279–329). New York: Guilford Press.

Albano, A. M., & Hack, S. (2004). Children and adolescents. In R. G. Heimberg, C. L. Turk, & D. S. Mennin (Eds.), *Generalized anxiety disorder: Advances in research and practice* (pp. 383–408). New York: Guilford Press.

Alford, B. A., & Beck, A. T. (1997). *The integrative power of cognitive therapy*. New York: Guilford Press.

Aliyev, N. A., & Aliyev, Z. N. (2008). Valproate (depakine-chrono) in the acute treatment of outpatients with generalized anxiety disorder without psychiatric comorbidity: Randomized, double-blind placebo-controlled study. *European Psychiatry, 23*(2), 109–114.

Allen, L. B., Ehrenreich, J. T., & Barlow, D. H. (2005). A unified treatment for emotional disorders: Application with adults and adolescents. *Japanese Journal of Behavior Therapy, 31*, 3–30.

Allen, L. B., McHugh, R. K., & Barlow, D. H. (2008). Emotional disorders: A unified protocol. In D. H. Barlow (Ed.), *Clinical handbook of psychological disorders: A step-by-step treatment manual* (4th ed., pp. 216–249). New York: Guilford Press.

Allgulander, C., Hackett, D., & Salinas, E. (2001). Venlafaxine extended release (ER) in the treatment of generalized anxiety disorder: Twenty-four week placebo-controlled dose-ranging study. *British Journal of Psychiatry, 179*, 15–22.

Allgulander, C., Dahl, A. A., Austin, C., Morris, P. L. P., Sogaard, J. A., Fayyad, R., Kutcher, S. P., & Clary, C. M. (2004). Efficacy of sertraline in a 12-week trial for generalized anxiety disorder. *American Journal of Psychiatry, 161*, 1642–1649.

Allgulander, C., Florea, I., & Trap Huusom, A. K. (2006). Prevention of relapse in generalized anxiety disorder by escitalopram. *International Journal of Neuropsychopharmacology, 9*, 495–505.

Allgulander, C. (2007). What our patient's want and need to know about generalized anxiety disorder? *Revista Brasileira de Psiquiatria, 29*(2), 172–176.

Allgulander, C., Hartford, J., Russell, J., Ball, S., Erickson, J., Raskin, J., & Rynn, M. (2007). Pharmacotherapy of generalized anxiety disorder: Results of duloxetine treatment from a pooled analysis of three clinical trials. *Current Medical Research and Opinion, 23*(6), 1245–1252.

Allgulander, C., Jorgensen, T., Wade, A., Francois, C., Despiegel, N., Aquier, P., & Toumi, M. (2007). Health-related quality of life (HRQOL) among patients with generalized anxiety disorder: Evaluation conducted alongside an escitalopram relapse prevention trial. *Current Medical Research and Opinion, 23*(10), 2543–2459.

American Psychiatric Association (APA). (1952). *Diagnostic and statistical manual of mental disorders.* Washington, DC: American Psychiatric Association Mental Health Service.

American Psychiatric Association (APA) (1968). *Diagnostic and statistical manual of mental disorders* (2nd ed.). Washington, DC: American Psychiatric Association.

American Psychiatric Association (APA) (1980). *Diagnostic and statistical manual of mental disorders* (3rd ed.). Washington, DC: American Psychiatric Association.

American Psychiatric Association (APA) (1987). *Diagnostic and statistical manual of mental disorders* (3rd ed., rev.). Washington, DC: American Psychiatric Association.

American Psychiatric Association (APA) (1994). *Diagnostic and statistical manual of mental disorders* (4th ed.). Washington, DC: American Psychiatric Association.

American Psychiatric Association (APA) (2000). *Diagnostic and statistical manual of mental disorders* (4th ed., text rev.) Washington, DC : American Psychiatric Association.

Anderson, D. J., Noyes, R., & Crowe, R. R. (1984). A comparison of panic disorder and generalized anxiety disorder. *American Journal of Psychiatry, 141,* 572–575.

Anderson, D. J., Williams, S., McGee, R., & Silva, P. A. (1987). DSM-III disorders in preadolescent children: Prevalence in a large sample from the general population. *Archives of General Psychiatry, 44*(1), 69–76.

Andreasen, N. (1984). *The broken brain: The biological revolution in psychiatry.* New York: Harper Collins.

Andreasen, N., & Black, D. W. (2001). *Introductory textbook of psychiatry* (3rd ed.). Washington, DC: American Psychiatric Association.

Andrews, G. (1990). Neuroses, personality, and cognitive behavior therapy. In M. McNaughton & G. Andrews (Eds.), *Anxiety* (pp. 3–14). New Zealand: University of Otago Press.

Andrews, G., Stewart, G., Allen, R., & Henderson, A. S. (1990). The genetics of six neurotic disorders: A twin study. *Journal of Affective Disorders, 19*(1), 23–29.

Andrews, G. (1996). Comorbidity and the general neurotic syndrome. *The British Journal of Psychiatry, 168,* 76–84.

Angst, J., & Vollrath, M. (1991). The natural history of anxiety disorders. *Acta Psychiatrica Scandinavica, 84,* 446–452.

Antony, M. M., Orsillo, S. M., & Roemer, L. (2001). *Practitioner's guide to empirically based measures of anxiety.* New York: Kluwer Academic.

Arana, G. W., & Rosenbaum, J. F., & Hyman, S.E. (2000). *Handbook of psychiatric drug therapy* (4th ed.). Philadelphia, PA: Lippincott Williams & Wilkins.

Argyropoulous, S. V., Ploubidis, G. B., Wright, T. S., Palm, M. E., Hood, S. D., Nash, J. R., Taylor, A. C., Forshall, S. W., Anderson, I. M., Nutt, D. J., & Potokar, J. P. (2007). Development and validation of the generalized anxiety disorder inventory (GADI). *Journal of Psychopharmacology, 21*(2), 145–152.

Arkowitz, H. (1997). Integrative theories of therapy. In P. L. Wachtel, S. B. Messer (Eds.), *Theories of psychotherapy: Origins and evolution* (pp. 227–288). Washington, DC: American Psychological Association.

Arnold, P., Banerjee, S. P., Bhandari, R., Lorch, E., Ivey, J., Rose, M., & Rosenberg, D. R. (2003). Childhood anxiety disorders and developmental issues in anxiety. *Current Psychiatry Reports, 5*(4), 252–265.

Ayers, C. R., Sorrell, J. T., Thorp, S. R., & Wetherell, J. L. (2007). Evidence-based psychological treatments or late-life anxiety. *Psychology and Aging, 22*(1), 8–17.

Bakhshani, N. M., Lashkaripour, K., & Sadjadi, S. A. (2007). Effectiveness of short term cognitive behavior therapy in patients with generalized anxiety disorder. *Journal Medical Sciences, 7*(7), 1076–1081.

Bakish, D. (1999). The patient with comorbid depression and anxiety: The unmet need. *Journal of Clinical Psychiatry, 60*(Suppl. 6), 20–24.

Baldwin, D. S., & Thompson, C. V. (2003). The future of antidepressant pharmacotherapy. *World Psychiatry*, *2*, 3–8.

Baldwin, D. S., Huusom, A. K. T., & Maehlum, E. (2004). Escitalopram and paroxetine compared to placebo in generalised anxiety disorder. *European Neuropsychopharmacology*, *14*(Suppl. 3), S311–S312.

Baldwin, D. S., & Nair, R. V. (2005). Escitalopram in the treatment of generalized disorder. *Expert Review of Neurotherapeutics*, *5*(4), 443–449.

Baldwin, D. S., & Polkinghorn, C. (2005). Evidence-based pharmacotherapy of generalized anxiety disorder. *International Journal of Neuropsychopharmacology*, *8*, 293–302.

Baldwin, D. S., Anderson, I. M., Nutt, D. J., Bandelow, B., Bond, A., Davidson, J. R. T., den Doer, J. A., Fineberg, N. A., Knapp, M., Scott, J., & Wittchen, H. U. (2005). Evidence-based guidelines for the pharmacological treatment of anxiety disorders: Recommendations from the British Association for Psychopharmacology. *Journal of Psychopharmacology*, *19*(6), 567–596.

Ball, S., Lightfoot, J., Goddard, A., & Shekhar, A. (2003). An introduction to the Indiana University Generalized Anxiety Measurement Scale (IU-GAMS). Paper presented at the Anxiety Disorders National Conference, Toronto, Canada.

Ball, S. G., Kuhn, A., Wall, D., Shekhar, A., & Goddard, A. W. (2005). Selective serotonin reuptake inhibitor treatment for generalized anxiety disorder: A double-blind, prospective comparison between paroxetine and sertraline. *Journal of Clinical Psychiatry*, *66*(1), 94–99.

Ballenger, J. (1999). Current treatment of the anxiety disorders in adults. *Biological Psychiatry*, *46*(11), 1579–1594.

Ballenger, J. C., Davidson, J. R., Lecrubier, Y., Nutt, D. J., Borkovec, T. D., Rickels, K., Stein, D. J., & Wittchen, H. U. (2001). Consensus statement on generalized anxiety disorder from the International Consensus Group on Depression and Anxiety. *Journal of Clinical Psychiatry, 62*, 53–58.

Bandelow, B. (2006). Defining response and remission in anxiety disorders: Toward an integrated approach. *CNS Spectrums*, *11*(10, Suppl. 12), 21–28.

Bandelow, B., Seidler-Brandler, U., Becker, A., Wedekind, D., & Ruther, E. (2007). Meta-analysis of randomized controlled comparisons of psychopharmacological and psychological treatments for anxiety disorders. *The World Journal of Biological Psychiatry*, *8*(3), 175–187.

Bandelow, B., Wedekind, D., & Leon, T. (2007). Pregabalin for the treatment of generalized anxiety disorder: A novel pharmacologic intervention. *Expert Review of Neurotherapeutics*, *7*(7), 769–781.

Barlow, D. H., Cohen, A. S., Waddell, M. T., Vermilyea, B. B., Klosko, J. S., Blanchard, E. B., & Di Nardo, P. A. (1984). Panic and generalized anxiety disorder: Nature and treatment. *Behavior Therapy*, *15*, 431–449.

Barlow, D. H. (1988). *Anxiety and its disorders*. The nature and treatment of anxiety and panic New York: Guilford Press.

Barlow, D. H. (1991). The nature of anxiety: Anxiety, depression, and emotional disorders. In R. M. Rapee & D. H. Barlow (Eds.), *Chronic anxiety: Generalized anxiety disorder and mixed anxiety-depression* (pp. 1–28). New York: Guilford Press.

Barlow, D. H., & Di Nardo, P. A. (1991). The diagnosis of generalized anxiety disorder: Development, current status and future directions. In R. M. Rapee & D. H. Barlow (Eds.), *Chronic anxiety: Generalized anxiety disorder and mixed anxiety-depression* (pp. 95–118). New York: Guilford Press.

Barlow, D. H., Rapee, R. M., & Brown, T. A. (1992). Behavioral treatment of generalized anxiety disorder. *Behavior Therapy*, *23*, 551–570.

Barlow, D. H., Lerner, J., & Esler, J. (1996). Behavioral healthcare in primary care settings: Recognition and treatment of anxiety disorders. In R. J. Resnick & R. H. Rozensky (Eds.), *Health Psychology through the life span: Practice and research opportunities* (pp. 133–148). Washington, DC: American Psychological Association.

Barlow, D. H. (2000). Unraveling the mysteries of anxiety and its disorders from the perspective of emotion theory. *American Psychologist*, *55*, 1245–1263.

Barlow, D. H. (2001). *Clinical handbook of psychological disorders: A step-by-step treatment manual* (3rd ed.). New York: Guilford Press.

Barlow, D. H. (2002). *Anxiety and its disorders: The nature and treatment of anxiety and panic* (2nd ed.). New York: Guilford Press.

Barlow, D. H., Allen, L. B., & Choate, M. L. (2004). Toward a unified treatment for emotional disorders. *Behavior Therapy, 35*, 205–230.

Barlow, D. H. (Eds.). (2008). *Clinical handbook of psychological disorders: A step-by-step treatment manual* (4th ed.). New York: Guilford Press.

Barrett, P. M., Dadds, M. R., & Rapee, R. M. (1996). Family treatment of childhood anxiety: A controlled trial. *Journal of Consulting and Clinical Psychology, 64*, 333–342.

Barrett, P. M. (1998). Evaluation of cognitive-behavioral group treatments for childhood anxiety disorders. *Journal of Clinical Child Psychology, 27*(4), 459–468.

Barrett, P. M., Duffy, A. L., Dadds, M. R., & Rapee, R. M. (2001). Cognitive-behavioral treatment of anxiety disorders in children. Long term (6 year) follow-up. *Journal of Consulting and Clinical Psychology, 69*, 135–141.

Barrowclough, C., King, P., Colville, J., Russell, E., Burns, A.S., & Tarrier, N. (2001). A randomized trial of the effectiveness of cognitive-behavioral therapy and supportive counseling for anxiety symptoms in older adults. *Journal of Consulting and Clinical Psychology, 69*, 756–762.

Beekman, A.T., Bremmer, M.A., Deeg, D.J., van Balkom. A.J., Smit, J.H., de Beurs, E., van Dyck, R., & Van Tilburg, W. (1998). Anxiety disorders in later life: A report from the Longitudinal Aging study Amsterdam. International Journal of Geriatric Psychiatry, 13, 717–726.

Beekman, A.T., de Beurs, E., van Balkom, A.J., Deeg, D.J., van Tilburg, W. (2000). Anxiety and depression in later life: Co-occurence in communality of risk factors. American Journal of Psychiatry, 157, 89–95.

Beck, A. T. (1976). *Cognitive therapy and the emotional disorders.* New York: International Universities Press.

Beck, A. T., Emery, G., & Greenberg, R.L. (1985). *Anxiety disorders and phobias: A cognitive perspective.* New York: Basic Books.

Beck A., Steer R. (1987). Manual for the Beck Depression Inventory. San Antonio, Texas: Psychological Corporation.

Beck, A. T., Epstein, N., Brown, G., & Steer, R. A. (1988). An inventory of measuring clinical anxiety: Psychometric properties. *Journal of Consulting and Clinical Psychology, 50*, 893–897.

Beck, A. T., & Steer, R. A. (1990). *Manual for the Beck Anxiety Inventory. San Antonio*, TX: The Psychological Corporation.

Beck, A. T., Steer, R. A., & Brown, G. K. (1996). *Beck Depression Inventory Manual* (2nd ed.). San Antonio, TX: Psychological Corporation.

Beck, A. T., & Clark, D. A. (1997). An information processing model of anxiety. Automatic and strategic processes. *Behaviour Research and Therapy, 35*, 49–58.

Beck, J. G., Stanley, M. A., & Zebb, B. J. (1996). Characterization of generalized anxiety disorder in older adults: A descriptive study. *Behaviour Research and Therapy, 34*, 225–234.

Beck, J. G., & Stanley, M. A. (2001). Assessment of anxiety disorders in older adults: Current concerns, future prospects. In M. M. Antony, S. M. Orsillo, & L. Roemer (Eds.), *Practitioner's guide to empirically based measures of anxiety* (pp. 43–48). New York: Kluwer Academic/Plenum Publishers.

Beck, J. G., & Averill, P. M. (2004). Older adults. In R. G. Heimberg, C. L. Turk, & D. S. Mennin (Eds.), *Generalized anxiety disorder: Advances in research and practice* (pp. 409–433). New York: Guilford Press.

Beck, J. S. (1995). *Cognitive therapy: Basics and beyond.* New York: Guilford Press.

Behar, E., & Borkovec, T. D. (2005). The nature and treatment of generalized anxiety disorder. In B. O. Rothbaum (Ed.), *Pathological anxiety: Emotional processing in etiology and treatment* (pp. 181–196). New York: Guilford Press.

Beidel, D. C., Christ, M. A., & Long, P. J. (1991). Somatic complaints in anxious children. *Journal of Abnormal Child Psychology, 19*, 659–670.

Beidel, D. C., & Stanley, M. A. (1992). Developmental issues in the measurement of anxiety. In C. G. Last (Ed.), *Anxiety across the lifespan: A developmental perspective* (pp. 167–203). New York: Springer.

Beidel, D. C., & Turner, S. M. (2005). *Childhood anxiety disorders: A guide to research and treatment.* New York: Routledge.

Beitchman, J. H., Wekerle, C., & Hood, J. (1987). Diagnostic continuity from preschool to middle childhood. *Journal of the American Academy of Child and Adolescent Psychiatry, 26*, 694–699.

Bellew, K. M., McCafferty, J. P., Iyengar, M., & Zaninelli, R. M. (2000). Paroxetine treatment of GAD: A double-blind, placebo-controlled trial. Paper presented at the Annual Meeting of the American Psychiatric Association, Chicago.

Belzer, K. D., & Schneier, F. R. (2006). Tools for assessing generalized anxiety disorder. *Psychiatric Times, 23*(3), 26, 28–29.

Ben-Noun, L. (1998). Generalized anxiety disorder in dysfunctional families. *Journal of Behavior Therapy and Experimental Psychiatry, 29*, 115–122.

Bernstein, G., Borchardt, C. M., & Perwien, A. R. (1996). Anxiety disorders in children and adolescents: A review of the past 10 years. *Journal of American Academy of Child and Adolescent Psychiatry, 35*, 1110–1119.

Bernstein, D. A., Borkovec, T. D., & Hazlett-Stevens, H. (2000). *New directions in progressive muscle relaxation training: A guideline for helping professionals.* Westport, CT: Praeger Publications.

Berrios, G. E., & Link, C. (1995). Anxiety disorders: Clinical section. In G. E. Berrios & R. Porter (Eds.). *A history of clinical psychiatry.* London: Athlone Press.

Bielski, R., Bose, A., Nil, R., & Chang, C. C. (2004). Double-blind comparison of escitalopram and paroxetine in the treatment of generalized anxiety disorder. *European Psychiatry, 19*(Suppl. 1), S223.

Birmaher, B., Waterman, G. S., Ryan, N., Cully, M., Balach, L., Ingram, J., & Brodsky, M. (1994). Fluoxetine for childhood anxiety disorders. *Journal of the American Academy of Child and Adolescent Psychiatry, 33*, 993–999.

Birmaher, B., Khetarpal, S., Brent, D. A., Cully, M., Balach, L., Kaufman, J., & McKenzie-Neer, S. (1997). The Screen for Child Anxiety Related Emotional Disorders (SCARED): Scale construction and psychometric characterization. *Journal of the American Academy of Child and Adolescent Psychiatry, 36*, 545–553.

Birmaher, B., Brent, D. A., Chiappetta, L., Bridge, J., Monga, S., & Baugher, M. (1999). Psychometric properties of the Screen for Child Anxiety Related Emotional Disorders (SCARED): A replication study. *Journal of the American Academy of Child and Adolescent Psychiatry, 38*, 1230–1236.

Birmaher, B., Axelson, D. A., Monk, K., Kalas, C., Clark, D. B., Ehmann, M., Bridge, J., Heo, J., & Brent, D. A. (2003). Fluoxetine for the treatment of childhood anxiety disorders. *Journal of American Academy of Child and Adolescent Psychiatry, 42*(4), 415–423.

Blank, S., Lenze, E. J., Mulsant, B. H., Dew, M. A., Karp, J. F., Shear, K. M., Houck, P. R., Miller, M. D., Pollock, B. G., Tracey, B., & Reynolds, C. F. (2006). Outcomes of late-life anxiety disorders during 32 weeks of citalopram treatment. *Journal of Clinical Psychiatry, 67*, 468–472.

Blashfield, R., Noyes, R., Reich, J., Woodman, C., Cook, B. L., & Garvey, M. J. (1994). Personality disorder traits in generalized anxiety and panic disorder patients. *Comprehensive Psychiatry, 35*, 329–334.

Blazer, D., George, L. K., & Hughes, D. (1991). The epidemiology of anxiety disorders: An age comparison. In C. Salzman & B. D. Lebowitz (Eds.), *Anxiety in the elderly and research* (pp. 17–30). New York: Springer.

Blazer, D. G., Hughes, D., George, L. K., Swartz, M., & Boyer, R. (1991). Generalized anxiety disorder. In L. N. Robins & D. A. Regier (Eds.), *Psychiatric disorders in America* (pp. 180–203). New York: Free Press.

Blowers, C., Cobb, J., & Matthews, A. (1987). Generalized anxiety disorder: A controlled treatment study. *Behaviour Research and Therapy, 25*, 493–502.

Bohart, A. C. (2000). Paradigm clash: Empirically supported treatments versus empirically supported psychotherapy practice. *Psychotherapy Research, 10*, 488–493.

Bohm, C., Robinson, D. S., Gammans, R. E., Shrotriya, R. C., Alms, D. R., Leroy, A., & Placchi, M. (1990). Buspirone therapy in anxious elderly patients: A controlled clinical trial. *Journal of Clinical Psychopharmacology, 10*, 47S–51S.

Borkovec, T. D., Robinson, E., Pruzinsky, T., & DePree, J. (1983). Preliminary exploration of worry: Some characteristics and processes. *Behaviour Research and Therapy, 21*, 9–16.

Borkovec, T. D., Matthews, A. M., Chambers, A., Ebrahim, S., Lytle, R., & Nelson, R. (1987). The effects of relaxation training with cognitive or non-directive therapy and the role of relaxation-induced anxiety in the treatment of generalized anxiety disorder. *Journal of Consulting and Clinical Psychology, 55*, 883–888.

Borkovec, T. D., & Inz, J. (1990). The nature of worry in generalized anxiety disorder: A predominance of thought activity. *Behavior Research and Therapy, 28*, 153–158.

Borkovec, T. D., Lyonfields, J. D., Wiser, S. L., & Deihl, L. (1993). The role of worrisome thinking in the suppression of cardiovascular response to phobic imagery. *Behaviour Research and Therapy, 31*, 321–324.

Borkovec, T. D., & Costello, E. (1993). Efficacy of applied relaxation and cognitive behavioral therapy in the treatment of generalized anxiety disorder. *Journal of Consulting and Clinical Psychology, 61*, 611–619.

Borkovec, T. D. (1994). The nature, functions, and origins of worry. In G. Davey & F. Tallis (Eds.), *Worry: Perspectives on theory, assessment, and treatment* (pp. 5–34). New York: Wiley.

Borkovec, T. D., Abel, J. L., & Newman, H. (1995). Effects of psychotherapy on comorbid conditions in generalized anxiety disorder. *Journal of Consulting and Clinical Psychology, 63*, 479–483.

Borkovec, T. D., & Roemer, L. (1995). Perceived functions of worry among generalized anxiety disorder subjects: Distraction from more emotional topics? *Journal of Behavior Therapy and Experimental Psychiatry, 26*, 25–30.

Borkovec, T. D., & Whisman, M. A. (1996). Psychosocial treatment for generalized anxiety disorder. In M. R. Mavissakalian & R. F. Prien (Eds.), *Long-term treatment of anxiety disorders* (pp. 171–199). Washington, DC: American Psychiatric Press.

Borkovec, T. D., & Newman, M. G. (1998). Worry and generalized anxiety disorder. In A. S. Bellack, M. Hersen (Series Eds.), & P. Salkovskis (Vol. Ed.), *Comprehensive clinical psychology: Vol. 6. Adults: Clinical formation and treatment* (pp. 439–459). New York: Pergamon Press.

Borkovec, T. D., & Castonguay, L. G. (1998). What is the scientific meaning of empirically supported therapy? *Journal of Consulting and Clinical Psychology, 66*, 136–142.

Borkovec, T. D., Ray, W. J., & Stober, J. (1998). Worry: A cognitive phenomenon intimately linked to affective, physiological, and interpersonal behavioral processes. *Cognitive Therapy and Research, 22*, 561–576.

Borkovec, T. D., Hazlett-Stevens, H., & Diaz, M. L. (1999). The role of positive beliefs about worry in generalized anxiety disorder and its treatment. *Clinical Psychology and Psychotherapy, 6*, 126–138.

Borkovec, T. D. (1999). The nature and psychosocial treatment of generalized anxiety disorder. Paper presented at the Annual Meeting of the American Psychological Society, Denver, CO.

Borkovec, T. D., & Ruscio, A. M. (2001). Psychotherapy for generalized anxiety disorder. *Journal of Clinical Psychiatry, 62*, 37–45.

Borkovec, T. D., Newman, M. G., Pincus, A. L., & Lytle, R. (2002). A component analysis of cognitive-behavioral therapy for generalized anxiety disorder and the role of interpersonal problems. *Journal of Consulting and Clinical Psychology, 70*(2), 288–298.

Borkovec, T. D., Newman, M. G., & Castonguay, L. G. (2003). Cognitive-behavioral therapy for generalized disorder with integrations from interpersonal and experiential therapies, *CNS Spectrums, 8*(5), 382–389.

Borkovec, T. D., & Sharpless, B. (2004). Generalized anxiety disorder: Bringing cognitive-behavioral therapy into the valued present. In S. C. Hayes, V. M. Follette, & M. M. Linehan (Eds.), *Mindfulness and acceptance* (pp. 209–242). New York: Guilford Press.

Borkovec, T. D., Alcaine, O. M., & Behar, E. (2004). Avoidance theory of worry and generalized anxiety disorder. In R. G. Heimberg, C. L. Turk, & D. S. Mennin (Eds.), *Generalized anxiety disorder: Advances in research and practice* (pp. 77–108). New York: Guilford Press.

Borkovec, T. D. (2006). Applied relaxation and cognitive therapy for pathological worry and generalized anxiety disorder. In G. C. L. Davey & A. Wells (Eds.), *Worry and its psychological disorders: Theory, assessment and treatment* (pp. 273–287). Chichester, UK: Wiley.

Bowen, R. C., Offord, D. R., & Boyle, M. H. (1990). The prevalence of overanxious disorder and separation anxiety disorder: Results from the Ontario Child Health Study. *Journal of the American Academy of Child and Adolescent Psychiatry, 29*, 753–758.

Boyd, R. C., Ginsburg, G. A., Lambert, S. F., Cooley, M. R., & Campbell, K. D. M. (2003). Screen for Child Anxiety Related Emotional Disorders (SCARED): Psychometric properties in an African American parochial high school sample. *Journal of the American Academy of Child and Adolescent Psychiatry, 42*, 1188–1196.

Brawman-Mintzer, O., Lydiard, R. B., Emmanuel, N., Payeur, R., Johnson, M., Roberts, J., Jarrell, M. P., & Ballenger, J. C. (1993). Psychiatric comorbidity in patients with generalized anxiety disorder. *American Journal of Psychiatry, 150*, 1216–1218.

Brawman-Mintzer, O. (2001). Generalized anxiety disorder. *The Psychiatric Clinics of North America, 24(1), Philadelphia, Pennsylvania: W. B. Saunders Company.*

Brawman-Mintzer, O., Knapp, R. G., & Niebert, P. J. (2005). Adjunctive risperidone in generalized anxiety disorder: A double-blind, placebo-controlled study. *Journal of Clinical Psychiatry, 66*, 1321–1325.

Brawman-Mintzer, O., Knapp, R. G., Rynn, M., Carter, R. E., & Rickels, K. (2006). Sertraline treatment for generalized anxiety disorder: A randomized, double-blind. Placebo-controlled study. *Journal of Clinical Psychiatry, 67*, 874–881.

Brazier, J., Roberts, J., & Deverill, M. (2002). The estimation of a preference based measure of health from the SF-36. *Journal of Health Economics, 21*, 271–292.

Breggin, P. R. (1994). *Toxic psychiatry: Why therapy, empathy and love must replace the drugs, electroshock, and biochemical theories of the "New Psychiatry".* New York: St. Martin's Griffin.

Breggin, P. R., & Cohen, D. (2000). *Your drug may be your problem: How and why to stop taking psychotropic medications.* New York: Da Capo Press.

Breitholtz, E., Johansson, B., & Ost, L. G. (1999). Cognitions in generalized anxiety disorder and panic disorder patients: A prospective approach. *Behavior Research and Therapy, 37*, 533–544.

Bresolin, N., Monza, G., Scarpini, E., Scarlato, G., Straneo, G., Martinazzoli, A., Beninca, G., Cattoni, C., De Candia, R., & Belloni, G. (1988). Treatment of anxiety with ketazolam in elderly patients. *Clinical Therapeutics, 10(5)*, 536–542.

Brown, T. A., Antony, M. M., & Barlow, D. H. (1992). Psychometric properties of the Penn State Worry Questionnaire in a clinical anxiety disorders sample. *Behaviour Research and Therapy, 30*, 33–37.

Brown, T. A., & Barlow, D. H. (1992). Comorbidity among anxiety disorders: Implications for treatment and DSM-IV. *Journal of Consulting and Clinical Psychology, 60*, 835–844.

Brown, T. A., Moras, K., Zinbarg, R. E., & Barlow, D. H. (1993). Diagnostic and symptom distinguishability of generalized anxiety disorder and obsessive-compulsive disorder. *Behavior Therapy, 24*, 227–240.

Brown, T. A., Di Nardo, P. A., & Barlow, D. H. (1994). *Anxiety Disorders Interview Schedule for DSM-IV.* New York: Oxford University Press.

Brown, T. A., Barlow, D. H., & Leibowitz, M. R. (1994). The empirical basis of generalized anxiety disorder. *American Journal of Psychiatry, 151*, 1272–1280.

Brown, T. A., Marten, P. A., & Barlow, D. H. (1995). Discriminant validity of the symptoms constituting the DSM-III-R and DSM-IV associated symptom criterion of generalized anxiety disorder. *Journal of Anxiety Disorders, 9*, 317–328.

Brown, T. A. (1997). The nature of generalized anxiety disorder and pathological worry: Current evidence and conceptual models. *Canadian Journal of Psychiatry, 42*, 817–825.

Brown, T. A., Chorpita, B. F., & Barlow, D. H. (1998). Structural relationships among dimensions of the DSM-IV anxiety and mood disorders and dimensions of negative affect, positive affect, and autonomic arousal. *Journal of Abnormal Psychology, 107*, 179–192.

Brown, T. A., Di Nardo, P. A., Lehman, C. L., & Campbell, L. A. (2001). Reliability of DSM-IV anxiety and mood disorders: Implications for the classification of emotional disorders. *Journal of Abnormal Psychology, 110*, 49–58.

Brown, T. A., O' Leary, T. A., & Barlow, D. H. (2001). Generalized anxiety disorder. In D. H. Barlow (Ed.), *Clinical handbook of psychological disorders: A step-by-step treatment manual* (3rd ed., pp. 154–208). New York: Guilford Press.

Brown, J. S. L., Elliot, S. A., Boardman, J., Ferns, J., & Morrison, J. (2004). Meeting the unmet need for depression services with psycho-educational self-confidence workshops: Preliminary report. *British Journal of Psychiatry, 185*, 511–515.

Brown, T. A., & Barlow, D. H. (2005). Dimensional versus categorical classification of mental disorders in the Fifth Edition of the Diagnostic and Statistical Manual of Mental Disorders and beyond: Comments on the special section. *Journal of Abnormal Psychology, 114*(4), 551–556.

Buhr, K., & Dugas, M. J. (2002). The Intolerance of Uncertainty Scale: Psychometric properties of the English version. *Behaviour Research and Therapy, 40*, 931–945.

Burns, D. D. (1999). *The feeling good handbook*. New York: Penguin.

Butler, G., Cullington, A., Hibbert, R., Klimes, I., & Gelder, M. (1987). Anxiety management for persistent generalized anxiety disorder. *British Journal of Psychiatry, 151*, 535–542.

Butler, G., Fennell, M., Robson, P., & Gelder, M. (1991). Comparison of behavior therapy and cognitive behavior therapy in the treatment of generalized anxiety disorder. *Journal of Consulting and Clinical Psychology, 59*, 167–175.

Campbell-Sills, L., & Barlow, D. H. (2007). Incorporating emotion regulation into conceptualizations and treatments of anxiety and mood disorders. In J. J. Gross (Ed.), *Handbook of emotion regulation* (pp. 542–559). New York: Guilford Press.

Cartwright-Hatton, S., & Wells, A. (1997). Beliefs about worry and intrusions. The Metacognitions Questionnaire and its correlates. *Journal of Anxiety Disorders, 11*, 279–296.

Cartwright-Hatton, S., Roberts, C., Chitsabesan, P., Fothergill, C., & Harrington, R. (2004). Systematic review of the efficacy of cognitive behavioral therapies for childhood and adolescent anxiety disorders. *British Journal of Clinical Psychiatry, 43*, 421–436.

Cartwright-Hatton, S. (2006). Worry in childhood and adolescence. In G. C. L. Davey & A. Wells (Eds.), *Worry and its psychological disorders: Theory, assessment and treatment* (pp. 81–97). Chichester, UK: Wiley.

Cassady, J. (1995). Attachment and generalized anxiety disorder. In D. Ciccheti & S. Toth (Eds.), *Rochester symposium on developmental psychopathology*: Vol. 6. Emotion, cognition and representation (pp. 343–370). Rochester, NY: University of Rochester Press.

Cassady, J. A., & Shaver, P. R. (Eds.). (1999). *Handbook of attachment: Theory, research, and clinical applications*. New York: Guilford Press.

Castaneda, J. O., & Segerstrom, S. C. (2004). Effect of stimulus and worry on physiological responses to fear. *Journal of Anxiety Disorders, 18*, 809–823.

Castonguay, L. G. (2000). A common factors approach to psychotherapy training. *Journal of Psychotherapy Integration, 10*, 263–282.

Castonguay, L. G., Newman, M. G., Borkovec, T. D., Grosse Holtforth, M. & Maramba, G. G. (2005). In J. C. Norcross & M. R. Goldfried (Eds.), *Handbook of psychotherapy integration* (2nd ed., pp. 241–260). New York: Oxford University Press.

Chambless, D. L., & Gillis, M. M. (1993). Cognitive therapy of anxiety disorders. *Journal of Consulting and Clinical Psychology, 61*, 248–260.

Chambless, D. L., & Hollon, S. D. (1998). Defining empirically supported therapies. *Journal of Consulting and Clinical Psychology, 66*, 7–18.

Chansky, T. E., & Kendall, P. C. (1997). Social expectancies and self perceptions in anxiety disordered children. *Journal of Anxiety Disorders, 11*, 347–363.

Chorpita, B. F., Tracey, S. A., Brown, T. A., Collica, T. J., & Barlow, D. H. (1997). Assessment of worry in children and adolescents: An adaptation of the Penn State Worry Questionnaire. *Behaviour Research and Therapy, 35*, 569–581.

Clark, D. B., Birmaher, B., Axelson, D., Monk, K., Kalas, C., Ehmann, M., Bridge, J., Wood, S., Muthen, B., & Brent, D. (2005). Fluoxetine for the treatment of childhood anxiety disorders: Open label, long-term extension to a controlled trial. *Journal of American Academy of Child and Adolescent Psychiatry, 44*(12), 1263–1270.

Clark, D. M. (1990). Anxiety states: Panic and generalized anxiety disorder. In K. Hawton, P. M. Salkovskis, J. Kirk, & P. M. Clark (Eds.), *Cognitive behavior therapy for psychiatric disorders: A practical guide (pp. 52–96)*. New York: Oxford Press.

Clark, L. A., Watson, D., & Mineka, S. (1994). Temperament, personality, and the mood and anxiety disorders. *Journal of Abnormal Psychology, 103*, 103–116.

Cobham, V. E., Dadds, M. R., & Spence, S. H. (1998). The role of parental anxiety in the treatment of childhood anxiety. *Journal of Consulting and Clinical Psychology, 66*(6), 893–905.

Compton, S. N., March, J. S., Brent, D., Albano, A. M., Weersing, R., & Curry, J. (2004). Cognitive-behavioral psychotherapy for anxiety and depressive disorders in children and adolescents: An evidence-based medicine review. *Journal of American Academy of Child and Adolescent Psychiatry, 43*(8), 930–959.

Compton, S. N., Kratochvil, C. J., & March, J. S. (2007). Pharmacotherapy for anxiety disorders in children and adolescents: An evidence-based medicine review. *Psychiatric Annals, 37*(7), 504–517.

Connolly, S. D., & Bernstein, G. A. (2007). Practice parameters for the assessment and treatment of children and adolescents with anxiety disorders. *Journal of American Academy of Child and Adolescent Psychiatry, 46*(2), 267–283.

Connor, K. M., & Davidson, J. R. (1998). Generalized anxiety disorder: Neurobiological and pharmacotherapeutic perspectives. *Biological Psychiatry, 44*, 1286–1294.

Coplan, J. D., Tiffon, L., & Gorman, J. M. (1993). Therapeutic strategies for the patient with treatment-resistant anxiety. *Journal of Clinical Psychiatry, 54*(Suppl.), 69–74.

Corcoran, J., & Walsh, J. (2006). *Clinical assessment and diagnosis in social work practice*. New York: Oxford.

Covin, R., Ouimet, A. J., Seeds, P. M., & Dozois, D. J. (2008). A meta-analysis of CBT for pathological worry among clients with GAD. *Journal of Anxiety Disorders, 22*(1), 108–116.

Craske, M. G., & Zucker, B. G. (2001). Prevention of anxiety disorders: A model for intervention. *Applied and Preventive Psychology, 10*, 155–175.

Craske, M. G., & Barlow, D. H. (2006). *Mastery of your anxiety and worry, Workbook* (2nd ed.). New York: Oxford University.

Crestani, F., Lorez, M., Baer, K., Essrich, C., Benke, D., Laurent, J. P., Belzung, C., Fritschy, J. M., Luscher, B., & Mohler, H. (1999). Deceased GABAA-receptor clustering results in enhanced anxiety and a bias for threat cues. *Nature Neuroscience, 2*, 833–839.

Crits-Christoph, P., Crits-Christoph, K., Wolf-Palacio, D., Fichter, M., & Rudick, D. (1995). Brief supportive-expressive psychodynamic therapy for generalized anxiety disorder. In J. P. Barber & P. Crits-Christoph (Eds.), *Dynamic therapies for psychiatric disorders (Axis I)* (pp. 43–83). New York: Basic Books.

Crits-Christoph, P., Connolly, M. B., Azarian, K., Crits-Christoph, K., & Shappell, S. (1996). An open trial of brief supportive-expressive psychotherapy in the treatment of generalized anxiety disorder. *Psychotherapy, 33*(3), 418–430.

Crits-Christoph, P., Connolly Gibbons, M. B., & Crits-Christoph, K. (2004). Supportive-expressive psychodynamic therapy. In R. G. Heimberg, C. L. Turk, & D. S. Mennin (Eds.), Generalized anxiety disorder: Advances in research and practice (pp. 293–319). New York: Guilford Press.

Crits-Christoph, P., Connolly Gibbons, M. B., Narducci, J., Schamberger, M., & Gallop, R. (2005). Interpersonal problems and the outcome of interpersonally oriented psychodynamic treatment of GAD. *Psychotherapy Theory, Research, Practice, Training, 42*(2), 211–224.

Culpepper, L. (2002). Generalized anxiety disorder in primary care: Emerging issues in management and treatment. *Journal of Clinical Psychiatry, 63*, 35–42.

Dada, F., Sethi, S., & Grossberg, G. T. (2001). Generalized anxiety disorder in the elderly. *The Psychiatric Clinics of North America, 24*(1), 155–164.

Dahl, A. A., Ravindran, A., Allgulander, C., Kutcher, S. P., Austin, C., & Burt, T. (2005). Sertraline in generalized anxiety disorder: Efficacy in treating psychic and somatic anxiety factors. *Acta Psychiatrica Scandinavica, 111*, 429–435.

Darcis, T., Ferreri, M., Burtin, B., & Deram, P. (1995). A multicentre double-blind placebo-controlled investigating the anxiolytic efficacy of hydroxyzine in patients with generalized anxiety disorder. *Human Psychopharmacology, 10*, 181–187.

Davey, G. C. L., Tallis, F., & Capuzzo, N. (1996). Beliefs about the consequences of worrying. *Cognitive Therapy and Research, 20*, 499–520.

Davey, G. C. L., & Wells, A. (2006). *Worry and its psychological disorders: Theory, assessment and treatment*. Chichester, UK: Wiley.

Davidson, J. R., DuPont, R. L., Hedges, D., & Haskins, J. T. (1999). Efficacy, safety and tolerability of venlafaxine extended release and buspirone in outpatients with generalized anxiety disorder. *Journal of Clinical Psychiatry, 60*, 528–535.

Davidson, J. R. (2001). Pharmacotherapy of generalized anxiety disorder. *Journal of Clinical Psychiatry, 62*(Suppl. 11), 46–52.

Davidson, J. R. T., Bose, A., Korotzer, A., & Zheng, H. (2004). Escitalopram in the treatment of generalized anxiety disorder: Double-blind, placebo controlled, flexible-dose study. *Depression and Anxiety, 19*, 234–240.

Davidson, J. R. T., Bose, A., & Wang, Q. (2005). Safety and efficacy of escitalopram in the long-term treatment of generalized anxiety disorder. *Journal of Clinical Psychiatry, 66*(11), 1441–1446.

Davidson, J. R., Wittchen, H. U., Llorca, P. M., Erickson, J., Detke, M., Ball, S. G., & Russell, J. M. (2008). Duloxetine treatment for relapse prevention in adults with generalized anxiety disorder: A double-blind, placebo-controlled trial. *European Neuropsychopharmacology, 18*(9), 673–681.

Davis, M. (2006). Neural systems involved in fear and anxiety measured with fear-potentiated startle. *American Psychologist, 61*, 741–756.

de Beurs, E., Beekman, A. T. F., van Balkom, A. J. L. M., Deeg, D. J. H., van Dyck, R., & van Tilburg, W. (1999). Consequences of anxiety in older persons: Its affects on disability, well-being, and use of health services. *Psychological Medicine, 29*, 583–593.

Decker, M. L., Turk, C. L., Hess, B., & Murray, C. E. (2008). Emotion regulation among individuals classified with and without generalized anxiety disorder. *Journal of Anxiety Disorders, 22*(3), 485–494.

Deffenbacher, J. L., & Suinn, R. M. (1987). Generalized anxiety disorder. In L. Michelson & L. M. Ascher (Eds.), *Anxiety and stress disorders* (pp. 332–360). New York: Guilford Press.

Derogatis, L., Lipman, R., Rickels, K., Uhlenhuth, E., & Covi, L. (1973). The Hopkins Symptom Checklist (HSCL): A self-report inventory. *Behavioral Science, 19*, 1–15.

Diefenbach, G. J., Stanley, M. A., & Beck, J. G. (2001). Worry content reported by older adults with and without generalized anxiety disorder. *Aging and Mental Health, 5*, 269–274.

Diefenbach, G. J., Hopko, D. R., Feigon, S., Stanley, M. A., Novy, D. M., Beck, J. G., & Averill, P. M. (2003). "Minor GAD": Characteristics of subsyndromal generalized anxiety disorder in older adults, Behaviour Research and Therapy, 41, 481–487.

Diefenbach, G. J., Robinson, J. T., Tolin, D. F., & Blank, K. (2004). Late-life anxiety disorders among Puerto Rican primary care patients: Impact on well-being, functioning, and service utilization. *Journal of Anxiety Disorders, 18*(6), 841–858.

Diener, E., Emmons, R. A., Larsen, R. J., & Griffin, S. (1985). The satisfaction with life scale. *Journal of Personality Assessment, 49*(1), 71–75.

Di Nardo, P. A. O'Brien, G.T., Barlow, D.H., Waddell, M.T., & Blanchard, E.B. (1983). Reliability of DSM-III anxiety disorder categories using a new structured interview. *Archives of General Psychiatry, 40*, 1070–1074.

Di Nardo, P. A., Brown, T. A., & Barlow, D. H. (1994). *Anxiety Disorders Interview Schedule for DSM-IV – Lifetime version (ADIS-IV-L)*. New York: Oxford University Press.

Doble, A., Martin, I., & Nutt, D. J. (2003). *Calming the brain: Benzodiazepines and related drugs from laboratory to clinic*. London, UK: Informa Healthcare.

Dong, Q., Yank, B., & Ollendick, T. H. (1994). Fears in Chinese children and adolescents and their relation to anxiety and depression. *Journal of Child Psychology and Psychiatry and Allied Disciplines, 35*, 351–363.

Doucet, C., Ladouceur, R., Freeston, M. H., & Dugas, M. J. (1998). Themes d'inquietudes et tendance a s'inquieter chez les aines [Worry themes and the tendency to worry in older adults]. *Canadian Journal on Aging, 17*, 361–371.

Dugas, M. J., Gagnon, F., Ladouceur, R., & Freeston, M. H. (1998). Generalized anxiety disorder: A preliminary test of a conceptual model. *Behaviour Research and Therapy, 36*, 215–226.

Dugas, M. J., Langlois, F., Rheaume, J., & Ladouceur, R. (1998). Intolerance of uncertainty and worry: Investigating causality: In J. Stober (Chair) (Ed.), Worry: New Findings in applied and clinical research. *Symposium conducted at the Annual Convention of the Association for Advancement of Behavior Therapy*, Washington, DC.

Dugas, M. J., Freeston, M. H., Ladouceur, R., Rheaume, J., Provencher, M., & Boisvert, J.-M. (1998). Worry themes in primary GAD, secondary GAD, and other anxiety disorders. *Journal of Anxiety Disorders, 12*, 253–261.

Dugas, M. (2000). Generalized anxiety disorder publications: So where do we stand? *Journal of Anxiety Disorders, 14*, 31–40.

Dugas, M. J., Gosselin, P., & Ladouceur, R. (2001). Intolerance of uncertainty and worry: Investigating specificity in a nonclinical sample. *Cognitive Therapy and Research, 25*, 551–558.

Dugas, M. J., Ladouceur, R., Leger, E., Freeston, M. H., Langlois, F., Provencher, M. A., & Boisvert, J.-M. (2003). Group cognitive therapy-behavioral therapy for generalized anxiety disorder: Treatment outcome and long-term follow up. *Journal and Consulting Clinical Psychology, 71*(4), 821–825.

Dugas, M. J., & Koerner, N. (2005). Cognitive-behavioral treatment for generalized anxiety disorder: Current status and future directions. *Journal of Cognitive Therapy. An International Quarterly, 19*(1), 61–81.

Dugas, M. J., Hedayati, M., Karavidis, A., Buhr, K., Francis, K., & Phillips, N. A. (2005). Intolerance of uncertainty and information processing: Evidence of biased recall and interpretations. *Cognitive Therapy and Research, 29*, 57–70.

Dugas, M. J., Marchand, A., & Ladouceur, R. (2005). Further validation of a cognitive-behavioral model of generalized anxiety disorder: Diagnostic and symptom specificity. *Journal of Anxiety Disorders, 19*, 329–343.

Dugas, M. J., & Robichaud, M. (2007). *Cognitive-behavioral treatment for generalized anxiety disorder: From science to practice*. New York: Routledge.

Dugas, M. J., Savard, P., Gaudet, A., Turcotte, J., Laugesen, N., Robichaud, M., Francis, K., & Koerner, N. (2007). Can the components of a cognitive model predict the severity of generalized anxiety disorder? *Behavior Therapy, 38*(2), 169–178.

Durham, R. C., Chambers, J. A., MacDonald, R. R., Power, K. G., & Major, K. (2003). Does cognitive-behavioral therapy influence the long term outcome of generalized anxiety disorder? An 8–14 year follow-up of two clinical trials. *Psychological Medicine, 33*, 499–509.

Durham, R. C. (2007). Treatment of generalized anxiety disorder. *Psychiatry, 6*(5), 183–187.

Durham, R., & Fisher, P. (2007). Generalised Anxiety Disorder. In C. Freeman & M. Power (Eds.), *Handbook of evidence-based psychotherapies: A guide for research and practice* (pp. 401–413). Chichester: Wiley.

Dworkin, R. W. (2006). *Artificial happiness: The dark side of the new happy class*. New York: Carrol & Graf Publishers.

Ehrenreich, J. T., & Gross, A. M. (2001). Treatment of childhood generalized anxiety disorder/overanxious disorder. In H. Orvaschel & J. Faust (Eds.), *Handbook of conceptualization and treatment of child psychopathology* (pp. 211–238). Amsterdam, the Netherlands: Elsevier Science.

Ehrenreich, J. T., Buzzella, B. A., & Barlow, D. H. (2007). General principles for the treatment of emotional disorders across the life span. In S. G. Hofman & J. Weinberger (Eds.), *The art and science of psychotherapy* (pp. 191–209). New York: Routledge.

Ehrenreich, J. T., Fairholme, C. P., Buzzella, B. A., Ellard, K. K., & Barlow, D. H. (2007). The role of emotion in psychological theory. *Clinical Psychology: Science Practice, 14*, 423–429.

Eisen, A. R., & Silverman, W. K. (1993). Should I relax or change my thoughts? *Journal of Cognitive Therapy, 7*, 265–279.

Eisen, A. R., & Engler, L. B. (1995). Chronic anxiety. In A. R. Eisen, C. A. Kearney, & C. A. Schaefer (Eds.), *Clinical handbook of anxiety disorders in children and adolescents* (pp. 223–250). Northvale, NJ: Aronson.

Eisen, A. R., & Silverman, W. K. (1998). Prescriptive treatment for generalized anxiety disorder in children. *Behavior Therapy, 29*, 105–121.

El-Khayat, R., & Baldwin, D. S. (1998). Anti-psychotic drugs for non-psychotic patients: Assessment of the benefit/risk ratio in generalized anxiety disorder. *Journal of Psychopharmacology, 12*, 323–329.

Ellis, A., & Becker, I. (1982). *A guide to personal happiness*. Hollywood, CA: Melvin Powers Wilshire Book Company.

Emmelkamp, P. M. G. (1974). The contours of positive human health. *Psychological Inquiry, 9*, 1–28.

Endicott, J., Nee, J., Harrison, W., & Blumenthal, R. (1993). Quality of Life Enjoyment and Satisfaction Questionnaire: A new measure. *Psychopharmacology Bulletin, 29*(2), 321–326.

Endicott, J., Russell, J. M., Raskin, J., Detke, M. J., Erickson, J., Ball, S. J., Marciniak, M., & Swindle, R. W. (2007). Duloxetine treatment for role functioning improvement in generalized anxiety disorder: Three independent studies. *Journal of Clinical Psychiatry, 68*, 518–524.

Enkelmann, R. (1991). Alprazalom versus buspirone in the treatment of outpatients with generalized anxiety disorder. *Psychopharmacology, 105*, 428–432.

Erickson, T. M., & Newman, M. G. (2005). Cognitive behavioral psychotherapy for generalized anxiety disorder: A primer. *Expert Review Neurotherapeutics, 5*(2), 247–257.

Evans, S., Ferrando, S., Findler, M., Stowell, C., Smart, C., & Haglin, D. (2008). Mindfulness-based cognitive therapy for generalized anxiety disorder. *Journal of Anxiety Disorders, 22*(4), 716–721.

Fairbanks, J. M., Pine, D. S., Tancer, N. K., Dummit, E. S., Kentgen, L. M., Martin, J., Asche, B. K., & Klein, R. G. (1997). Open fluoxetine treatment of mixed anxiety disorders in children and adolescents. *Journal of Child and Adolescent Psychopharmacology, 7*, 17–29.

Fava, G. A. (1999). Well-being therapy. *Psychotherapy & Psychosomatics, 68*, 171–178.

Fava, G. A. (2000). Cognitive behavioral therapy. In M. Fink (Ed.), *Encyclopedia of stress* (pp. 484–487). San Diego, CA: Academic Press.

Fava, G. A., Ruini, C., Rafanelli, C., Finos, L., Salmaso, L., Mangelli, L., & Sirigatti, S. (2005). Well-being therapy of generalized anxiety disorder. *Psychotherapy and Psychosomatics, 74*(1), 126–130.

Feehan, M., McGee, R., Raja, R., & Williams, S. (1994). DSM-III-R disorders in New Zealand 18 year olds. *Australian and New Zealand Journal Psychiatry, 28*, 87–99.

Feltner, D. E., Crockatt, J. G., Dubovksy, S. J., Cohn, C. K., Shrivastava, R. K., Targum, S. D., Liu-Dumaw, M., Carter, C. M., & Pande, A. C. (2003). A randomized, double-blind, placebo-controlled, fixed-dose, multicenter study of pregabalin in patients with generalized anxiety disorder. *Journal of Clinical Psychopharmacology, 23*(3), 240–249.

Feltner, D., Wittchen, H.-U., Kavoussi, R., Brock, J., Baldinetti, F., & Pande, A. C. (2008). Long-term efficacy of pregabalin in generalized anxiety disorder. *International Clinical Psychopharmacology, 23*(1), 18–28.

Ferreri, M., & Hantouche, E. G. (1998). Recent clinical trials of hydroxyzine in generalized anxiety disorder. *Acta Psychiatrica Scandinavica, 98*(Suppl. 393), 102–108.

Figueira, M. L. (1995). Alprazalom extended release in the management of anxiety. *Current Therapeutic Research, 56*(9), 957–965.

Finn, R. (2004). Escitalopram effective for long term treatment of GAD. *Clinical Psychiatry News, 32*(9), 42(1).

First, M. B., Spitzer, R. L., Gibbon, M., & Williams, J. B. (1997). *Structured clinical Interview for DSM-IV Axis I disorders-clinician version (SCID-CV)*. Washington, DC: American Psychiatric Association.

First, M. B., Spitzer, R. L., Gibbons, M., & Williams, J. B. W. (2001). *Structured clinical interview for DSM-IV-TR Axis I disorders-research version, patient edition (SCID-I/P)*. New York: Biometrics Department: New York State Psychiatric Institute.

Fisher, J. E., & Noll, J. (1996). Anxiety Disorders. In L. Carstensen, B. Edelstein, & L. Dornbrand (Eds.), *The practical handbook of clinical gerontology* (pp. 304–323). Thousand Oaks, CA: Sage.

Fisher, P. H., Tobkes, J. L., Kotcher, L., & Masia-Warner, C. (2006). Psychosocial and pharmacological treatment for pediatric anxiety disorders. *Expert Review of Neurotherapeutics, 6*(11), 1707–1719.

Fisher, P. L., & Durham, R. C. (1999). Recovery rates in generalized anxiety disorder following psychological therapy: An analysis of clinically significant change on STAI-T across outcomes studies since 1990. *Psychological Medicine, 29*, 1425–1434.

Flannery-Schroeder, E. C., & Kendall, R. C. (2000). Group and individual cognitive-behavioral treatments for youth with anxiety disorders: A randomized clinical trial. *Cognitive Therapy and Research, 24*, 251–278.

Flannery-Schroeder, E. C. (2004). Generalized anxiety disorder. In T. L. Morris & J. S. March (Eds.), *Anxiety disorders in children and adolescents* (pp. 125–140). New York: Guilford Press.

Flint, A. (1994). Epidemiology and comorbidity of anxiety disorders in the elderly. *American Journal of Psychiatry, 151*, 640–649.

Flint, A. (1999). Anxiety disorders in late-life. *Canadian Family Physician, 45*, 2672–2679.

Flint, A. J. (2005). Generalised anxiety disorder in elderly patients: Epidemiology, diagnosis and treatment options. *Drugs and Aging, 22*(2), 101–114.

Foa, E. B., Franklin, M. E., & Moser, J. (2002). Context in the clinic: how well do cognitive-behavioral therapies and medications work in combination? *Biological Psychiatry, 52*, 987–997.

Fonseca, A. C., Yule, W., & Erol, N. (1994). Cross-cultural issues. In T. Ollendick, N. King, & W. Yule (Eds.), *International handbook of phobic and anxiety disorders in children and adolescents* (pp. 67–84). New York: Plenum Press.

Fosha, D. (2000). *The transforming power of affect: A model of accelerated change*. New York: Basic Books.

Frampton, J. E., & Foster, R. H. (2006). Pregabalin in the treatment of generalized anxiety disorder. *CNS Drugs, 20*(8), 685–693.

Francis, K., & Dugas, M. J. (2004). Assessing positive beliefs about worry: Validation of a structured interview. *Personality and Individual Differences, 37*, 405–415.

Frattola, L., Piolti, R., Bassi, S., Albizzati, M. G., Cesana, B. M., Bottani, M. S., Priore, P., & Morselli, P. L. (1992). Effects of alpidem in anxious elderly outpatients: A double-blind, placebo-controlled trial. *Clinical Neuropharmacology, 15*(6), 477–487.

Freeston, M. H., Rheaume, J., Letarte, H., Dugas, M., & Ladouceur, R. (1994). Why do people worry? *Personality and Individual Differences, 17*, 791–802.

Freeston, M. H., Dugas, M. J., & Ladouceur, R. (1996). Thoughts, images, worry, and anxiety. *Cognitive Therapy and Research, 20*, 265–273.

Freud, S. (1894). *The justification for detaching neurasthenia a particular syndrome: The anxiety neurosis. Collected papers, 1953* (Vol. 1, pp. 76–106). London: Hogarth.

Fricchione, G. (2004). Generalized anxiety disorder. *New England Journal of Medicine, 351*, 675–682.

Friedman, S. (1990). Assessing the marital environment of agoraphobics. *Journal of Anxiety Disorders, 4*, 335–340.

Frisch, M. B. (1994). *Manual and treatment guide for the Quality of Life Inventory*. Minneapolis, MN: NCS Pearson, Inc.

Garb, H. N. (1998). *Studying the clinician: Judgment, research and psychological assessment*. Washington, DC: American Psychological Association.

Garcia-Compayo, J., Sanz-Carrillo, C., Claraco, L. M., Arana, A., & Monton, C. (1997). The challenge of somatizations: The need for liaison units primary care-mental health. *Primary Psychiatry, 3*, 163–169.

Gelenberg, A. J., Lydiard, R. B., Rudolph, R. L., Aguiar, L., Haskins, J. T., & Salinas, E. (2000). Efficacy of venlafaxine extended-release capsules in nondepressed outpatients with generalized anxiety disorder: A 6-month randomized controlled trial. *Journal of the American Medical Association, 287*, 3082–3088.

Ginsburg, G. S., & Drake, K. L. (2002). School-based treatment for anxious African-American adolescents: A controlled pilot study. *Journal of the American Academy of Child and Adolescent Psychiatry, 41*, 768–775.

Gitlin, M. (1996). *The psychotherapist's guide to psychopharmacology* (2nd ed.). New York: Free Press.

Glass, C. R., Victor, B. J., & Arnkoff, D. B. (1993). Empirical research on integrative and eclectic psychotherapies. In G. Stricker & J. Gold (Eds.), *Comprehensive handbook of psychotherapy integration* (pp. 9–25). New York: Plenum.

Glass, C. R., Arnkoff, D. B., & Rodriguez, B. F. (1998). An overview of directions in psychotherapy integration research. *Journal of Psychotherapy Integration, 8*, 187–209.

Gleason, P. P., Schulz, R., Smith, N. L., Newson, J. T., Kroboth, P. O., Kroboz, F. J., & Psaty, B. M. (1998). Correlates and prevalence of benzodiazepines use in community-dwelling elderly. *Journal of General Internal Medicine, 13*(4), 243–250.

Gliatto, M. F. (2000). Generalized anxiety disorder. *American Family Physician, 62*(7), 1591–1600, 1602.

Goldberg, D., & Goodyear, I. (2005). *The origins and course of common mental disorders*. New York: Routledge Press.

Goldberg, R. J., & Posner, D. A. (2000). Anxiety in the medically ill. In A. Stoudemire, D. S. Fogel, & D. R. Greenberg (Eds.), *The psychiatric care of the medical patient* (pp. 165–180). New York: Oxford University Press.

Goldfried, M. R. (1971). Systematic desensitization as training in self-control. *Journal of Consulting and Clinical Psychology, 32*(2), 228–234.

Goldfried, M. R. (1980). Toward the delineation of therapeutic change principles. *American Psychologist, 35*, 991–999.

Goldfried, M. R., & Padawer, W. (1982). Current status and future directions in psychotherapy. In M. R. Goldfried (Ed.), *Converging themes in psychotherapy* (pp. 3–49). New York: Springer.

Goldstein, C. R., & Ehrenreich, J. T. (2005). Unified protocol for the treatment of emotional disorders in adolescents: A pilot study. Unpublished manuscript.

Goodman, W. K., Bose, A., & Wang, Q. (2005). Treatment of generalized anxiety disorder with escitalopram: Pooled results from double-blind, placebo-controlled trials. *Journal of Affective Disorders, 87*, 161–167.

Gorenstein, E. E., Papp, L. A., & Kleber, M. S. (1999). Cognitive behavioral treatment of anxiety in later life. *Cognitive and Behavioral Practice, 6*, 305–320.

Gorenstein, E. E., Kleber, M. S., Mohlman, J., DeJesus, M., Gorman, J. M. & Papp, L.A., (2005). Cognitive-behavioral therapy for management of anxiety and medication taper in older adults. *American Journal of Geriatric Psychiatry, 13*, 901–909.

Gorman, J. M. (2002). Treatment of generalized anxiety disorder. *Journal of Clinical Psychiatry, 63*(Suppl. 8), 17–23.

Gosch, E. A., Flannery-Schroeder, E., Mauro, C. F., & Compton, S. N. (2006). Principles of cognitive-behavioral therapy for anxiety disorders in children. *Journal of Cognitive Psychotherapy: An International Quarterly, 20*(3), 247–262.

Gould, R. A., Safren, S. A., Washington, D. O., & Otto, M. W. (2004). A meta-analytic review of cognitive-behavioral treatments. In R. G. Heimberg, L. C. Turk, & D. S. Mennin (Eds.), *Generalized anxiety disorder: Advances in research and practice* (pp. 248–264). New York: Guilford.

Grados, M. A., Leung, D., Ahmed, K., & Anega, A. (2005). Obsessive-compulsive disorder and generalized anxiety disorder: A common diagnostic dilemma. *Primary Psychiatry, 12*(3), 40–46.

Grant, B. F., Hasin, D. S., Stinson, F. S., Dawson, D. A., Chou, P. S., Ruan, J. W., & Huang, B. (2005). Co-occurrence of 12-month mood and anxiety disorders and personality disorders in the US: Results from the national epidemiologic survey on alcohol and related conditions. *Journal of Psychiatric Research, 39*(1), 1–9.

Gray, S. L., Eggen, A. E., Blough, D., Buchner, D., & La Croix, A. (2003). Benzodiazepine use in older adults enrolled in a health maintenance organization. *American Journal of Geriatric Psychiatry, 11*(5), 568–576.

Greenberg, L. S., & Safran, J. D. (1987). *Emotion in psychotherapy: Affect, cognition, and the process of change.* New York: Guilford Press.

Greenberg, L. S., Rice, C. N., & Elliot, R. K. (1996). *Facilitating emotional change: The moment-by-moment process.* New York: Guilford Press.

Greenberg, P. E., Sisitsky, T., Kessler, R. C., Finkelstein, S. N., Berndt, E. R., Davidson, J. R., Ballenger, J. L., & Fyer, A. J. (1999). The economic burden of anxiety disorders in the 1990's. *Journal of Clinical Psychiatry, 60,* 427–435.

Guitierrez, M. A., Stimmel, G. L., & Aiso, J. Y. (2003). Venlafaxine: A 2003 update. *Clinical Therapy, 25*(8), 2138–2154.

Gullone, E., & King, N. J. (1993). The fears of youth in the 1990's: Contemporary normative data. *Journal of Genetic Psychology, 154,* 137–153.

Guy, W. (1976). The clinician global severity and impression scales. In: *ECDEU Assessment Manual for Psychopharmacology.* US Department of Health, Education, and Welfare, MD, USA, 218–222.

Halbreich, U. (2003). Anxiety disorders in woman: A developmental and life cycle perspective. *Depression and Anxiety, 17,* 107–110.

Hales, R. E., Hilty, D. A., & Wise, M. G. (1997). A treatment algorithm for the management of anxiety in primary care practice. *Journal of Clinical Psychiatry, 58*(Suppl. 3), 76–80.

Hallowell, E. M. (2002). Worry. New York: Random House.

Hamilton, M. (1959). The assessment of anxiety states by rating. *The British Journal of Medical Psychology, 32*(1), 50–55.

Hamilton, M. (1960). A rating scale for depression. *Journal of Neurology, Neurosurgery and Psychiatry, 23,* 56–62.

Hammad, T. A. (2004). Review and evaluation of clinical trials data: Relationship between psychotropic drugs and pediatric suicide. Online document: http://www.fda.gov/ahrms/dockets/ac/04/briefing/2004-4065bi-10-TAB08-Hammads-Review.Pdf

Hartford, J., Kornstein, S., Liebowitz, M., Pigott, T., Russell, J., Detke, M., Walker, D., Ball, S., Dunayevich, E., Dinkel, J., & Erickson, J. (2007). Duloxetine as an SNRI treatment for generalized anxiety disorder: Results from a placebo and active-controlled trial. *International Clinical Psychopharmacology, 22*(3), 167–174.

Harvey, A. G., & Rapee, R. M. (1995). Cognitive-behavior therapy for generalized anxiety disorder. *The Psychiatric Clinics of North America, 18,* 859–870.

Harvey, A., Watkins, E., Mansell, W., & Shafran, R. (2004). *Cognitive behavioural processes across psychological disorders: A transdiagnostic approach to research and treatment.* New York: Oxford University Press.

Havens, L. (2004). The best kept secret: How to form an effective alliance. *Harvard Review of Psychiatry, 12,* 56–62.

Hayes, S. C., Wilson, K. G., Gifford, E. V., Follette, V. M., & Strosahl, K. (1996). Experiential avoidance and behavior disorders: A functional dimension approach to diagnosis and treatment. *Journal of Consulting and Clinical Psychology, 64,* 1152–1168.

Hayes, S. C., Strosahl, K. D., & Wilson, K. G. (1999). *Acceptance and commitment therapy: An experiential approach to behavior change. New York*: Guilford Press.

Hayes, S. C., Strosahl, K. D., Wilson, K. G., Bissett, R. T., Pistorello, J., Toarmino, D., Polansky, M. A., Dykstra, T. A., Batten, S. V., Bergan, J., Stewart, S. H., Zvolensky, M. J., Eifert, G. H., Bond, F. W., Forsyth, J. P., Karekla, M., & McCurry, S. M. (2004). Measuring experiential avoidance: A preliminary test of a working model. *The Psychological Record, 54,* 533–578.

Hazlett-Stevens, H. (2008). *Psychological approaches to generalized anxiety disorder: A clinician's guide to assessment and treatment.* New York: Springer Verlag.

Healy, D. (1999). *The antidepressant era.* Boston, MA: Harvard University Press.

Healy, D. (2004). Let them eat prozac: *The unhealthy relationship between the pharmaceutical industry and depression.* New York: New York University Press.

Henning, E. R., Turk, C. L., Mennin, D. S., Fresco, D. M., & Heimberg, R. G. (2007). Impairment and quality of life in individuals with generalized anxiety disorder. *Depression and Anxiety, 24*(5), 342–349.

Hettema, J. M., Neale, M. C., & Kendler, K. S. (2001). A review and meta-analysis of the genetic epidemiology of anxiety disorders. *American Journal of Psychiatry, 158*(10), 1568–1578.

Hettema, J. M., Prescott, C. A., & Kendler, K. S. (2004). Genetic and environmental sources of covariation between generalized anxiety disorder and neuroticism. *American Journal of Psychiatry, 161*(9), 1581–1587.

Hettema, J. M. (2008). The nosologic relationship between generalized anxiety disorder and major depression. *Depression and Anxiety, 25,* 300–316.

Hoehn-Saric, R., & McLeod, D. R. (1988). The peripheral sympathetic nervous system: Its role in normal and pathological anxiety. *The Psychiatric Clinics of North America, 11,* 375–386.

Hoehn-Saric, R., McLeod, D. R., & Zimmerli, W. D. (1989). Somatic manifestations in woman with generalized anxiety disorder: *Psychophysiological responses to psychological stress. Archives of General Psychiatry, 46,* 1113–1119.

Hoehn-Saric, R., & McLeod, D. R. (1991). Clinical management of generalized anxiety disorder. In W. Coryell & G. Winokur (Eds.), *The clinical management of anxiety disorders* (pp. 79–100). New York: Oxford University Press.

Hoehn-Saric, R., Hazlett, R. L., & McLeod, D. R. (1993). Generalized anxiety disorder with early and late onset of anxiety symptoms. *Comprehensive Psychiatry, 34,* 291–298.

Hoehn-Saric, R., Borkovec, T. D., & Nemiah, J. C. (1995). Generalized anxiety. In G. O. Gabbard (Ed.), Treatment of psychiatric disorders: The DSM-IV edition (pp. 1537–1567). Washington, DC: American Psychiatric Association.

Hoehn-Saric, R. (2005). Generalized anxiety disorder in medical practice. *Primary Psychiatry, 12*(3), 30–34.

Hoehn-Saric, R. (2007). Treatment of somatic symptoms in generalized anxiety disorder. *Psychiatric Times, 24*(3), 34–36.

Hoffman, D. L., Dukes, E. M., & Wittchen, H. U. (2008). Human and economic burden of generalized anxiety disorder. *Depression and Anxiety, 25*(1), 72–90.

Hoge, E. A., Oppenheimer, J. E., & Simon, N. M. (2004). Generalized anxiety disorder. *Focus: The Journal of Lifelong Learning in Psychiatry, 2*(3), 346–359.

Hoge, E. A., Tamrakar, S. M., Christian, K. M., Mahara, N., Nepal, M. K., Pollack, M. H., & Simon, N. M. (2006). Cross-cultural differences in somatic presentation in patients with generalized anxiety disorder. *The Journal of Nervous and Mental Disease, 194*(12), 962–966.

Hoge, E. A., Worthington, J. J., Kaufman, R. E., Delong, H. R., Pollack, M. H., & Simon, N. M. (2008). Aripiprazole as augmentation treatment of refractory generalized anxiety disorder and panic disorder. *CNS Spectrums, 13*(6), 522–527.

Hollifield, M., Katon, W., Spain, D., & Pule, L. (1990). Anxiety and depression in a village in Lesotho, Africa: A comparison with the United States. *British Journal of Psychiatry, 156,* 343–350.

Holmes, M., & Newman, M. G. (2006). Generalized anxiety disorder. In F. Andrasik, M. Hersen, & J. C. Thomas (Eds.), Comprehensive handbook of personality and psychopathology, Volume 2, adult psychopathology (pp. 101–120). Hoboken, NJ: Wiley.

Holowka, D. W., Dugas, M. J., Francis, K., & Laugesen, N. (2000). *Measuring beliefs about worry: A psychometric evaluation of the Why Worry II Questionnaire.* Poster presented at the Annual Meeting of the Association for Advancement of Behavior Therapy, New Orleans, LA.

Hopko, D. R., Stanley, M. A., Reas, D. L., Wetherell, J. L., Beck, J. G., Novy, D. M., & Averill, P. M. (2003). Assessing worry in older adults: Confirmatory factor analysis of the Penn State Worry Questionnaire and psychometric properties of an abbreviated model. Psychological Assessment, 15, 173–183.

Howard, B. L., & Kendall, P. C. (1996). Cognitive-behavioral family therapy for anxiety disordered children: A multiple-baseline evaluation. *Cognitive Therapy and Research, 20,* 423–443.

Hoyer, J., Becker, E. S., & Roth, W. T. (2001). Characteristics of worry in GAD patients, social phobics, and controls. *Depression and Anxiety, 13,* 89–96.

Hsu, L. K., & Folstein, M. F. (1997). Somatoform disorders in Caucasian and Chinese Americans. *Journal of Nervous and Mental Disease, 185,* 382–387.

Hsu, S. I. (1999). Somatization among Asia refugees and immigrants as a culturally-shaped illness behaviour. *Annals Academy Medicine Singapore, 28,* 841–845.

Hunt, C., Issakidis, C., & Andrews, G. (2002). DSM-IV generalized anxiety disorder in the Australian National Survey of mental health and well-being. *Psychological Medicine, 32,* 649–659.

Hunt, S., Wisocki, P., & Yanko, J. (2003). Worry and use of coping strategies among older and younger adults. *Anxiety Disorders, 7,* 547–560.

In-Albon, T., & Schneider, S. (2007). Psychotherapy of childhood anxiety disorders: A meta-analysis. *Psychotherapy and Psychosomatics, 76,* 15–24.

Jensen, J. P., Bergin, A. E., & Greaves, D. W. (1990). The meaning of eclectism: New Survey and analysis of components. *Professional Psychology: Research and Practice, 21,* 124–130.

Jetty, P. V., Charney, D. S., & Goddard, A. W. (2001). Neurobiology of generalized anxiety disorder. *Psychiatrics Clinics of North America, 24*(1), 75–97.

Johnstone, E. C., Cunninghams, D. G., Frith, C. D., McPherson, K., Dowie, C., Riley, G., & Gold, A. (1980). Neurotic illness and its response to anxiolytic and antidepressant treatment. *Psychological Medicine, 10*(2), 321–328.

Jones, G. N., Ames, S. C., Jeffries, S. K., Scarinci, I. C., & Brantley, P. J. (2001). Utilization of medical services and quality of life among low income patients with generalized anxiety disorder attending primary care clinics. *International Journal of Psychiatry in Medicine, 31*(2), 193–198.

Joorman, J., & Stober, J. (1999). Somatic symptoms of generalized anxiety disorder from the DSM-IV: Associations with pathological worry and depression symptoms in a nonclinical sample. *Journal of Anxiety Disorders, 13,* 491–503.

Judd, L. L., Kessler, R. C., Paulus, M. P., Zeller, P. V., Wittchen, H. U., & Kunovac, J. L. (1998). Comorbidity as a fundamental feature of generalized anxiety disorders: Results from the National Comorbidity Study (NCS). *Acta Psychiatrica Scandinavica. Supplementum, 393,* 6–11.

Kabat-Zinn, J. (1990). *Full catastrophe living: Using the wisdom of your body and mind to face stress, pain and illness.* New York: Delacorte.

Kabat-Zinn, J., Massion, A. O., Kristeller, J. L., Peterson, L. G., Fletcher, K. E., Pbert, L., Lenderking, W. R., & Santorelli, S. F. (1992). Effectiveness of a meditation-based stress reduction program in the treatment of anxiety disorders. *American Journal of Psychiatry, 149,* 936–943.

Kabat-Zinn, J. (1994). *Wherever you go there you are.* New York: Hyperion.

Kahn, C., & Henderson, C. W. (2000). Venlafaxine significantly effective for children and adolescents. *Pain and Central Nervous System Week,* 11–14.

Kahn, R. J., McNair, D. M., Lipman, R. S., Covi, L., Rickels, K., Downing, R., Fisher, S., & Frankenthaler, L. M. (1986). Imipramine and chlordiazepoxide in depressive and anxiety disorders: II. Efficacy in anxious outpatients. *Archives of General Psychiatry, 43*(1), 79–85.

Kane, M. T., & Kendall, P. C. (1989). Anxiety disorders in children: A multiple-baseline evaluation of cognitive-behavioral treatment. *Behavioral Therapy, 20,* 499–508.

Kaplan, A. (2007). Practice parameters provides guidance on childhood anxiety. *Psychiatric Times, 24*(9), 1, 7–9.

Kasper, S. (2004). *Recent advances in the treatment of generalized anxiety disorder. Programs and abstracts of the International Congress of Biological Psychiatry.* Sydney, Australia, Symposium 120.

Katon, W., von Korff, M., Lin, E., Lipscomb, P., Russo, J., Wagner, E., & Polk, E. (1990). Distressed high utilizers of medical care: DSM-III-R diagnoses and treatment needs. *General Hospital Psychiatry, 12*, 355–362.

Katz, I. R., Reynolds, C. F., Alexopoulos, G. S., & Hackett, D. (2002). Venlafaxine ER as a treatment for generalized anxiety disorder in older adults: Pooled analysis of five randomized placebo-controlled clinical trials. *Journal of American Geriatric Society, 50*, 18–25.

Keller, M. B. (2002). The long-term clinical course of generalized anxiety disorder. *Journal of Clinical Psychiatry, 63*(Suppl. 8), 11–16.

Kellner, R. (1987). A symptom questionnaire. *Journal of Clinical Psychiatry, 48*, 269–274.

Kendall, P. C. (1994). Treating anxiety disorders in children: Results of a randomized clinical trial. *Journal of Consulting and Clinical Psychology, 62*, 100–110.

Kendall, P.C., & Chansky, T.E. (1991). Considering cognition in anxiety-disordered children. Journal of Anxiety Disorders, 5, 167–185.

Kendall, P. C., & Southam-Gerow, M. A. (1996). Long-term follow up a cognitive behavioral therapy for anxious youth. *Journal of Consulting and Clinical Psychology, 62*, 724–730.

Kendall, P. C., & Warman, M. J. (1996). Anxiety disorders in youth: Diagnostic consistency across DSM-III-R and DSM-IV. *Journal of Anxiety Disorders, 10*, 453–463.

Kendall, P. C., Flannery-Schroeder, E., Panichelli-Mindel, S., Southam-Gerow, M., Henin, A., & Warman, M. (1997). Therapy for youths with anxiety disorders: A second randomized clinical trial. *Journal of Consulting and Clinical Psychology, 65*, 366–380.

Kendall, P., Krain, A., & Treadwell, K. (1999). Generalized anxiety disorder. In R. T. Ammerman, M. Hersen, & C. G. Last (Eds.), Handbook of prescriptive treatments for children and adolescents (2nd ed., pp. 155–171). Needham, MA: Allyn & Bacon.

Kendall, P. C., Safford, S., Flannery-Schroeder, E., & Webb, A. (2004). Child anxiety treatment: Outcomes in adolescence and impact on substance use and depression at 7.4 years follow-up. *Journal of Consulting and Clinical Psychology, 72*, 276–287.

Kendall, P. C., Hudson, J. L., Gosch, E., Flannery-Schroeder, E., & Suveg, C. (2008). Cognitive-behavioral therapy for anxiety disordered youth: A randomized clinical trial evaluating child and family modalities. *Journal of Consulting and Clinical Psychology, 76*(2), 282–297.

Kendler, K. S., Neale, M. C., Kessler, R. C., Heath, A. C., & Eaves, L. J. (1992a). Major depression and generalized anxiety disorder: Same genes (partly) different environments? *Archives of General Psychiatry, 49*, 716–722.

Kendler, K. S., Neale, M. C., Kessler, R. C., Heath, A. C., & Eaves, L. J. (1992b). Generalized anxiety disorder in woman: A population-based twin study. *Archives of General Psychiatry, 49*, 267–272.

Kendler, K. S., Walters, E. E., Neale, M. C., Kessler, R. C., Heath, A. C., & Eaves, L. J. (1995). The structure of the genetic and environmental risk factors for six major psychiatric disorders in woman: Phobia, generalized anxiety disorder, panic disorder, bulimia, major depression, and alcoholism. *Archives of General Psychiatry, 52*, 374–383.

Kendler, K. S. (1996). Major depression and generalized anxiety disorder: Same genes (partly) different environments – revisited. *British Journal of Psychiatry, 168*(Suppl. 30), 68–75.

Kendler, K. S., & Prescott, C. A. (2006). *Genes, Environment and Psychopathology: Understanding the cause of psychiatric and substance abuse disorders.* New York: Guilford Press.

Kendler, K. S., Gardner, C. D., Gatz, M., & Pedersen, N. C. (2007). The source of comorbidity between major depression and generalized anxiety disorder in a Swedish National twin sample. *Psychological Medicine, 37*(3), 455–462.

Kennedy, B. L., & Schwab, J. J. (1997). Utilization of medical specialists by anxiety disorder patients. *Psychosomatics, 38*, 109–112.

Kessler, R. C., McGonagle, K. A., Zhao, S., Nelson, C. B., Hughes, M., Eshelman, S., Wittchen, H. U., & Kendler, K. S. (1994). Lifetime and 12-month prevalence of DSM-III-R psychiatric disorders in the United States: Results from the National Comorbidity Survey. *Archives of General Psychiatry, 51*, 8–19.

Kessler, R. C., Berglund, P., Dewit, D. J., Ustun, T., Wang, P. S., & Wittchen, H. (1999). Distinguishing generalized anxiety disorder from major depression: Prevalence and impairment from current pure and comorbid disorders in the US and Ontario. *International Journal of Methods in Psychiatric Research, 11*, 99–111.

Kessler, R. C., Keller, M. B., & Wittchen, H. U. (2001). The epidemiology of generalized anxiety disorder. *Psychiatric Clinics of North America, 24*(1), 19–39.

Kessler, R. C., Walters, E. E., & Wittchen, H. U. (2004). Epidemiology. In R. G. Heimberg, C. L. Turk & D. S. Mennin (Eds.), *Generalized anxiety disorder:* Advances in research and practice (pp. 29–50). New York: Guilford Press.

Kessler, R. C., Berglund, P., Demler, O., Jin, R., Merikangas, K. R., & Walters, E. E. (2005). Lifetime prevalence and age-of-onset distribution of DSM-IV disorders in the National Comorbidity Survey Replication. *Archives of General Psychiatry, 62*, 593–602.

Kessler, R. C., Brandenburg, N., Lane, M., Roy-Byrne, P., Stang, P. D., Stein, D. J., & Wittchen, H. U. (2005). Rethinking the duration requirement for generalized anxiety disorder: Evidence from the National Comorbidity Survey Replication. *Psychological Medicine, 35*, 1073–1082.

Kessler, R. C., Gruber, M., Hettema, J. M., Hwang, I., Sampson, N., & Yonkers, K. A. (2008). Co-morbid major depression and generalized anxiety disorder in the National Comorbidity Survey follow-up. *Psychological Medicine, 38*(3), 365–374.

King, N. J., Gullone, E., & Ollendick, T. H. (1992). Manifest anxiety and fearfulness in children and adolescents. *Journal of Genetic Psychology, 153*, 63–73.

Klein, D. F. (1964). Delineation of two drug-responsive anxiety syndromes. *Psychopharmacologia, 5*, 397–408.

Koepke, H. H., Gold, R. L., Linden, M. E., Lion, J. R., & Rickels, K. (1982). Multicenter controlled trial of oxazepam in anxious elderly outpatients. *Psychosomatics, 23*, 641–645.

Koerner, N., & Dugas, M. J. (2006). A cognitive model of generalized anxiety disorder: The role of intolerance of uncertainty. In G. C. L. Davey & A. Wells (Eds.), *Worry and its psychological disorders: Theory, assessment and treatment* (pp. 201–216). Chichester, UK: Wiley.

Kogan, J. N., Edelstein, B. A., & McKee, D. R. (2004). Assessment of anxiety in older adults: Current status. *Journal of Anxiety Disorders, 14*, 109–132.

Kogan, J. N., & Edelstein, B. A. (2004). Modification and psychometric examination of a self-report measure of fear in older adults. *Journal of Anxiety Disorders, 18*, 397–409.

Koponen, H., Allgulander, C., Erickson, J., Dunayevich, E., Pritchett, Y., Detke, M. J., Ball, S. G., & Russell, J. M. (2007). Efficacy of duloxetine for the treatment of generalized anxiety disorder: Implications for primary care physicians. *Primary Care Companion Journal of Clinical Psychiatry, 9*(2), 100–107.

Kratochvil, C., Kutcher, S., Reiter, S., & March, J. S. (1999). Pharmacotherapy of pediatric anxiety disorders. In S. W. Russ & J. Ollendick (Eds.), *Handbook of psychotherapies with children and families* (pp. 345–366). New York: Kluwer Academic.

Krueger, R. F., Markon, K. E., Patrick, C. J., & Iacono, W. G. (2005). Externalizing psychopharmacology in adulthood: A dimensional-spectrum conceptualization and its implication for DSM-IV. *Journal of Abnormal Psychology, 114*(4), 537–550.

Kutcher, S. P., Reiter, S., Gardner, D. M., & Klein, R. G. (1992). The pharmacotherapy of anxiety in children and adolescents. *Psychiatric Clinics of North America, 15*, 41–67.

Laakman, G., Schule, C., Lorkowski, G., Banghai, T., Kuhn, K., & Enrentraut, S. (1998). Buspirone and lorazepam in the treatment of generalized anxiety disorder in out-patients. *Psychopharmacology, 136*, 357–366.

Lader, M., & Scotto, J. C. (1998). A multicentre double-blind comparison of hydroxyzine, buspirone and placebo in patients with generalized anxiety disorder. *Psychopharmacology, 139*, 402–406.

Ladouceur, R., Blais, F., Freeston, M. H., & Dugas, M. J. (1998). Problem solving and problem orientation in generalized anxiety disorder. *Journal of Anxiety Disorders, 12*, 139–152.

Ladouceur, R., Dugas, M. J., Freeston, M. H., Rheaume, J., Blais, F., Boisvert, J. M., Gagnon, F., & Thibodeau, N. (1999). Specificity of generalized anxiety disorder symptoms and processes. *Behavior Therapy, 30*, 191–207.

Ladouceur, R., Dugas, M. J., Freeston, M. H., Leger, E., Gagnon, F., & Thibodeau, N. (2000). Efficacy of cognitive-behavioral treatment for generalized anxiety disorder: Evaluation in a controlled clinical trial. *Journal of Consulting and Clinical Psychology, 68*(6), 957–964.

Ladouceur, R., Leger, E., Dugas, M., & Freeston, M. H. (2004). Cognitive-behavioral treatment of generalized anxiety disorder (GAD) for older adults. *International Psychogeriatrics, 16*(2), 195–207.

Lampe, L. (2004). *Take control of your worry: Managing generalized anxiety disorder.* Australia: Simon & Schuster.

Lang, A. T. (2004). Treating generalized anxiety disorder with cognitive-behavioral therapy. *The Journal of Clinical Psychiatry, 65*(Suppl. 13), 14–19.

Last, C. G., Hersen, M., Kazdin, A. E., Finkelstein, R., & Strauss, C. C. (1987). Comparison of DSM-III separation anxiety and generalized anxiety disorders: Demographic characteristics and patterns of comorbidity. *Journal of the American Academy of Child and Adolescent Psychiatry, 26,* 527–531.

Last, C. G., Strauss, C. C., & Francis, G. (1987). Comorbidity among childhood anxiety disorders. *Journal of Nervous and Mental Disease, 175,* 726–730.

Ledley, D. R., Marx, B. P., & Heimberg, R. G. (2005). *Making cognitive-behavioral therapy work: Clinical process of new practitioners.* New York: Guilford Press.

Le Roux, H., Gatz, M., & Wetherell, J. L. (2005). Age of onset of generalized anxiety disorder in older adults. *American Journal of Geriatric Psychiatry, 13,* 23–30.

Leahy, R. L. (2004). Cognitive-behavioral therapy. In R. G. Heimberg, L. C. Turk, & D. S. Mennin (Eds.), *Generalized anxiety disorder: Advances in research and practice* (pp. 265–292). New York: Guilford Press.

Leahy, R. L. (2005). The worry cure: Seven steps to stop worry from stopping you. New York: Harmony Books.

Leff, J. (1994). *Psychiatry around the globe.* London: Gaskell/Royal College of Psychiatrists.

Leighton, A. H. (1987). Primary prevention of psychiatric disorders. *Acta Psychiatrica Scandinavica, 76,* 7–13.

Lenze, E. J., Karp, J. F., Mulsant, B. H., Blank, S., Shear, K. M., Houck, P. R., & Reynolds, C. F. (2005). Somatic symptoms in late-life anxiety: Treatment issues. *Journal of Geriatric Psychiatry and Neurology, 18,* 89–96.

Lenze, E. J., Mulsant, B. H., Shear, M. K., Dew, M. A., Miller, M. D., Pollock, B. G., Houck, P., Tracey, B., & Reynolds, C. F. (2005). Efficacy and tolerability of citalopram in the treatment of late-life anxiety disorders: Results from an 8-week randomized, placebo-controlled trial. *American Journal of Psychiatry, 162,* 146–150.

Lenze, E. J., Mulsant, B. H., Mohlman, J., Shear, M. K., Dew, M. A., Schulz, R., Miller, M. D., Tracey, B., & Reynolds, C. F. (2005). Generalized anxiety disorder in late-life: Life-time course and comorbidity with major depressive disorder. *American Journal of Geriatric Psychiatry, 13,* 77–80.

Leonard, H. A. (Ed.). (2007, April). Pediatric generalized anxiety disorder: Differing results in trials leave uncertainty on venlafaxine ER for generalized anxiety disorder. *The Brown University Child and Adolescent Psychopharmacology Update, 9*(4), 1, 6–7.

Levant, R. F. (2004). The empirically-validated treatments movement: A Practitioner/educator perspective. *Clinical Psychology: Science and Practice, 11,* 219–224.

Lewinsohn, P. M., Hops, H., Roberts, R. E., Seeley, J. R., & Andrews, J. A. (1993). Adolescent psychopathology: I. Prevalence and incidence of depression and other DSM-III-R disorders in high school students. *Journal of Abnormal Psychology, 102,* 133–144.

Linden, M., Zubraegel, D., Baer, T., Franke, U., & Schlattmann, P. (2005). Efficacy of cognitive behavioral therapy in generalized anxiety disorders. *Psychotherapy & Psychosomatics, 74*(1), 36–42.

Lindsay, W. R., McLaughlin, E., Hood, E. H., Espie, C. A., & Gamsu, C. V. (1987). A controlled trial of treatments for generalized anxiety disorder. *British Journal of Clinical Psychology, 26,* 3–15.

Linehan, M. M. (1993). *Cognitive-behavioral treatment of borderline personality disorder.* New York: Guilford Press.

Linehan, M. M. (1994). Acceptance and change: The central dialectic in psychotherapy. In S. C. Hayes, N. S. Jacobsen, V. M. Follette, & M. J. Dougher (Eds.), *Acceptance and change: Content and context in psychotherapy* (pp. 73–86). Reno, NV: Context Press.

Lipschitz, A. (1988). Diagnosis and classification of anxiety disorders. In C. G. Last & M. Hersen (Eds.), *Handbook of anxiety disorders* (pp. 41–65). New York: Pergamon Press.

Llorca, P. M., Spadone, C., Sol, O., Danniau, A., Bougerol, T., Corruble, E., Faruch, M., Macher, J. P., Sermet, E., & Servant, D. (2002). Efficacy and safety of hydroxyzine in the treatment of generalized anxiety disorder: A 3-month double-blind study. *Journal of Clinical Psychiatry, 63*, 1020–1027.

Lovibond, S. H., & Lovibond, P. F. (1995). *Manual for the Depression Anxiety Stress Scales* (2nd ed.). Sydney: Psychology Foundation.

Luborsky, L. C. (1984). *Principles of psychoanalytic psychotherapy: A manual for supportive-expressive treatment.* New York: Basic Books.

Lydiard, R. B. (2000). An overview of generalized anxiety disorder: Disease-state appropriate therapy. *Clinical Therapeutics, 22*(Suppl. A), A3–A19.

Lydiard, R. B., & Monnier, J. (2004). Pharmacological treatment. In R. G. Heimberg, L. C. Turk, & D. S. Mennin (Eds.), *Generalized anxiety disorder: Advances in research and practice* (pp. 351–379). New York: Guilford Press.

Maier, W., Gansicke, M., Freyberger, H. J., Linz, H., Heun, R., & Lecrubier, Y. (2000). Generalized anxiety disorder (ICD-10) in primary care from a cross cultural perspective: A vague diagnostic entity? *Acta Psychiatrica Scandinavica.*

Manassis, K., Mendlowitz, S. L., Scapillato, D., Avery, D., Fiksenbaum, L., Friere, M., Monga, S., & Owens, M. (2002). Group and individual cognitive-behavioral therapy for childhood anxiety disorders: A randomized trial. *Journal of the American Academy of Child and Adolescent Psychiatry, 41*, 1423–1430.

Manela, M., Katona, C., & Livingston, G. (1996). How common are the anxiety disorders in old age? *International Journal of Geriatric Psychiatry, 11*, 65–70.

March, J. S., Parker, J. D. A., Sullivan, K., Stallings, P., & Connors, C. K. (1997). The Multidimensional Anxiety Scale for Children (MASC): Factor, structure, reliability, and validity. *Journal of the American Academy of Child and Adolescent Psychiatry, 36*, 554–565.

March, J. S., & Sullivan, K. (1999). Test-retest reliability of the Multidimensional Anxiety Scale for Children. *Journal of Anxiety Disorders, 13*, 349–358.

March, J. S., & Albano, A. M. (2002). Anxiety disorders in children and adolescents. In D. J. Stein & E. Hollander (Eds.), *Textbook of anxiety disorders* (pp. 415–427). Washington, DC: American Psychiatric Association.

Marks, I. M., & Matthews, A. M. (1979). Brief standard self-rating for phobic patients. *Behaviour Research and Therapy, 17*, 263–267.

Marten, P. A., Brown, T. A., Barlow, D. H., Borkovec, T. D., Shear, M. K., & Lydiard, R. B. (1993). Evaluation of the ratings comprising the associated symptom criteria of DSM-III-R generalized anxiety disorder. *The Journal of Nervous and Mental Disease, 181*(11), 676–682.

Masi, G., Mucci, M., Favilla, L., Romano, R., & Poli, P. (1999). Symptomatology and comorbidity of generalized anxiety disorder in children and adolescents. *Comprehensive Psychiatry, 40*, 210–215.

Masi, G., Favilla, L., Mucci, M., & Millepiedi, S. (2000). Depressive comorbidity in children and adolescents with generalized anxiety disorder. *Child Psychiatry and Human Development, 30*, 205–215.

Masi, G., Millepiedi, S., Mucci, M., Poli, P., Bertini, N., & Milantoni, L. (2004). Generalized anxiety disorder in referred children and adolescents. *Journal of the American Academy of Child and Adolescent Psychiatry, 43*, 752–760.

Matthew, R. J., Ho, B. T., Francis, P. J., Taylor, D. L., & Weinman, M. L. (1982). Catecholamines and anxiety. *Acta Psychiatrica Scandinavica, 65*(2), 142–147.

Mathew, S. J., Price, R. B., & Charney, D. S. (2008). Recent advances in the neurobiology of anxiety disorders: Implications for novel therapeutics. *American Journal of Medical Genetics, 148*(2), 89–98.

McCullough, L., Kuhn, N., Andrews, S., Kaplan, A., Wolf, J., & Hurley, C. L. (2003). *Treating affect phobia: A manual for short-term dynamic psychotherapy.* New York: Guilford Press.

McGee, R., Feehan, M., Williams, S., & Partridge, F. (1990). DSM-III disorders in a large sample of adolescents. *Journal of the American Academy of Child and Adolescent Psychiatry, 29,* 611–619.

McHorney, C. A., Ware, J. E., Lu, J. F., & Sherbourne, C. D. (1994). The MOS 36-item Short-Form Health Survey (SF-36): III: Tests of data quality, scaling assumptions, and reliability across diverse patient groups. *Medical Care, 32,* 40–66.

McHugh, P. R. (1999, December). How psychiatry lost its way. *Commentary Magazine, 108*(5), 32–38.

McHugh, P. R., & Slavney, P. R. (1998). *The perspectives of psychiatry* (2nd ed.). Baltimore, MD: The Johns Hopkins Press.

McHugh, P. R. (2001). Beyond DSM-IV: From appearances to essences. *Psychiatric Research Paper, 17,* 2–5.

McHugh, P. R. (2005). *The mind has mountains: Reflections on society and psychiatry.* Baltimore, MD: Johns Hopkins Press.

McHugh, P. R. (2008). Try to remember: Psychiatry's clash over meaning, memory and mind. Washington, DC. Dana Press.

McLellarn, R. W., & Rosenzweig, J. (2004). Generalized anxiety disorder. In B. A. Thyer & J. A. Wodarski (Eds.), *Handbook of empirical social work, Vol. 1, Mental Disorders* (pp. 385–397). Hoboken, NJ: Wiley.

McLeod, J. D. (1994). Anxiety disorders and marital quality. *Journal of Abnormal Psychology, 103,* 767–776.

McQuaide, S., & Ehrenreich, J. H. (1997). Assessing clients' strengths. Families in Society. *The Journal of Contemporary Human Services, 78*(2), 201–212.

Meehl, P. E. (1975). Hedonic capacity: Some conjectures. *Bulletin of Menninger Clinic, 39,* 295–307.

Mendlowitz, S. L., Manassis, K., Bradley, S., Scapillato, D., Muezitis, S., & Shaw, B. F. (1999). Cognitive-behavioral group treatments in childhood anxiety disorders: The role of personal involvement. *Journal of the American Academy of Child and Adolescent Psychiatry, 38*(10), 1223–1229.

Mennin, D. S. (2001). *Examining the relationship between emotion and worry: A test of the avoidance theory of generalized anxiety disorder.* Doctoral dissertation, Temple University, Philadelphia, PA.

Mennin, D. S. (2004). Emotion regulation therapy for generalized anxiety disorder. *Clinical Psychology and Psychotherapy, 11,* 17–29.

Mennin, D. S. (2006). Emotion regulation therapy: An integrative approach to treatment-resistant anxiety disorders. *Journal of Contemporary Psychotherapy, 36,* 95–105.

Mennin, D. S., Heimberg, R. G., & Turk, C. L. (2004). Clinical presentation and diagnostic features. In R. G. Heimberg, C. L. Turk, & D. S. Mennin (Eds.), *Generalized anxiety disorder: Advances in research and practice* (pp. 3–28). New York: Guilford Press.

Mennin, D. S., Turk, C. L., Heimberg, R. G., & Carmin, C. N. (2004). Focusing on the regulation of emotion: A new direction for conceptualizing and treating generalized anxiety disorder. In M. A. Reinecke & D. A. Clark (Eds.), *Cognitive therapy across the life span: Evidence and practice* (pp. 60–89). New York: Cambridge University Press.

Mennin, D.S., Heimberq, R.G., Turk, C.L., & Fresco, D.M. (2002). Applying an emotion regulation framework to integrative approaches to generalized anxiety disorders. Clinical Psychology: Science and Practice, 9, 85–90.

Mennin, D. S., Heimberg, R. G., Turk, C. L., & Fresco, D. M. (2005). Preliminary evidence for an emotion dysregulation model of generalized anxiety disorder. *Behavioural Research and Therapy, 43,* 1281–1310.

Menza, M. M., Dobkin, R. D., & Marin, H. (2007). An open-label trial of aripiprazole augmentation for treatment resistant generalized anxiety disorder. *Journal of Clinical Psychopharmacology, 22*(2), 207–210.

Meoni, P., Hackett, D., & Lader, M. (2004). Pooled analysis of venlafaxine XR efficacy on somatic and psychic symptoms of anxiety in patients with generalized anxiety disorder. *Depression and Anxiety, 19*(2), 127–132.

Merikangas, K. R., & Low, N. C. (2005). Genetic epidemiology of anxiety disorders. *Handbook of Experimental Pharmacology, 169,* 163–179.

Messer, S. B. (2001). Empirically supported treatment: What's a non-behaviorist to do? In B. D. Slife, R. N. Williams, & D. H. Barlow (Eds.), *Critical issues in psychotherapy: Translating new ideas into practice* (pp. 3–19). Thousand Oaks, CA: Sage.

Messer, S. B. (2002). Empirically supported treatments: Cautionary notes. *Medscape General Medicine, 4,* 1–4.

Messer, S. B. (2004). Evidence-based practice: Beyond empirically supported treatments. *Professional Psychology: Research and Practice, 35*(6), 580–588.

Meyer, T. J., Miller, M. L., Metzger, R. L., & Borkovec, T. D. (1990). Development and validation of the Penn State Worry Questionnaire. *Behaviour Research and Therapy, 28,* 487–495.

Miller, C. (2003). Interviewing strategies. In M. Hersen & S. M. Turner (Eds.), Diagnostic interviewing (3rd ed., pp. 47–66). New York: Kluwer Academic.

Miller, J. J., Fletcher, K., & Kabat-Zinn, J. (1995). Three-year follow up and clinical implications of a mindfulness meditation-based stress reduction intervention in the treatment of generalized anxiety disorders. *General Hospital Psychiatry, 17,* 192–200.

Miller, P. R., Dasher, R., Collins, R., Griffiths, P., & Brown, F. (2001). Inpatient diagnostic assessments: 1. Accuracy of structured vs. unstructured interviews. *Psychiatry Research, 105,* 255–264.

Mitte, K., Noack, P., Steel, R., & Hautzinger, M. (2005). A meta-analytic review of the efficacy of drug treatment in generalized anxiety disorder. *Journal of Clinical Psychopharmacology, 25,* 141–150.

Moffitt, T. E., Harrington, H., Caspi, A., Kim-Cohen, J., Goldberg, D., Gregory, A. M., & Poulton, R. (2007). Depression and generalized anxiety disorder: Cumulative and sequential comorbidity in a birth cohort followed prospectively to age 32 years. *Archives of General Psychiatry, 64,* 651–660.

Mohlman, J., Gorenstein, E. E., Kleber, M., deJesus, M., Gorman, J. M., & Papp, L. A. (2003). Standard and enhanced cognitive-behavior therapy for late-life generalized anxiety disorder: Two pilot investigations. *American Journal of Geriatric Psychiatry, 11,* 24–32.

Mohlman, J. (2004). Psychosocial treatment of late-life generalized anxiety: Current status and future directions. *Clinical Psychology Review, 24,* 149–169.

Mohlman, J., & Gorman, J. M. (2005). The role of executive functioning in CBT: A pilot study with anxious older adults. *Behaviour Research and Therapy, 43,* 447–465.

Mohlman, J., & Price, R. (2006). Recognizing and treating late-life generalized anxiety disorder: Distinguishing features and psychosocial treatment. *Expert Review of Neurotherapeutics, 6*(10), 1–7.

Moller, H. J., Volz, H. P., Reimann, I. W., & Stoll, K. D. (2001). Opipramol for the treatment of generalized anxiety disorder: A placebo-controlled trial including an alprazalom-treated group. *Journal of Clinical Psychopharmacology, 21,* 59–65.

Montgomery, S. A., & Asberg, M. (1979). A new depression scale designed to be sensitive to change. *British Journal of Psychiatry, 134,* 382–389.

Montgomery, S. A. (2006). Pregabalin for the treatment of generalized anxiety disorder. *Expert Opinion Pharmacotherapy, 7,* 2139–2154.

Montgomery, S. A., Tobias, K., Zornberg, G. L., Kasper, S., & Pande, A. C. (2006). Efficacy and safety of pregabalin in the treatment of generalized anxiety disorder: A 6-week, multicenter, randomized. Double-blind, placebo-controlled comparison of pregabalin and venlafaxine. *Journal of Clinical Psychiatry, 67,* 771–782.

Montgomery, S., Chatamra, K., Pauer, L., Whalen, E., & Baldinetti, E. (2008). Efficacy and safety of pregabalin in elderly patients with generalized anxiety disorder. British Journal of Psychiatry, 193, 389–394.

Montorio, I., Nuevo, R., Marquez, M., Izal, M., & Losada, A. (2003). Characterization of worry according to the severity of anxiety. *Aging and Mental Health, 7,* 334–341.

Morris, T. L., Hirshfeld-Becker, D. R., Hennin, A., & Storch, E. A. (2004). Developmentally sensitive assessment of social anxiety. *Cognitive and Behavioral Practice, 11*, 13–28.

Moses, E. B., & Barlow, D. H. (2006). A new unified treatment approach emotional disorders based on emotion science. *Current Directions in Psychological Science, 15*(3), 146–150.

Muller, N. (2001). *Risiken und vulnerabilitaten der sozialen angs tstorung.* Doctoral dissertation, Banberg.

Mumford, G. K., Evans, S. M., Fleishaker, J. C., & Griffiths, R. R. (1995). Alprazalom absorption kinetics affects abuse liability. *Clinical Pharmacology and Therapeutics, 57*(3), 356–365.

Munjack, D. J., Baltazar, P. L., DeQuattro, V., Sobin, P., Palmer, R., Zulueta, A., Crocker, B., Usigli, R., Buckwalter, G., & Leonard, M. (1990). Generalized anxiety disorder: Some biochemical aspects. *Psychiatry Research, 32*(1), 35–43.

Muris, P., Mayer, B., Bartfelds, E., Tierney, S., & Bogie, N. (2001). The revised version of the Screen for Child Anxiety Related Emotional Disorders (SCARED-R): Treatment sensitivity in an early intervention for childhood anxiety disorders. *British Journal of Clinical Psychology, 40*, 323–336.

Nauta, M. H., Scholing, A., Emmelkamp, P. M., & Minderaa, R. B. (2003). Cognitive-behavioral therapy for children with anxiety disorders in a clinical setting: No additional effect of a cognitive parent training. *Journal of the American Academy of Child and Adolescent Psychiatry, 42*, 1270–1278.

Newman, M. J., & Borkovec, T. (1995). Cognitive-behavioral treatment of generalized anxiety disorder. *The Clinical Psychologist, 48*, 5–7.

Newman, M. G., Castonguay, L. G., & Borkovec, J. D. (1999). *New dimensions in the treatment of generalized anxiety disorder: Interpersonal focus and emotional deepening.* Paper presented at the Society of the Exploration of Psychotherapy Integration, Miami, FL.

Newman, M. G. (2000a). Generalized anxiety disorder. In M. Hersen & M. Biaggio (Eds.), *Effective brief therapies: A clinician's guide* (pp. 157–178). San Diego, CA: Academic Press.

Newman, M. G. (2000b). Recommendations for a cost-offset model of psychotherapy allocation using generalized anxiety disorder as an example. *Journal of Consulting and Clinical Psychology, 68*(4), 549–555.

Newman, M. G., & Borkovec, T. D. (2002). Cognitive-behavioural therapy for worry and generalized anxiety disorder. In G. Simos (Ed.), *Cognitive behaviour therapy: A guide for the practicing clinician* (pp. 150–172). New York: Taylor and Francis.

Newman, M. G., Zuellig, A. R., Kachin, K. E., Constantino, M. J., Przeworski, A., Erickson, T., & Cashman-Grath, L. (2002). Preliminary reliability and validity of the Generalized Anxiety Disorder Questionnaire-IV: A revised self-report diagnostic measure of generalized anxiety disorder. *Behavior Therapy, 33*, 215–233.

Newman, M. G., Castonguay, L. G., Borkovec, T. D., & Molnar, C. (2004). Integrative psychotherapy. In R. G. Heimberg, C. L. Turk, & D. S. Mennin (Eds.), *Generalized anxiety disorder: Advances in research and practice* (pp. 320–350). New York: Guilford Press.

Newman, M. G., Castonguay, L. G., Borkovec, T. D., Fisher, A. J., & Nordberg, S. S. (2008). An open trial of integrative therapy for generalized anxiety disorder. *Psychotherapy: Theory, Research, Practice, Training, 45*(2), 135–147.

Nimatoudis, I., Zissis, N. P., Kogeorgos, J., Theodoropoulous, S., Vidalis, A., & Kaprinis, G. (2004). Remission rates with venlafaxine extended release in Greek outpatients with generalized anxiety disorder: A double-blind, randomized, placebo controlled study. *International Clinical Psychopharmacology, 19*, 331–336.

Ninan, P. T. (2002). New insights into the diagnosing and pharmacologic management of generalized anxiety disorder. *Psychopharmacology Bulletin, 36*(2), 105–122.

Norcross, J. C. (2002). *Psychotherapy relationships that work.* New York: Oxford University Press.

Norcross, J. C., Hedges, M., & Castle, P. H. (2002). Psychologists conducting psychotherapy in 2001: A study of the Division 29 membership. *Psychotherapy, 39*, 97–102.

Norcross, J. C. (2005). A primer on psychotherapy integration. In J. C. Norcross & M. R. Goldfried (Eds.), *Handbook of psychotherapy integration* (2nd ed., pp. 3–23). New York: Oxford.

Nordhus, I. H., & Pallesen, S. (2003). Psychological treatment of late-life anxiety: An empirical review. *Journal of Consulting and Clinical Psychology, 71*, 643–651.

Norton, P. J., Asmundson, G. J. G., Cox, B. J., & Norman, G. R. (2000). Future directions in anxiety disorders: Profiles and perspectives of leading contributors. *Journal of Anxiety Disorders, 14*, 69–95.

Norton, P. J., & Price, E. C. (2007). A meta-analytic review of adult cognitive-behavioral treatment outcome across the anxiety disorders. *The Journal of Nervous and Mental Disease, 195*(6), 521–531.

Novick-Kline, P., Turk, C. L., Mennin, D. S., Hoyt, E. A., & Gallagher, C. L. (2005). Level of emotional awareness as a differentiating variable between individuals with and without generalized anxiety disorder. *Journal of Anxiety Disorders, 19*, 557–572.

Noyes, R., Clarkson, C., Crowe, R. R., Yates, W. R., & McChesney, C. M. (1987). A family study of generalized anxiety disorder. *American Journal of Psychiatry, 144*(8), 1019–1024.

Noyes, R., Woodman, C., Garvey, M. J., Cook, B. L., Suelzer, M., Clancy, J., & Anderson, D. J. (1992). Generalized anxiety disorder vs. panic disorder: Distinguishing characteristics and patterns of comorbidity. *The Journal of Nervous and Mental Disease, 180*, 369–379.

Noyes, R. (2001). Comorbidity in generalized anxiety disorder. *Psychiatric Clinics of North America, 24*(1), 41–55.

Nutt, D. J. (2001). Neurobiological mechanisms in generalized anxiety disorder. *Journal of Clinical Psychiatry, 62*(Suppl. 11), 22–27.

Nutt, D., Argyropoulous, S. V., & Forshall, S. (2001). *Generalized anxiety disorder: Diagnosis, treatment and its relationship to other anxiety disorders* (3rd ed.). London, UK: Martin Dunitz/Informa Healthcare.

Nutt, D., Rickels, K., & Stein, D. J. (Eds.). (2002). *Generalized anxiety disorder: Symptomatology, pathogenesis and management*. London, UK: Martin Dunitz.

Nutt, D. J., & Ballenger, J. C. (Eds.). (2003). *Anxiety Disorders*. London, UK: Blackwell.

Nutt, D. J. (2005). Overview of diagnosis and drug treatments of anxiety disorders. *CNS Spectrums, 10*(1), 49–56.

Ohara, G. E., Suzuki, Y., Ochiai, M., Tsukamoto, T., & Tani, K. (1999). A variable-number-tandem-repeat of the serotonin transporter gene and anxiety disorders. *Progress in Neuro-Psychopharmacology and Biological Psychiatry, 23*(1), 55–65.

Olajide, D., & Lader, M. (1987). A comparison of buspirone, diazepam, and placebo in patients with chronic anxiety states. *Journal of Clinical Psychopharmacology, 7*, 148–152.

Olfson, M., Weissman, M. M., Leon, A. C., Sheehan, D. V., & Farber, L. (1996). Suicidal ideation in primary care. *Journal of General Internal Medicine, 11*, 447–453.

Orlinsky, D. A., Grawe, K., & Parks, B. K. (1994). Process and outcome in psychotherapy: Noch einmal. In A. E. Bergin & S. L. Garfield (Eds.), Handbook of psychotherapy and behavior change (4th ed., pp. 270–376). New York: Wiley.

Ormel, J., Von Korff, M., Ustun, B., Dini, S., Korten, A., & Oldenhinkel, T. (1994). Common mental disorders and disabilities across cultures: Results from the WHO Collaborative Study on psychological problems in general health care. *Journal of the American Medical Association, 272*, 1741–1748.

Orsillo, S. M., Roemer, L., & Barlow, D. H. (2003). Integrating acceptance and mindfulness into existing cognitive-behavioral treatment for GAD: A case study. *Cognitive and Behavioral Practice, 10*, 222–230.

Orsillo, S. M., Roemer, L., Lerner, J. B., & Tull, M. T. (2004). Acceptance, mindfulness, and cognitive-behavioral therapy. In S. C. Hayes, V. M. Follette, & M. M. Linehan (Eds.), *Mindfulness and acceptance: Expanding the cognitive-behavioral tradition* (pp. 66-95). New York: Guilford Press.

Ost, L. G., & Breitholtz, E. (2000). Applied relaxation vs. cognitive therapy in the treatment of generalized anxiety disorder. *Behaviour Research and Therapy, 38*, 777–790.

Owen, R. T. (2007). Pregabalin: Its efficacy, safety and tolerability profile in generalized anxiety. *Drugs of Today*, *43*(9), 601–610.

Pande, A. C., Crockatt, J. G., Feltner, D. E., Liu-Dumaw, M., & Werth, J. L. (2000). Pregabalin GAD study group: Three randomized, placebo-controlled double-blind trials of pregabalin treatment of generalized anxiety disorder (GAD). *European Neuropsychopharmacology*, *10*(Suppl. 3), 344.

Pande, A. C., Crockatt, J. G., Feltner, D. E., Janney, C. A., Smith, W. T., Weisler, R., Londborg, P. D., Bielski, R. J., Zimbroff, D. L., Davidson, J. R. T., & Liu-Dumaw, M. (2003). Pregabalin in generalized anxiety disorder: A placebo-controlled trial. *American Journal of Psychiatry*, *160*, 533–540.

Parloff, M. B. (1979). Can psychotherapy research guide the policy maker? A little knowledge may be a dangerous thing. *American Psychologist, 34,* 296–306.

Paykel, E. S. (1985). The clinical interview for depression: Development, reliability and validity. *Journal of Affective Disorders*, *9*, 85–96.

Pecknold, J. C., Matas, M., Howarth, B. G., Ross, C., Swinson, R., Vezeau, C., & Ungar, W. (1989). Evaluation of buspirone as an antianxiety agent: Buspirone and diazepam versus placebo. *Canadian Journal of Psychiatry*, *34*, 766–771.

Pestle, S. L., Chorpita. B. F., & Schiffman, J. E. Psychometric properties of the Penn State Worry Questionnaire for children in a large clinical sample. *Journal of Clinical Child and Adolescent Psychology* (in press).

Pincus, A. L., & Borkovec, T. D. (1994). *Interpersonal problems in generalized anxiety disorder: Preliminary clustering of patients' interpersonal dysfunction.* Paper presented at the Annual Meeting of the American Psychological Society, New York.

Pinquart, M., & Duberstein, P. R. (2007). Treatment of anxiety disorders in older adults: A meta-analytic comparison of behavioral and pharmacological interventions. *American Journal of Geriatric Psychiatry*, *15*(8), 639–651.

Pohl, R. B., Feltner, D. E., Fieve, R. R., & Pande, A. C. (2005). Efficacy of pregabalin in the treatment of generalized anxiety disorder. Double-blind, placebo-controlled comparison of BID versus TID dosing. *Journal of Clinical Psychopharmacology*, *25*, 151–158.

Pollack, M. H., Worthington, J. J., Manfro, G. G., Otto, M. W., & Zucker, B. G. (1997). Abecarnil for the treatment of generalized anxiety disorder: A placebo-controlled comparison of two dosage ranges of abecarnil and buspirone. *Journal of Clinical Psychiatry*, *58*(Suppl. 11), 19–23.

Pollack, M. H., Smoller, J. W., & Lee, D. K. (1998). Approaches to the anxious patient. In T. A. Stern, J. B. Herman, & P. L. Slavin (Eds.), *The MGH guide to psychiatry in primary care (pp. 23–37),* New York: McGraw-Hill.

Pollack, M. H. (2001). Optimizing pharmacotherapy of generalized anxiety disorder to achieve remission. *Journal of Clinical Psychiatry*, *62*(Suppl. 19), 20–25.

Pollack, M. H., Zaninelli, R., Goddard, A., McCafferty, J. B., Bellew, K. M., Burham, D. B., & Iyengar, M. K. (2001). Paroxetine in the treatment of generalized anxiety disorder: Results of a placebo-controlled, flexible-dosage trial. *Journal of Clinical Psychiatry*, *62*, 350–357.

Pollack, M. H. (2002). *Generalized anxiety disorder: Long-term treatment to improve outcome.* Paper presented at the Annual Meeting of the American Psychiatric Association, Philadelphia.

Pollack, M. H., Roy-Byrne, P. P., Van Ameringen, M. V., Snyder, H., Brown, C., Ondrasik, J., & Rickels, K. (2005). The selective GABA reuptake inhibitor tiagabine for the treatment of generalized anxiety disorder: Results of a placebo-controlled study. *Journal of Clinical Psychiatry*, *66*, 1401–1408.

Pollack, M. H. (2006). Generalized anxiety disorder – Overview and case history. *Medscape*, 1–13.

Pollack, M. H., Simon, N. M., Zalta, A. K., Worthington, J. J., Hoge, E. A., Mick, E., Kinrys, G., & Oppenheimer, J. (2006). Olanzapine augmentation of fluoxetine for refractory generalized anxiety disorder: A placebo controlled study. *Biological Psychiatry*, *59*, 211–215.

Pollack, M. H., Otto, M. W., Roy-Byrne, P. P., Coplan, J. D., Rothbaum, B. O., Simon, N. M., & Gorman, J. M. (2007). Novel treatment approaches for refractory anxiety disorders. *Depression and Anxiety, 25*(6), 467–476.

Pollack, M. H., Tiller, J., Xie, F., & Trivedi, M. (2008). Tiagabine in adult patients with generalized anxiety disorder: results from 3 randomized, double-blind, placebo-controlled, parallel-group studies. *Journal of Clinical Psychopharmacology, 28*(3), 308–316.

Pollack, M., Kinrys, G., Krystal, A., Vaughn, W. M., Roth, T., Schaefer, K., Rubens, R., Roach, J., Huang, H., & Krishnan, R. (2008). Eszopiclone coadministered with escitalopram in patients with insomnia and comorbid generalized anxiety disorder. *Archives of General Psychiatry, 65*(5), 551–562.

Pollock, R., & Kuo, I. (2004). Treatment of anxiety disorders: An update. *Medscape*, 1–17.

Portman, M. (1995). *Generalized anxiety disorder: Enigmas and paradoxes*. Final paper. Unpublished manuscript. The Ohio State University, Columbus, OH.

Powers, C. B., Wisocki, P. A., & Whitbourne, S. K. (1992). Age difference and correlates of worrying in young and elderly adults. *The Gerontologist, 32*, 82–88.

Preston, J., & Johnson, J. (2004). *Clinical psychopharmacology made ridiculously simple* (5th ed.). Miami, FL: MedMaster.

Rapee, R. M. (1985). Distinctions between panic disorder and generalized anxiety disorder: Clinical presentation. *Australian and New Zealand Journal of Psychiatry, 19*, 227–232.

Rapee, R. M. (1991). Generalized anxiety disorder: A review of clinical features and theoretical concepts. *Clinical Psychology Review, 11*, 419–440.

Rapee, R. M., Barrett, D. M., Dadds, M. R., & Evans, L. (1994). Reliability of the DSM-III-R childhood anxiety disorders using structured interview: Interrater and parent-child agreement. *Journal of the American Academy of Child and Adolescent Psychiatry, 33*, 984–992.

Rapee, R. M. (2000). Group treatment of children with anxiety disorders: Outcome and predictors of treatment response. *Australian Journal of Psychology, 52*, 125–129.

Reinblatt, S. P., & Riddle, M. A. (2007). The pharmacological management of childhood anxiety disorders: A review. *Psychopharmacology, 191*, 67–86.

Reynolds, C. R., & Richmond, B. O. (1979). Factor, structure, and construct validity of "What I think and feel": The Revised Children's Manifest Anxiety Scale. *Journal of Personality Assessment., 43*, 281–283.

Rickels, K., Weisman, K., Norstad, N., Singer, M., Stoltz, D., Brown, A., & Danton, J. (1982). Buspirone and diazepam in anxiety: A controlled study. *Journal of Clinical Psychiatry, 43*, 81–86.

Rickels, K., Case, W. G., Schweizer, E., Garcia-Espana, F., & Fridman, R. (1991). Long-term benzodiazepine users after 3 years in a discontinuation program. American Journal of Psychiatry, 148, 757–761.

Rickels, K., Downing, R., Schweizer, E., & Hassman, H. (1993). Antidepressants for the treatment of generalized anxiety disorder: A placebo-controlled comparison of imipramine, trazadone and diazepam. *Archives of General Psychiatry, 50*(11), 884–895.

Rickels, K., Pollack, M. H., Sheehan, D. V., & Haskins, J. T. (2000). Efficacy of extended-release venlafaxine in non-depressed outpatients with generalized anxiety disorder. *American Journal of Psychiatry, 157*, 968–974.

Rickels, K., & Rynn, M. (2001). Overview and clinical presentation of generalized anxiety disorder. *The Psychiatric Clinics of North America, 24*(1), 1–17.

Rickels, K., & Rynn, M. (2002). Pharmacotherapy of generalized anxiety disorder. *Journal of Clinical Psychiatry, 63*(Suppl. 14), 9–16.

Rickels, K., Pollack., M. H., Lydiard, R. B., Bielski, R. J., Feltner, D. E., Pande, A. C., & Kavoussi, R. J. (2002). *Efficacy and safety of pregabalin and alprazalom in generalized anxiety disorder.* Paper presented at the Annual Meeting of the American Psychiatric Association, Philadelphia.

Rickels, K., Zaninelli, R., McCafferty, J., Bellew, K., Iyengar, M., & Sheehan, D. (2003). Paroxetine treatment of generalized anxiety disorder: A double blind, placebo-controlled study. *American Journal of Psychiatry, 160*, 749–756.

Rickels, K., Pollack, M. H., Feltner, D. E., Lydiard, R. B., Zimbroff, D. L., Bielski, R. J., Tobias, K., Brock, J. D., Zornberg, G. L., & Pande, A. C. (2005). Pregabalin for treatment of generalized anxiety disorder: A 4-week, multicenter, double-blind, placebo-controlled trial of pregabalin and alprazalom. *Archives of General Psychiatry, 62*, 1022–1030.

Rickels, K., Rynn, M., Iyengar, M., & Duff, D. (2006). Remission of generalized anxiety disorder: A review of the paroxetine clinical trials database, *Journal of Clinical Psychiatry, 67*, 41–47.

Riskind, J. H., Williams, N. L., Gessner, T., Chrosniak, L. D., & Cortina, J. (2000). The looming maladaptive style: Anxiety, danger, and schematic processing. *Journal of Personality and Social Psychology, 79*, 837–852.

Riskind, J. H. (2004). Cognitive theory and research on generalized anxiety disorder. In R. L. Leahy (Ed.), *Contemporary cognitive therapy: Theory, research and practice* (pp. 62–85). New York: Guilford Press.

Riskind, J. H. (2005). Cognitive mechanisms in generalized anxiety disorder: A second generation of theoretical perspectives. *Cognitive Therapy and Research, 29*(1), 1–5.

Riskind, J. H., & Williams, N. L. (2005). The looming cognitive style and generalized anxiety disorder: Distinctive danger schemas and cognitive phenomenology. *Cognitive Therapy and Research, 29*(1), 7–27.

Riskind, J. H., & Williams, N. L. (2006). A unique vulnerability common to all anxiety disorders: The looming maladaptive style. In L. B. Alloy & J. H. Riskind (Eds.), *Cognitive vulnerability to emotional disorders* (pp. 175–206). Mahwah, NJ: Lawrence Erlbaum Associates.

Riskind, J. H., Williams, N. L., & Joiner, E. T. (2006). The looming cognitive style: A cognitive vulnerability for anxiety disorders. *Journal of Social and Clinical Psychology, 25*(7), 779–801.

Robichaud, M., & Dugas, M. J. (2006). A cognitive-behavioral treatment targeting intolerance of uncertainty. In G. C. L. Davey & A. Wells (Eds.), *Worry and its psychological disorders: Theory, assessment and treatment* (pp. 289–304). Chichester, UK: Wiley.

Robins, L. N., & Regier, D. A. (Eds.). (1991). *Psychiatric disorders in America: The Epidemiologic Catchment Area Study*. New York: Free Press.

Rocca, P., Fonzo, V., Scotta, M., Zanalda, E., & Ravizza, L. (1997). Paroxetine efficacy in the treatment of generalized anxiety disorder. *Acta Psychiatrica Scandinavica, 95*, 444–450.

Rocca, P., Beoni, A. M., Eva, C., Ferrero, P., Zanalda, E., & Ravizza, L. (1998). Peripheral benzodiazepine receptors messenger RNA is deceased in lymphocytes of generalized anxiety disorder patients. *Biological Psychiatry, 43*(10), 767–773.

Roemer, L., Molina, S., & Borkovec, T. D. (1997). An investigating of worry content among generally anxious individuals. *Journal of Nervous and Mental Disease, 185*, 314–319.

Roemer, L., Molina, S., Litz, B. T., & Borkovec, T. D. (1997). Preliminary investigation of the role of previous exposure to potentially traumatizing events in generalized anxiety disorder. *Depression and Anxiety, 4*, 134–138.

Roemer, L., & Medaglia, E. (2001). Generalized anxiety disorder: A brief review guide to assessment. In M. M. Antony, S. M. Orsillo, & L. Roemer (Eds.), *Practitioner's guide to empirically based measures of anxiety* (pp. 189–195). New York: Kluwer Academic.

Roemer, L., & Orsillo, S. M. (2002). Expanding our conceptualization of and treatment for generalized anxiety disorder: Integrating mindfulness/acceptance-based approaches with existing cognitive-behavioral models. *Clinical Psychology: Science and Practice, 9*, 54–68.

Roemer, L., Orsillo, S. M., & Barlow, D. H. (2002). Generalized anxiety disorder. In D. H. Barlow (Ed.), *Anxiety and its disorder: The nature and treatment of anxiety and panic* (2nd ed., pp. 477–515). New York: Guilford Press.

Roemer, L., & Orsillo, S. M. (2005). Acceptance-based behavior therapy for generalized anxiety disorder. In S. M. Orsillo & L. Roemer (Eds.), *Acceptance and mindfulness-based approaches to anxiety: Conceptualization and treatment* (pp. 213–240). New York: Springer.

Roemer, L., Salters, K., Raffa, S.D., & Orsillo, S.M. (2005). Fear and avoidance of internal experiences in GAD: Preliminary tests of a conceptual model. Cognitive Therapy and Research, 29(1), 71–88.

Roemer, L., Salters-Pedneault, K., & Orsillo, S. M. (2006). Incorporating mindfulness and acceptance-based strategies in the treatment of generalized anxiety disorder. In R. A. Baer (Ed.), *Mindfulness-based treatment approaches: Clinician's guide to evidence base and applications* (pp. 51–74). Boston: Academic Press.

Roemer, L., & Orsillo, S. M. (2007). An open trial of an acceptance-based behavior therapy for generalized anxiety disorder. *Behavior Therapy, 38*, 72–85.

Roemer, L., Orsillo, S. M., & Salters-Pedneault, K. (2008) Efficacy of an acceptance-based behavior therapy for generalized anxiety disorder: Evaluation in a randomized controlled trial. *Journal of Consulting and Clinical Psychology*76(6), 1083–1089.

Roe-Sepowitz, D. E., Bedard, L. E., & Thyer, B. A. (2005). Anxiety. In C. N. Dulmus & L. A. Rapp-Paglicci (Eds.), *Handbook of preventive interventions for adults* (pp. 13–26). Hoboken, NJ: Wiley.

Rogers, M. P., Warshaw, M. G., Goisman, R. M., Goldenberg, I., Rodriquez-Villa, F., Mallya, G., Freeman, S. A., & Keller, M. B. (1999). Comparing primary and secondary generalized anxiety disorder in a long-term naturalistic study of anxiety disorders. *Depression and Anxiety, 10*, 1–7.

Rosenbaum, J. F., Pollack, M. H., Otto, M. W., & Berstein, J. G. (1997). Anxious patients. In N. H. Cassem, T. A. Stern, J. F. Rosenbaum, & M. S. Jellinek (Eds.), *Massachusetts General Hospital handbook of general hospital psychiatry* (4th ed., pp. 173–210). St. Louis: Mosby-Year Book.

Rosenthal, M. (2003). Tiagabine for the treatment of generalized anxiety disorder: A randomized, open-label, clinical trial with paroxetine as a positive control. *Journal of Clinical Psychiatry, 64*, 1245–1249.

Roth, W. T., Doberenz, S., Dietel, A., Conrad, A., Mueller, A., Wollburg, E., Meuret, A. E., Taylor, C. B., & Kim, S. (2008). Sympathetic activation in broadly defined generalized anxiety disorder. *Journal of Psychiatric Research, 42*(3), 205–212.

Roy, M.-A., Neale, M. C., Pedersen, N. C., Mathe, A. A., & Kendler, K. S. (1995). A twin study of generalized anxiety disorder and major depression. *Psychological Medicine, 25*, 1037–1049.

Roy-Byrne, P. P. (1996). Generalized anxiety and mixed-anxiety depression: Association with disability and health care utilization. *Journal of Clinical Psychology, 57*, 86–91.

Roy-Byrne, P. P., & Katon, N. (1997). Generalized anxiety disorder in primary care: The precursor modifier pathway to increased health care utilization. *Journal of Clinical Psychiatry, 58*, 34–38.

Roy-Bryne, P., & Cowley, D. S. (1998). Clinical approach to treatment-resistant panic disorder: In J. F. Rosenbaum & M. H. Pollack (Eds.), *Panic disorder and its treatment* (pp. 205–227). New York: Marcel Dekker.

Rubio, G., & Lopez-Ibor, J. J. (2006). Generalized anxiety disorder: A 40-year follow up study. *Acta Psychiatrica Scandinavica, 115*, 372–379.

Ruini, C., & Fava, G. A. (2004). Clinical applications of well-being therapy. In G. P. Linley & S. Joseph (Eds.), *Positive psychology in practice* (pp. 371–387). New York: Wiley.

RUPP Anxiety Study Group (2001). Fluvoxamine for the treatment of anxiety disorders in children and adolescents. *New England Journal of Medicine, 344*(17), 1279–1285.

RUPP (2002). Treatment of pediatric anxiety disorders: An open-label extension of the research units on pediatric psychopharmacology anxiety study: *Journal of Child and Adolescent Psychopharmacology, 12*, 175–188.

Ruscio, A. M., Lane, M., Roy-Byrne, P., Stang, P. E., Stein, D. J., Wittchen, H. U., & Kessler, R. C. (2005). Should excessive worry be required for a diagnosis of generalized anxiety disorder? Results from the US National Comorbidity Survey Replication. *Psychological Medicine, 35*, 1761–1772.

Ryff, C. D. (1989). Happiness is everything, or is it? Explorations in the meaning of psychological well-being. *Journal of Personality and Social Psychology, 57*, 1069–1081.

Ryff, C. D., & Singer, B. H. (1996). Psychological well-being, meaning, measurement and implications for psychotherapy research. *Psychotherapy and Psychosomatics, 65*, 14–23.

Rygh, J. L., & Sanderson, W. C. (2004). *Treating generalized anxiety disorder: Evidenced-based strategies, tools, and techniques.* New York: Guilford Press.

Rynn, M. A., Siqueland, L., & Rickels, K. (2001). Placebo-controlled trial of sertraline in the treatment of children with generalized anxiety disorder. *American Journal of Psychiatry, 158*(12), 2008–2014.

Rynn, M. A., & Franklin, M. (2002). Generalized anxiety disorder in children and adolescents. In D. Nutt, K. Rickels, & D. J. Stein (Eds.), *Generalized anxiety disorder: Symptomatology, pathogenesis and management* (pp. 155–170). London, UK: Martin Dunitz.

Rynn, M. A., & Brawman-Mintzer, O. (2004). Generalized anxiety disorder: Acute and chronic treatment. *CNS Spectrums, 9*(10), 716–723.

Rynn, M. A., Riddle, M. A., Yeung, P. P., & Kunz, N. R. (2007). Efficacy and safety of extended release venlafaxine in the treatment of generalized anxiety disorder in children and adolescents: Two placebo-controlled trials. *American Journal of Psychiatry, 164*, 290–300.

Rynn, M., Russell, J., Erickson, J., Detke, M. J., Ball, S., Dinkel, J., Rickels, K., & Raskin, J. (2008). Efficacy and safety of duloxetine in the treatment of generalized anxiety disorder: A flexible-dose, progressive-titration, placebo-controlled trial. *Depression and Anxiety, 25*(3), 182–189.

Saarni, C. (1990). Emotional competence: How emotions and relationships become integrated. In R. A. Thompson (Ed.), (1988). *Socioemotional development. Nebraska symposium on motivation* (pp. 115–182). Lincoln, NE: University of Nebraska Press.

Saarni, C. (1999). *The development of emotional competence.* New York: Guilford Press.

Safran, J. D., Crocker, P., McMain, S., & Murray, P. (1990). Therapeutic alliance rupture as a therapy event for empirical investigation. *Psychotherapy, 27*, 154–165.

Safran, J. D., Muran, J. C., & Samstag, L. W. (1994). Resolving therapeutic alliance ruptures: A task analytic investigation. In A. O. Horvath & L. S. Greenberg (Eds.), *The working alliance: Theory, research and practice* (pp. 225–255). Oxford, UK: Wiley.

Safran, J. D., & Segal, Z. V. (1990). *Interpersonal process in cognitive therapy.* New York: Basic Books.

Safran, J. D. (1998). *Widening the scope of cognitive therapy: The therapeutic relationship, emotion, and the process of change.* Northvale, NJ: Jason Aronson.

Safran, J. D., & Muran, J. C. (2000). *Negotiating the therapeutic alliance.* New York: Guilford Press.

Salters-Pedneault, K., Roemer, L., Tull, M. T., Rucker, L., & Mennin, D. S. (2006). Evidence of broad deficits in emotion regulation associated with chronic worry and generalized anxiety disorder. *Cognitive Therapy Research, 3*, 469–480.

Salzman, C., Goldenberg, I., Bruce, S. E., & Keller, M. B. (2001). Pharmacologic treatment of anxiety disorders in 1989 versus 1996. Results from the Harvard Brown Anxiety Disorders Research Program. *Journal of Clinical Psychiatry, 62*, 149–152.

Sanavio, E. (1988). Obsession and compulsions: The Padua Inventory. *Behaviour Research and Therapy, 26*, 169–177.

Sanderson, K., & Andrews, G. (2002). Prevalence and severity of mental-health related disability and relationship to diagnosis. *Psychiatric Services, 53*, 80–86.

Sanderson, W. C., & Barlow, D. H. (1990). A description of patients diagnosed with DSM-III-R generalized anxiety disorder. *The Journal of Nervous and Mental Disease, 178*, 588–591.

Sanderson, W. C., Wetzler, S., Beck, A. T., & Betz, F. (1994). Prevalence of personality disorders among patients with anxiety disorders. *Psychiatry Research, 51*, 167–174.

Sanderson, W. C., & Rego, S. A. (2000). Movement toward evidence-based psychotherapies. *Trends in Evidence-Based Neuropsychiatry, 2*, 50–55.

Schaller, J. L., Thomas, J., & Rawlings, D. (2004). Low-dose tiagabine effectiveness in anxiety disorders. *Medscape General Medicine, 6*(3), 8.

Scharko, A. M. (2004). Selective serotonin reuptake inhibitor – individual sexual dysfunction in adolescents: A review. *Journal of the American Academy of Child and Adolescent Psychiatry, 43*, 1071–1079.

Scherrer, J. F., True, W. R., Ian, H., Lyons, M. J., Eisen, S. A., Goldberg, J., Lin, N., & Tsuang, M. T. (2000). Evidence for genetic influence common and specific to symptoms of generalized anxiety and panic. *Journal of Affective Disorders, 57*, 25–35.

Schniering, C. A., Hudson, J. L., & Rapee, R. M. (2000). Issues in the diagnosis and assessment of anxiety disorders in children and adolescents. *Clinical Psychology Review*, *20*, 453–478.

Schonfeld, W. H., Verboncoeur, C. J., Fifer, S. K., Lipschutz, R. C., Lubek, D. P., & Buesching, D. P. (1997). The functioning and well-being of patients with unrecognized anxiety disorders and major depressive disorder. *Journal of Affective Disorders*, *43*, 105–119.

Schottenbauer, M. A., Glass, C. R., & Arnkoff, D. B. (2005). Outcome research on psychotherapy integration. In J. C. Norcross & M. R. Goldfried (Eds.), *Handbook of Psychotherapy Integration* (pp. 459–493). New York: Oxford University Press.

Schulz, J., Gotto, J. G., & Rapaport, M. H. (2005). The diagnosis and treatment of generalized anxiety disorder. *Primary Psychiatry*, *12*(11), 58–67.

Schut, A. J., Castonguay, L. G., & Borkovec, T. D. (2001). Compulsive checking behaviors in generalized anxiety disorder. *Journal of Clinical Psychology*, *57*(6), 705–715.

Schuurmans, J., Comijs, H. C., Beekman, A. T. F., de Beurs, E., Deeg, D. J. H., Emmelkamp, P. M. G., & van Dyck, R. (2005). The outcome of anxiety disorders in older people at 6-year follow-up: Results from the Longitudinal Aging Study Amsterdam. *Acta Psychiatrica Scandinavica*, *111*, 420–428.

Schuurmans, J., Comijs, H., Emmelkamp, P. M. G., Gundy, C. M. M., Weijnen, I., van den Hout, M., & van Dyck, R. (2006). A Randomized controlled trial of the effectiveness of cognitive-behavioral therapy and sertraline versus a waitlist control group for anxiety disorders in older adults. *American Journal of Geriatric Psychiatry*, *14*, 255–263.

Schweizer, E. (1995). Generalized anxiety disorder: Longitudinal course and pharmacologic treatment. *Psychiatric Clinics of North America*, *18*, 843–857.

Scogin, F. R. (1998). Anxiety in old age. In I. H. Norhus, G. R. VandenBos, S. Berg, & P. Fromholt (Eds.), *Clinical geropsychology* (pp. 205–209). Washington, DC: American Psychological Association.

Segal, Z. V., Williams, J. M., & Teasdale, J. D. (2002). *Mindfulness-based cognitive therapy for depression: A new approach to preventing relapse*. New York: Guilford Press.

Seligman, M. E. P., Schulman, P., DeRubeis, R. J., & Hollon, S. D. (1999). *The prevention of depression and anxiety. Prevention and Treatment, 2*. Retrieved January 22, 2004, from http://journals.apa.org/prevention/volume2/pre0020008a.html

Seligman, M. E. P. (2002). Positive psychology, positive prevention, and positive therapy. In C. R. Snyder & S. J. Lopez (Eds.), *Handbook of positive psychology* (pp. 3–9). London: Oxford University Press.

Sevy, S., Papadimitriou, G. N., Surmount, D. W., Goldman, S., & Mendlewicz, J. (1989). Noradrenergic function in generalized anxiety, major depressive disorder, and healthy subjects. *Biological Psychiatry*, *25*(2), 141–152.

Shader, R. I., & Greenblatt, D. J. (1993). Use of benzodiazepines in anxiety disorders. *New England Journal of Medicine*, *328*(19), 1398–1405.

Shapiro, D. (1965). *Neurotic styles*. New York: Basic Books.

Shapiro, D. (1989). *Psychotherapy of the neurotic character*. New York: Basic Books.

Shear, K., Belnap, B. H., Mazumdar, S., Houck, P., & Rollman, B. L. (2006). Generalized anxiety disorder severity scale (GADSS): A preliminary validation study. *Depression and Anxiety*, *23*(2), 77–82.

Sheehan, D. V. (1983). The anxiety disease. New York: Scribners.

Sheehan, D. V., Harnett-Sheehan, K., & Raj, B. A. (1996). The measurability of disability. *International Clinical Psychopharmacology*, *11*(Suppl. 3), 89–95.

Sheikh, J. I., & Cassidy, E. L. (2000). Treatment of anxiety disorders in the elderly: Issues and strategies. *Journal of Anxiety Disorders*, *14*(2), 173–190.

Sherbourne, C. D., Wells, K. B., Meredith, L. S., Jackson, C. A., & Camp, P. (1996). Comorbid anxiety disorder and the functioning and well-being of chronically ill patients of general medical providers. *Archives of General Psychiatry*, *53*, 889–895.

Sherbourne, C. D., Wells, K., & Sturm, R. (1997). Measuring health outcomes for depression. *Evaluation & The Health Profession*, *20*, 47–64.

Shortt, A. L., Barrett, P. M., & Fox, T. L. (2001). Evaluating the FRIENDS program: A cognitive behavioral group treatment for anxious children and their parents. *Journal of Clinical Child Psychology*, *30*(4), 525–535.

Sibrava, N. J., & Borkovec, T. D. (2006). The cognitive avoidance theory of worry. In G. C. L. Davey & A. Wells (Eds.), *Worry and its psychological disorders: Theory, assessment and treatment* (pp. 239–256). Chichester, UK: Wiley.

Siev, J., & Chambless, D. L. (2007). Specificity of treatment effects: Cognitive therapy and relaxation for generalized anxiety and panic disorders. *Journal of Consulting and Clinical Psychology, 75*(4), 513–522.

Silva, R. R., Gallagher, R., & Minani, H. (2006). Cognitive-behavioral treatments for anxiety disorders in children and adolescents. *Primary Psychiatry, 13*(5), 68–76.

Silverman, W. K., & Nelles, W. B. (1988). The Anxiety Disorders Interview Schedule for Children. *Journal of the American Academy of Child and Adolescent Psychiatry, 27*, 772–778.

Silverman, W. K., & Albano, A. M. (1996). *The Anxiety Disorders Interview Schedule for DSM-IV, child revision*. San Antonio, TX: Psychological Corporation.

Silverman, W. K., Kurtines, W. M., Ginsburg, G. S., Weems, C. F., Lumpkin, P. W., & Carmichael, D. H. (1999). Treating anxiety disorders in children with group cognitive-behavioral therapy: A randomized clinical trial. *Journal of Consulting and Clinical Psychology, 67*, 995–1003.

Silverman, W. K., Saavedra, L. M., & Pina, A. A. (2001). Test-retest reliability of anxiety symptoms and diagnosis with the Anxiety Interview Schedule for DSM-IV: Child and parent versions. *Journal of the American Academy of Child and Adolescent Psychiatry, 40*, 937–944.

Simeon, J. G., & Ferguson, H. B. (1987). Alprazolom effects in children with anxiety disorders. *Canadian Journal of Psychiatry, 32*, 570–574.

Simeon, J. G., Ferguson, H. B., Knott, V., Roberts, N., Gauthier, B., Dubois, C., & Wiggins, D. (1992). Clinical, cognitive, and neurophysiological effects of alprazalom in children and adolescents with overanxious and avoidant disorders. *Journal of the American Academy of Child and Adolescent Psychiatry, 31*, 29–33.

Simeon, J. G., Knott, V. J., Dubois, C., & Wiggins, D. (1994). Buspirone therapy of mixed anxiety disorders in childhood and adolescence: A pilot study. *Journal of Child and Adolescent Psychopharmacology, 4*, 159–170.

Simon, N. M., Zalta, A. K., Worthington, J., Hoge, E. A., Christian, K. M., Stevens, J. C., & Pollack, M. H. (2006). Preliminary support for gender differences in response to fluoxetine for generalized anxiety disorder. *Depression and Anxiety, 23*(6), 373–376.

Simon, N. M., Hoge, E. M., Fischman, D., Worthington, J. J., Christian, K. M., Kinrys, G., & Pollack, M. H. (2006). An open-label trial of risperidone augmentation for refractory anxiety disorders. *Journal of Clinical Psychiatry, 67*, 381–385.

Simon, N. M., Connor, K. M., Lebeau, R. T., Hoge, E. A., Worthington, J. J., Zhang, W., Davidson, J. R., & Pollack, M. H. (2008). Quetiapine augmentation of paroxetine CR for the treatment of refractory generalized anxiety disorder: Preliminary findings. *Psychopharmacology, 197*(4), 675–681.

Siqueland, L., Rynn, M., & Diamond, G. S. (2005). Cognitive behavioral and attachment based family therapy for anxious adolescents: Phase I and II studies. *Journal of Anxiety Disorders, 19*(4), 361–381.

Skre, I., Onstad, S., Edvardsen, J., Torgersen, S., & Kringlen, E. (1994). A family study of anxiety disorders: Familial transmission and relationship to mood and psychoactive substance use disorder. *Acta Psychiatrica Scandinavica, 90*(5), 366–374.

Snyder, C., Ilardi, S., Michael, S., & Cheavens, J. (2000). Hope theory: Updating a common process for psychological change. In C. R. Synder & R. E. Ingram (Eds.), *Handbook of psychological change: Psychotherapy, processes and practices for the 21st century* (pp. 128–153). New York: Wiley.

Snyderman, S. H., Rynn, M. A., & Rickels, K. (2005). Open-label pilot study of ziprasidone for refractory generalized anxiety disorder. *Journal of Clinical Psychopharmacology, 25*(5), 497–498.

Spielberger, C. D. (1983). Manual for the State-Trait Anxiety Inventory. STAI (Form Y). Palo Alto, CA: Mind Garden, Inc.

Spitzer, R., Williams, J., & Skodol, A. (1980). DSM-III: The major achievements and an overview. *American Journal of Psychiatry, 137*, 151–164.

Spitzer, R. L., Kroenke, K., Williams, J. B. W., & Lowe, B. (2006). A brief measure for assessing generalized anxiety disorder: The GAD-7. *Archives of Internal Medicine, 166*, 1092–1097.

Stahl, S. M., Ahmed, S., & Handiquet, V. (2007). Analysis of the rate of Improvement of specific psychic and somatic symptoms of generalized anxiety disorder during long-term treatment with venlafaxine ER. *CNS Spectrums, 12*(9), 703–711.

Stanley, M.A., Beck, J.G., & Glassco, J.D. (1996). Treatment of generalized anxiety in older adults: A preliminary comparison of cognitive-behavioral and supportive approaches, Behavior Therapy, 27, 565–581.

Stanley, M. A., Beck, J. G., & Zebb, B. J. (1996). Psychometric properties of four anxiety measures in adults. *Behaviour Research and Therapy, 34*, 827–838.

Stanley, M., Novy, D., Bourland, S., Beck, J. G., & Averill, P. (2001). Assessing adults with generalized anxiety disorder: A replication and extension. *Behaviour Research and Therapy, 39*, 221–235.

Stanley, M. A. (2002). Generalized anxiety disorder in later life. In D. Nutt, K. Rickels, & D. J. Stein (Eds.), *Generalized anxiety disorder: Symptomatology, pathogenesis and management* (pp. 171–183). London, UK: Martin Dunitz.

Stanley, M. A., Beck, J. G., Novi, D. M., Averill, P. M., Swann, A. C., Diefenbach, J. G., & Hopko, D. R. (2003). Cognitive-behavioral treatment of late-life generalized anxiety disorder. Journal of Consulting and Clinical Psychology, 71(2), 309–319.

Stanley, M. A., Hopko, D. R., Diefenbach, G. J., Bourland, S. L., Rodriquez, H., & Wagener, P. (2003). Cognitive-behavior therapy for late-life generalized anxiety disorder in primary care. *American Journal of Geriatric Psychiatry, 11*(1), 92–96.

Starcevic, V., & Bogojevic, G. (1999). The concept of generalized anxiety disorder: Between the too narrow and too wide diagnostic criteria. *Psychopathology 32*, 5–11.

Starcevic, V. (2005). *Anxiety disorders in adults.* New York: Oxford University Press.

Stein, D. J., & Hollander, E. (2002). *The American psychiatric textbook of anxiety disorders* (1st ed.). Washington, DC: American Psychiatric Association.

Stein, D. J. (2004). *Clinical manual of anxiety disorders* (1st ed.). Washington, DC: American Psychiatric Association.

Stein, D. J. (2005). Generalized anxiety disorder: Rethinking diagnosis and rating. *CNS Spectrums, 10*(12), 930–934.

Stein, D. J., Andersen Frus, H., & Goodman, W. K. (2005). Escitalopram for the treatment of GAD: Efficacy across different subgroups and outcomes. *Annals of Clinical Psychiatry, 17*(2), 71–75.

Stein, D. J., Lerer, B., & Stahl, S. M. (2005). *Evidence-based psychopharmacology.* Cambridge, UK: Cambridge University Press.

Stein, M. B., & Heimberg, R. G. (2004). Well-being and life satisfaction in generalized anxiety disorder: Comparison to major depressive disorder in a community sample. *Journal of Affective Disorders, 79*, 161–166.

Steiner, M., Allgulander, C., Ravindran, A., Kosar, H., Burt, T., & Austin, C. (2005). Gender differences in clinical presentation and responses to sertraline treatment of generalized anxiety disorder. *Human Psychopharmacology, 20*, 3–13.

Steketee, G., Van Noppen, B., Cohen, I., & Clary, L. (1998). Psychopathology of anxiety disorders. In J. B. W. Williams & K. Ell (Eds.), *Recent advances in mental health research* (pp. 118–156). Washington, DC: NASW Press.

Stocchi, F., Nordera, G., Jokinen, R. H., Lepola, U. M., Hewett, K., Brysoin, H., Iyengar, M. K., & The Paroxetine Generalized Anxiety Workgroup (2003). Efficacy and tolerability of paroxetine for the long-term treatment of generalized anxiety disorder. *Journal of Clinical Psychiatry, 64*, 250–258.

Strauss, C. C. (1988). Behavioral assessment and treatment of overanxious disorder in children and adolescents. *Behavior Modification, 12*, 234–251.

Strauss, C. C., Lahey, B. B., Frick, P., Fram, C. L., & Hynd, G. W. (1988). Peer social status of children with anxiety disorders. *Journal of Consulting and Clinical Psychology, 56*, 137–141.

Strauss, C. C., Lease, C. A., Kazdin, A. E., Dulcan, M. K., & Last, C. G. (1989). Multimethod assessment of the social competence of children with anxiety disorders. *Journal of Clinical Child Psychology, 18,* 184–189.

Strauss, C. C. (1990). Overanxious disorder in childhood. In M. Hersen & C. G. Last (Eds.), *Handbook of child and adult psychopathology: A longitudinal perspective* (pp. 237–246). New York: Pergamon Press.

Struzik, L., Vernani, M., Coonerty-Femiano, A., & Katzman, M. A. (2004). Treatments for generalized anxiety disorder: *Expert Review Neurotherapeutics, 4*(2), 285–294.

Suarez, L., Bennett, S. M., Goldstein, C., & Barlow, D. H. (2009). Understanding anxiety disorders from a "triple vulnerability" framework. In M. M. Antony & M. B. Stein (Eds.), *Oxford handbook of anxiety and related disorders* (pp. 153–172). New York: Oxford University Press.

Sylvester, B. (2003). Escitalopram treatment leads to remission in GAD. *Clinical Psychiatry News, 31*(4), 25(1).

Szasz, T. S. (1984). *The myth of mental illness: Foundations of a theory of personal conduct* (rev. ed.). New York: Harper Paperbacks.

Tafet, G. E., Idoyaga-Vargas, V. P., Abulafia, D. P., Calandria, J. M., Roffman, S. S., Chiovetta, A., & Shinitzky, M. (2001). Correlation between cortisol and serotonin uptake in patients with chronic stress and depression. *Cognitive, Affective and Behavioral Neuroscience, 1*(4), 388–393.

Tafet, G. E., Toister-Achituv, M., & Shinitzky, M. (2001). Enhancement of serotonin uptake by cortisol: A possible link between stress and depression. *Cognitive, Affective and Behavioral Neuroscience, 1*(1), 96–104.

Tallis, F., Eysenck, M., & Matthews, A. (1992). A questionnaire for the measurement of nonpathological worry. *Personality and Individual Differences, 13,* 161–168.

Tiihonen, J., Kuikka, J., Rasanen, P., Lepola, U., Koponen, H., Liuska, A., Lehmusvaara, A., Vainio, P., Kononen, M., Bergstrom, K., Yu, M., Kinnunen, I., Akerman, K., & Karhu, J. (1997). Cerebral benzodiazepines receptor binding distribution in generalized anxiety disorder: A fractal analysis. *Molecular Psychiatry, 2*(6), 463–471.

Tracey, S. A., Chorpita, B. F., Douban, J., & Barlow, D. H. (1997). Empirical evaluation of DSM-IV generalized anxiety disorder criteria in children and adolescents. *Journal of Clinical Child Psychology, 26,* 404–414.

Trull, T. J., & Sher, K. J. (1994). Relationship between the Five Factor Model of Personality and Axis I disorders in a nonclinical sample. *Journal of Abnormal Psychology, 103,* 350–360.

Tseng, W. S. (1973). The development of psychiatric concepts in traditional Chinese medicine. *Archives of General Psychiatry, 29,* 569–575.

Turk, C. L., Mennin, D. S., Fresco, D. M., & Heimberg, R. G. (2000). *Impairment and quality of life among individuals with generalized anxiety disorder.* Poster presented at the Annual Meeting of the Association for Advancement of Behavior Therapy, New Orleans.

Turk, C. L., Heimberg, R. G., & Mennin, D. S. (2004). Assessment. In R. G. Heimberg, C. L. Turk, & D. S. Mennin (Eds.). *Generalized anxiety disorder: Advances in research and practice* (pp. 219–247). New York: Guilford Press.

Turk, C.L., Heimberg, R.G., Luterek, J.A., Mennin, D.S., & Fresco, D.M. (2005). Emotion Dysregulation in Generalized Anxiety Disorder: A Comparison with soical Anxiety Disorder. *Cognitive Therapy and Research, 29*(1), 89–106.

Turk, C. L., & Wolanin, A. T. (2006). Assessment of generalized anxiety disorder. In G. C. L. Davey & A. Wells (Eds.), *Worry and its psychological disorders: Theory, assessment and treatment* (pp. 137–155). Chichester, UK: Wiley.

Tyrer, P. (1989). *Classification of neurosis.* Oxford, UK: Wiley.

Tyrer, P. (1999). *Anxiety: A multidisciplinary review.* London: Imperial College Press.

Tyrer, P. (2001). The case for cothymia: Mixed anxiety and depression as a single diagnosis. *British Journal of Psychiatry, 179,* 191–193.

Tyrer, P., Seivewright, H., & Johnson, T. (2004). The Nottingham Study of Neurotic Disorder: Predictors of 12 year outcome of dysthymic, panic and generalized anxiety disorder. *Psychological Medicine, 34,* 1385–1394.

Tyrer, P., & Baldwin, D. (2006). Generalised anxiety disorder. *Lancet, 368*, 2156–2166.

Uhlenhuth, E. H., Balter, M. B., Ben, T. A., & Yang, K. (1999). International study of expert judgment on therapeutic use of benzodiazepines and other psychotherapeutic medication: IV. Therapeutic dose dependence and abuse liability of benzodiazepines in the long-term treatment of anxiety disorders. *Journal of Clinical Psychopharmacology, 19*(Suppl. 2), 23S–29S.

Vasey, M. W. (1993). Development and cognition in childhood anxiety: The example of worry. *Advances in Clinical Child Psychology, 15*, 1–39.

Vasey, M. W., & Daleiden, E. L. (1994). Worry in children. In G. Davey & F. Tallis (Eds.), *Worrying: Perspectives on theory, assessment and treatment* (pp. 185–208). Chichester, UK: Wiley.

Walkup, J., & Labellarte, M. (2001). Complications of SSRI treatment. *Journal of Child and Adolescent Psychopharmacology, 11*, 1–4.

Wampold, B. E. (2001). *The great psychotherapy debate: Models, methods, and findings.* Mahwah, NJ: Lawrence Erlbaum Associates.

Ware, J. E. (1994). *SF-36 physical and mental health summary scales: A user's manual.* Boston: The Health Institute, New England Medical Center.

Weems, C. F., Silverman, W. K., & La Greca, A. M. (2000). What do youth referred for anxiety problems worry about? Worry and its relation to anxiety and anxiety disorders in children and adolescents. *Journal of Abnormal Child Psychology, 28*, 63–72.

Wells, A. (1994). A multi-dimensional measure of worry: Development and preliminary evaluation of the anxious thoughts inventory. *Anxiety, Stress, and Coping, 6*, 289–299.

Wells, A. (1995a). Attention and the control of worry. In G. C. L. Davey & F. Tallis (Eds.), *Worrying: Perspectives on theory, assessment and treatment* (pp. 91–114). Chichester, UK: Wiley.

Wells, A. (1995b). Metacognition and worry: A cognitive model of generalized anxiety disorder. *Behavioural and Cognitive Psychotherapy, 23*, 301–320.

Wells, A. (1997). *Cognitive therapy of anxiety disorders: A practice manual and conceptual guide.* Chichester, UK: Wiley.

Wells, A., & Papageorgiou, C. (1998). Relationships between worry, obsessive compulsive symptoms, and metacognitive beliefs. *Behavior Research and Therapy, 36*, 899–913.

Wells, A. (1999). A metacognitive model and therapy for generalized anxiety disorder. Clinical Psychology and Psychotherapy, 6, 86–95.

Wells, A., & Carter, K. (2001). Further tests of a cognitive model of generalized anxiety disorder: Metacognitions and worry in GAD, panic disorder, social phobia, depression and non-patients. *Behavior Therapy, 32*, 85–102.

Wells, A. (2002). GAD, metacognition, and mindfulness: An information processing analysis. *Clinical Psychology: Science and Practice, 9*, 95–100.

Wells, A. (2004). A cognitive model of GAD: Metacognitions and pathological worry. In R. G. Heimberg, C. L. Turk, & D. S. Menniname (Eds.), Generalized anxiety disorder: Advances in research and practice (pp. 164–186). New York: Guilford Press.

Wells, A. (2005). The metacognitive model of GAD: Assessment of meta-worry and relationship with DSM-IV generalized anxiety disorder. *Cognitive Therapy and Research, 29*(1), 107–121.

Wells, A. (2006a). Metacognitive therapy for worry and generalized anxiety disorder. In G. C. L. Davey & A. Wells (Eds.), *Worry and its psychological disorders: Theory, assessment and treatment* (pp. 259–272). Chichester, UK: Wiley.

Wells, A. (2006b). The metacognitive model of worry and generalized anxiety disorder. In G. C. L. Davey & A. Wells (Eds.), *Worry and its psychological disorders: Theory, assessment and treatment* (pp. 179–199). Chichester, UK: Wiley.

Wells, A., & Carter, K. (2006). Generalized anxiety disorder. In A. Carr & M. McNulty (Eds.), *The handbook of adult clinical psychology: An evidence-based practice approach* (pp. 423–457). East Sussex: Routledge.

Wells, A., & King, P. (2006). Metacognitive therapy for generalized anxiety disorder: An open trial. *Journal of Behavior Therapy and Experimental Psychiatry, 37*, 206–212.

Wells, A. (2007). Cognition about cognition: Metacognitive therapy and change in generalized anxiety disorder and social phobia. *Cognitive and Behavioral Practice, 14*, 18–25.

Wells, A., Welford, M., King, P., Papageoriou, C., Wisely, J., & Mendel, E. A randomized trial of metacognitive therapy versus applied relaxation in the treatment of GAD (in prep.).

Werry, J. S. (1991). Overanxious disorder: A review of its taxonomic properties. *Journal of the American Academy of Child and Adolescent Psychiatry, 30*, 533–544.

Westen, D., & Morrison, K. (2001). A multidimensional metaanalysis of treatments for depression, panic and generalized anxiety disorder: An empirical examination of the status of empirically supported therapies. *Journal of Consulting and Clinical Psychology, 69*, 875–899.

Westra, H. A., Arkowitz, H., & Dozois, D. J. A. (2007). *Motivational interviewing as a pretreatment for CBT in generalized anxiety disorder: Preliminary results of a controlled clinical trial.* Paper presented at the Annual Meeting of the Association for Behavioral and Cognitive Psychotherapies, Philadelphia, USA.

Wetherell, J. L., Gatz, M., & Craske, M. G. (2003). Treatment of generalized anxiety disorder in older adults. *Journal of Consulting and Clinical Psychology, 71*(1), 31–40.

Wetherell, J. L., Le Roux, H., & Gatz, M. (2003). DSM-IV criteria for generalized anxiety disorder in older adults: Distinguishing the worried from the well. *Psychology and Aging, 18*(3), 622–627.

Wetherell, J. L., Thorp, S. R., Patterson, T. L., Goldshan, S., Jeste, D. V., & Gatz, M. (2004). Quality of life in geriatric generalized anxiety disorder: A preliminary investigation. *Journal of Psychiatric Research, 38*, 305–312.

Wetherell, J. L., Lenze, E. J., & Stanley, M. A. (2005). Evidence-based treatment of geriatric anxiety disorders. *Psychiatric Clinics of North America, 28*, 871–896.

Wetherell, J. L., Hopko, D. R., Diefenbach, G. J., Averill, P. M., Beck, J. G., Craske, M. G., Gatz, M., Novy, D. M., & Stanley, M. A. (2005). Cognitive-behavioral therapy for late-life generalized anxiety disorder: Who gets better? *Behavior Therapy, 36*, 147–156.

Wetherell, J. L., Sorrell, J. T., Thorp, S. R., & Patterson, T. J. (2005). Psychological interventions for late-life anxiety: A review and early lessons from the CALM study. *Journal of Geriatric Psychiatry and Neurology, 18*, 72–82.

Wetherell, J. L. (2006). Worry in older adults. In G. C. L. Davey & A. Wells (Eds.), *Worry and its psychological disorders: Theory, assessment and treatment* (pp. 69–80). Chichester, UK: Wiley.

Whisman, M. A., Sheldon, C. T., & Guering, P. (2000). Psychiatric disorders and satisfaction with social relationships. Does type of relationship matter? *Journal of Abnormal Psychology, 109*, 803–808.

Williams, D. D., & McBride, A. (1998). Benzodiazepines: Time for reassessment. *British Journal of Psychiatry, 173*, 361.

Williams, K. E., Chambless, P. L., & Ahrens, A. (1997). Are emotion frightening? An extension of the fear of fear construct. *Behaviour Research and Therapy, 35*, 239–248.

Williams, N. L., & Riskind, J. H. (2004). Adult romantic attachment and cognitive vulnerabilities to anxiety and depression: Examining the interpersonal bias of vulnerability models. *Journal of Cognitive Psychotherapy: An International Quarterly, 18*, 7–24.

Wisocki, P. A., Handen, B., & Morse, C. K. (1986). The worry scale as a measure of anxiety among homebound and community active elderly. *The Behavior Therapist, 5*, 91–95.

Wisocki, P. A. (1988). Worry as a phenomenon relevant to the elderly. *Behaviour Therapy, 19*, 369–379.

Wisocki, P. A. (1994). The experience of worry among the elderly. In G. C. L. Davey & F. Tallis (Eds.), *Worrying: Perspectives on theory, assessment, and treatment* (pp. 247–261). New York: Wiley.

Wittchen, H. U., Zhao, S., Kessler, R. C., & Eaton, W. W. (1994). DSM-III-R generalized anxiety disorder in the National Comorbidity Survey. *Archives of General Psychiatry, 51*, 355–364.

Wittchen, H. U., Nelson, C. B., & Lochner, G. (1998). Prevalence of mental disorders and psychosocial impairments in adolescents and young adults. *Psychological Medicine, 28*, 109–126.

Wittchen, H. U., Carter, R. M., Pfister, H., Montgomery, S. A., & Kessler, R. C. (2000). Disabilities and quality of life in pure and comorbid generalized anxiety disorder and major depression in a national survey. *International Clinical Psychopharmacology, 15*, 319–328.

Wittchen, H. U., Krause, P., Hoyer, J., Beesdo, K., Jacobi, F., Hofler, W., & Winter, S. (2001). Prevalence and correlates of GAD in primary care. *MMW Fortschritte der Medizin, 143*, 17–25.

Wittchen, H. U., Kessler, R. C., Beesdo, K., Krause, P., Hoffler, M., & Hoyer, J. (2002). Generalized anxiety disorder and depression in primary care: Prevalence, recognition and management. *Journal of Clinical Psychiatry, 63*, 24–24.

Wittchen, H. U. (2002). Generalized anxiety disorder: Prevalence, burden, and costs to society. *Depression and Anxiety, 16*, 162–171.

Wittchen, H. U., & Jacobi, F. (2005). Size and burden of mental disorders in Europe–a critical review and appraisal of 27 studies. *European Neuropsychopharmacology, 15*, 357–376.

Wolfe, B. E. (1992). Self-experiencing and the integrative treatment of the anxiety disorders. *Journal of Psychotherapy Integration, 2*, 29–43.

Wolfe, B. E. (1994). Adapting psychotherapy outcome research to clinical reality. *Journal of Psychotherapy Integration, 4*, 160–166.

Wolfe, B. E. (1995). Self pathology and psychotherapy integration. *Journal of Psychotherapy Integration, 5*, 293–312.

Wolfe, B. E. (2001). A message to assimilative integrationists: Its time to become accommodative integrationists: A commentary. *Journal of Psychotherapy Integration, 11*, 123–131.

Wolfe, B. E. (2003). Knowing the self: Building a bridge from basic research to clinical practice. *Journal of Psychotherapy Integration, 13*, 83–91.

Wolfe, B. E. (2005). Integrative psychotherapy of the anxiety disorders. In J. C. Norcross & M. R. Goldfried (Eds.), *Handbook of psychotherapy integration* (2nd ed., pp. 263–280). New York: Oxford University Press.

Wolfe, B. E. (2005). *Understanding and treating anxiety disorders: An integrative approach to healing the wounded self.* Washington, DC: American Psychological Association.

Woodman, C. L., Noyes, R., Black, D. W., Schlosser, S., & Yagla, S. J. (1999). A 5-year follow-up study of generalized anxiety disorder and panic disorder. *Journal of Nervous and Mental Disease, 187*, 3–9.

World Organization Health. (2007). *The ICD-10 (revision version) classification of mental and behavioural disorders: Clinical descriptions and diagnostic guidelines.* Geneva: World Health Organization.

Yonkers, K. A., Warshaw, M. G., Massion, A. O., & Keller, M. B. (1996). Phenomenology and course of generalized anxiety disorder. *British Journal of Psychiatry, 168*, 308–313.

Yonkers, K. A., Dyck, I. R., Warshaw, M., & Keller, M. B. (2000). Factors predicting the clinical course of generalized anxiety disorder. *British Journal of Psychiatry, 176*, 544–549.

Yoon, K. L., & Zinbarg, R. E. (2007). Generalized anxiety disorder and entry into marriage or a marriage like relationship. *Journal of Anxiety Disorders, 21*, 955–965.

Zanarini, M. C., Skodol, A. E., Bender, D., Dolan, R., Sanislow, C., Schaefer, E., Morey, L. C., Grilo, C. M., Shea, M. T., McGlashan, T. H., & Gunderson, J. G. (2000). The collaborative longitudinal personality disorder study: Reliability of axis I and II diagnoses. *Journal of Personality Disorders, 14*, 291–299.

Zimmerman, M., & Chelminski, I. (2003). Generalized anxiety disorder in patients with major depression: Is DSM-IV's hierarchy correct? *American Journal of Psychiatry, 160*, 504–512.

Zimmerman, M., Rothschild, L., & Chelminski, I. (2005). The prevalence of DSM-IV personality disorders in psychiatric outpatients. *American Journal of Psychiatry, 162*(10), 1911–1918.

Zinbarg, R. E., & Barlow, D. H. (1996). Structure of anxiety and anxiety disorders: A hierarchical model. *Journal of Abnormal Psychology, 105*, 181–193.

Zinbarg, R. E., Craske, M. G., & Barlow, D. H. (2006). Mastery of your own anxiety and worry (MAW), *Therapist guide* (2nd ed.). New York: Oxford University.

Zuellig, A. R., Newman, M. G., Alcaine, O. A., & Behar, E. S. (1999). *Childhood history of post-traumatic stress disorder in adults with generalized anxiety disorder, panic disorder, and non-disordered controls.* Poster presented at the Annual Meeting of the Association of Advancement of Behavior Therapy, Toronto.

Zung, W. C. (1971). A rating instrument for anxiety disorders. *Psychosomatics, 12*, 371–379.

Index

Printed in the United States
141470LV00001BD/10/P